D0824188

Welcome to the Big Leagues

A Big League Welcome For A Big League Grand Slam

"I cannot begin to express the profound impact that *Welcome to the Big Leagues* has had in my life. In telling the story of Darrel Chaney and opening up to tell his own, Dan Hettinger has crafted a powerful testimony that revealed to me the heart of my Heavenly Father and His divine purpose for my life. I realize the hyperbole of such a statement, but the truth of God's love often defies description; much like the Big League dreams of a small town kid coming true."

—**Richard B.**, Worship Leader & sports geek.

"*Welcome to the Big Leagues* has very encouraging applications to real life lessons. Darrel, in baseball and Dan, in ministry, experienced the same kind of things that I experienced in my career and, in fact, all men face during their lives. We may not be All-Stars, but our lives matter to our families, our friends, ourselves, but most of all to God. This book encouraged me to measure my worth as if through God's eyes and not my own. After all, it is His plan, not ours."

—**Carl K.**, Chemist, cancer and heart attack survivor
and Giants fan—even before they called San Francisco "home"

"A true gem. This book helps me see that God loves me more than I love myself."

—**Bob D.**, retired Golf Pro

"Welcome to the Big Leagues addresses the spiritual void in every man in this country. It encourages in the areas of struggle and disappointment where we have been hit the hardest. As the dad of an 11 year old and having coached 100's of kids with some success, I can relate to Darrel"s struggles. Add to that my work tribulations and this book is just what I need to keep encouraging me."

—**Doug B.**, Wealth Advisor, Rockies fan and Little League coach

"I love *Welcome to the Big Leagues*, especially the chapters about dreams and heroes. Looking back at my life I can see those moments where a significant person really made the difference as a hero in my life to help me fulfill my dreams. Now I more clearly see the need and want to be the hero

God has made me to be for my son and daughter as well as in the lives of others. It is amazing to think that God made me to be a hero. I can really believe in that idea, when I understand my God given significance."

—**Steve M.**, Aero Space Process Improvement Leader,
aka Rocket Scientist and lifelong Dodgers fan

"In *Welcome to the Big Leagues*, Dan has uncovered a unique niche to anyone who has been competitive in their life. Through the career of a baseball player, Dan has displayed the essence of perseverance and struggles that build character. In these challenges we can realize the never ending pursuit of that our Creator has for us that leads to our pursuit of Him. It is a riveting tail of the incredible grace and love the Father has for us. Through his writing Dan has provided an arena for the reader to see how faithful the Creator of the universe is to us."

—**Peter F.**, Wealth Creation, Transformation and Contribution Specialist

"A great read for any sports fan. I was inspired and encouraged as I read the true story of Darrel Chaney, a baseball player with 'The Big Red Machine' and Atlanta Braves, and the life lessons drawn out of his journey—I think it could work for every man. Darrel's story combined with Dan's parallel spiritual lessons make for a powerful and engaging read. I wish I had this book 20 years ago!"

—**Thom R.**, Biotech Executive and long time Atlanta Braves fan

Welcome
to the
Big Leagues

Every Man's Journey to Significance

THE DARREL CHANEY STORY

DAN HETTINGER

New York

Welcome to the Big Leagues
THE DARREL CHANEY STORY
Every Man's Journey to Significance

© 2013 **DAN HETTINGER**. All rights reserved.

No part of this publication may be reproduced or transmitted in any form or by any means, mechanical or electronic, including photocopying and recording, or by any information storage and retrieval system, without permission in writing from author or publisher (except by a reviewer, who may quote brief passages and/or show brief video clips in a review).

Disclaimer: The Publisher and the Author make no representations or warranties with respect to the accuracy or completeness of the contents of this work and specifically disclaim all warranties, including without limitation warranties of fitness for a particular purpose. No warranty may be created or extended by sales or promotional materials. The advice and strategies contained herein may not be suitable for every situation. This work is sold with the understanding that the Publisher is not engaged in rendering legal, accounting, or other professional services. If professional assistance is required, the services of a competent professional person should be sought. Neither the Publisher nor the Author shall be liable for damages arising herefrom. The fact that an organization or website is referred to in this work as a citation and/or a potential source of further information does not mean that the Author or the Publisher endorses the information the organization or website may provide or recommendations it may make. Further, readers should be aware that internet websites listed in this work may have changed or disappeared between when this work was written and when it is read.

Scriptures taken from the Holy Bible, New International Version®, NIV®. Copyright © 1973, 1978, 1984, 2011 by Biblica, Inc.™ Used by permission of Zondervan. All rights reserved worldwide. www.zondervan.com The "NIV" and "New International Version" are trademarks registered in the United States Patent and Trademark Office by Biblica, Inc.™

Darrel Chaney provided pictures and granted license for the publicity and privacy rights to the use of his stories and pictures in this book and in speaking engagements, seminars, retreats or workshops that might result from the authoring of this book. Pictures are also used with the permission of the Cincinnati Reds and the Atlanta Braves.

Initial cover design was created by Chad Reiling, Highlands Ranch, CO. The picture is adapted from a 1975 Topps Baseball Card.

ISBN 978-1-61448-366-3 paperback
ISBN 978-1-61448-451-6 hard cover
ISBN 978-1-61448-367-0 eBook
Library of Congress Control Number: 2012948151

Morgan James Publishing
The Entrepreneurial Publisher
5 Penn Plaza, 23rd Floor,
New York City, New York 10001
(212) 655-5470 office • (516) 908-4496 fax
www.MorganJamesPublishing.com

Cover Design by:
Rachel Lopez
www.r2cdesign.com

Interior Design by:
Bonnie Bushman
bonnie@caboodlegraphics.com

In an effort to support local communities, raise awareness and funds, Morgan James Publishing donates a percentage of all book sales for the life of each book to Habitat for Humanity Peninsula and Greater Williamsburg.

Get involved today, visit
www.MorganJamesBuilds.com.

Habitat
for Humanity®
Peninsula and
Greater Williamsburg
Building Partner

This book is dedicated to my sons,
Danny and Andrew,
who have made baseball more than a game.

TABLE OF CONTENTS

FOREWORD

My baseball career had ended and I was starting a new career in business and struggling with what I really wanted to do with the rest of my life. That is when I met Dan Hettinger. He was starting a church in Gwinnett County, Georgia. Right away, I saw that Dan and I had a couple of things in common. One was our belief in Jesus Christ as Our Lord and Savior and the other, our love of baseball. I knew the game of baseball pretty well. I didn't know the Lord's game very well.

I was looking to grow in my knowledge of the Bible so Dan and I started a Men's Bible Study shortly after we met. We also invested about a year in 1 to 1 Discipleship in his office or at Waffle House early one morning a week.

I shared a lot of baseball stories with Dan over the years. Good ones and not so good ones. As time went by, Dan said he was going to write a book of encouragement based on my life and experiences in baseball. So, we put it on our prayer list. I kept telling Dan we had a couple of things going against us. Dan was an unknown writer and I was a "not so famous, old ballplayer" that many people may not remember since my career wasn't one for the record books. Dan kept saying, "If the Lords want this book to be written, He'll take care of it." So He did and this is my story.

I come from middle America. We never had much growing up but, we were never in need either. My dad was a hard working pipe fitter in an oil refinery. From my days growing up, to my career in baseball to my transition into the business world to retirement, it seems I've always been the guy in the middle. Every championship team I played on and successful business I was involved in would not have succeeded without "the middle man."

But being in the middle does not mean mediocre. I always wanted to be the best and I dreamed big, trained hard and competed intensely and I made it to the Big Leagues—even the World Series three times! Every man wants success, dignity and respect—to make it to the Big Leagues or to the top of his profession. He wants to be significant.

Dan said that there is often a difference between those who inspire and those who encourage. Inspiration comes from the stars in position of strength and success. Encouragement comes from those who are defined by struggle and empathy. I believe the latter best describes my life.

Through this book project, I've come to realize in a deeper way that, even though I was not the most famous baseball player, my career and my life mattered to God. I was significant for who I was and when I lived that way, my life made an impact. Now I want to be an encourager for those who know me and hear me speak or read about my life. I want others to discover their God given significance. I pray that reading this book will encourage you as much as working on it with Dan, has given me a clearer belief in my God given significance.

—**Darrel Chaney**

ACKNOWLEDGEMENTS

A book and a baseball game have at least one thing in common. They both require a team!

Thom Rowland, Charley Heard and Carl Kollmar, board members of The Jakin Group, gave me focus, accountability and organization.

Richard Balagot, Connie Lambert and Susan Hettinger corrected me—a lot. I really needed it!

Gary Foster believed in this book before anyone else did. Steve McNeal, Doug Bartolff and Bob Douma encouraged me with their enthusiasm for baseball and ideas for this project. Alan Harris and Jason Gray provided perspective on the desire to write, especially when the size of the project grew and the finish was much farther away than it seemed at first. The Altomaris, the Jeffreys and the Deitrichs opened the doors to their mountain-get-aways, so that I would have a place to get-away and pray and think and write. Mike and Alice Aldredge-Dennis introduced me to writing resources and groups. Larry Sears did too. Through his efforts I met Patricia Raybon and heard of <u>Bird by Bird</u> by Anne Lammont and found instruction just when I needed it most.

Kevin Black, Rob Knox, Eric Slagle and the men's ministry of New Hope Presbyterian Church gave me an incubator to cultivate the inspiration and grow the ideas. My Life Group supported me with prayer and hope that I was doing something important. Thanks Steve and Tracey,

Eric and Allison, Darren and Leslie, Jim and Marvel, Troy and Kathy and Sterling and Jonnie! AnnMarie Spero and her prayer partners prayed for me faithfully. Tom Melton helped me feel that my life mattered.

Darrel and Cindy Chaney lived lives worth knowing. Thanks for letting me into your story.

My wife, Susan, has been in every inning with me. She has cheered for me, even when I struck out. I am also thankful that she really likes baseball.

So here is a tipping of my cap to people who blessed and helped me more than they know. Immeasurably more!

As God reveals His extravagant love for me and His tireless presence in every moment and event in my life, I love Him more and I run toward home, knowing He will be there celebrating with me.

BATTING PRACTICE

Introduction

Your life matters a lot more than you know.

It does not matter because of what you have done, are doing, or will do. Nor does it matter because of how much you have or someday hope to have. Your life matters because of who you are—a hard lesson for most men to learn.

Darrel Chaney played professional baseball in the Big Leagues for eleven years, which included four National League Championship Series and three World Series. This run was with one of the greatest baseball teams to ever take the field—the Cincinnati Reds, also known as The Big Red Machine.

Darrel was traded to the Atlanta Braves where he played for four years. Following that, he was a color commentator and play-by-play broadcaster with TBS during the early years of the Braves' televised games.

When I got to know Darrel, I recognized a trait that I did not understand. He used self-deprecating humor as though his career had no significance. He did not brag but seemed to be embarrassed that he did not do better or achieve higher.

"Darrel! I am proud just to know you. You hit your first Big League home run off of Juan Marichal. You hit a Big League grand slam. You batted against Luis Tiant in what is arguably the best World Series game of the last fifty years. When the Reds beat the Red Sox in the seventh game of that series, you were in the pile of celebrating ball players at Fenway Park.

Do you know my first Big League World Series? I was walking around the outside of Atlanta-Fulton County Stadium holding two fingers up in the air while trying to buy two tickets from a scalper so a buddy and I could watch the Atlanta Braves play the Minnesota Twins. I could not even get into the stadium. You have nothing to be ashamed of or embarrassed about. I know you did not make the Hall of Fame, the All-Star team or a million bucks, but you were good enough to be there for eleven years and you had a lot of awesome (and for me, enviable) experiences."

Sports are a great platform for teaching life's lessons. Darrel's career is a great metaphor summarizing the battles of every man. Every man experiences the same kind of discouragement and tends to lose sight of his dream when he is getting banged up in the battles of life. It is natural to measure his significance by comparing his accomplishments to the other guy's. Often, he looks at what he does not have or did not accomplish and live with an accusing voice inside his head that says, "You are not important. Your life does not matter. You are a loser."

That was the pattern of my life. I was a pastor of small churches during the era of church growth and mega-churches. My measurement system was in the number of parishioners and monetary worth. There was not very much of either. I could have been enjoying relationships more and making the most of every opportunity but I was fighting insecurity and self-doubt.

When I was telling Darrel how much I admired his baseball accomplishments and esteemed him as a winner in baseball and life—a man of great significance—the voice of God began to get through to me, as well. "Dan, I made you, called you and placed you. I died on the cross for you. I work through your life, even when you do not know it. Why would you put your life down and minimize the impact of your ministry? You have accomplished things that are beyond measure."

Some great books for men deal with the words, success and significance. They talk about significance as if it is better than success. It is as if there is the time when he graduates to significance. In this book, I look at those words differently. For guys like Darrel and me, we felt success eluded us because we felt insignificant. Men, who measure themselves incorrectly by comparing themselves to others, calculating what they own, or listing their achievements, usually have the feeling that they are not all they were meant to be. They feel insignificant.

But when a man knows he is significant in the eyes of God because of who he is, he will be successful. He will live with enthusiasm and strength. His relationships will be healthier. Winning is a certainty and failure is not an option. There is a different measurement and source to his life because, no matter what, his life matters and the simplest and smallest things have unlimited potential. The man who discovers his significance is a powerful man—one who knows he has a place in history, has encountered the Eternal and is being directed by God. The impact of his life is greater than he will know in this lifetime. He is a man who has the potential to change the world. We need more men like that today.

Writing this book about Darrel also became a book about my, and every other man's, journey to significance. There is much uncertainty in our world with turmoil and enemies of the good. But we were made for this time in history. I pray we recognize our God-given significance so we experience the Big League life He intends for us to live. Your life matters, more than you know! You are in the Big Leagues.

The Early Innings

Getting In the Game

The First Inning

Dreams

First Spring Training, The Dream
comes true at the age of 18.

Top of the First

DARREL'S BIG LEAGUE
DREAM STARTED EARLY

"Take delight in the Lord and He will give you the desires of your heart."
Psalm 37:4

"A winner is a person who becomes all that God intends for him to become.
He's given us all talents and abilities to use, not to abuse.
He hasn't given you dreams to dream so he can taunt you.
He's placed those dreams in your heart."
Lewis Timberlake

The Big Leagues are filled with dreams that began with little boys. Everybody has to start somewhere. The first two innings get Darrel, and every man, in the game.

• • • • •

When did Darrel Chaney become a Big Leaguer?

Officially, it was when the Cincinnati Reds called him up from the minors in 1969. In Darrel's boyhood imagination, it began the day Mr. Chaney got tired of the fighting between his two sons and did something about it. Larry Chaney was older, but only by 11 months, which made him just big enough and strong enough to come out on top whenever Larry and Darrel competed.

Tension was always present and consequently it didn't take much for them to get into an argument or fight. One evening, the elder Chaney, after almost a decade's worth of brotherly bickering, had enough. Being of modest means, the Chaney brothers not only shared a bedroom, but also the same bed, up until they were 10 and 11. When the boys turned in for the night, they did not settle down quickly. On this night, Dad would have none of that. "Quiet now! Not another peep," he ordered as he closed the door. He made sure to give his two charges a firm "I mean business" look before retiring to the living room. He didn't get very far when he heard, "peep."

"Now you've done it, Larry!" Darrel hissed. He could hear his Dad's heavy and fast-approaching steps coming down the hall and he knew that they were both in big trouble.

• • • • •

Carlos Chaney grew up in an orphanage, served in the Army, and worked as a pipe fitter at Sinclair Oil Refinery. He had converted to Catholicism to marry Eleanore "Ellie" Binsfeld. He was a strict disciplinarian who practiced tough love with his two sons. Larry and Darrel had little doubt about what their father considered to be right and wrong, and what was expected of them. Punishment for bad behavior was determined by which end of the belt was used on the "back-side" of the perpetrator. Minor offenses received the smooth end of the leather belt, while more serious transgressions—like throwing eggs at passing neighbors' cars, allegedly occurring when they were 12 and 13, respectively—the buckle end was used for emphasis. Regarding the egg-throwing incident, they never got caught but one of their more "sensitive" accomplices confessed to his dad who then made a quick visit to the Chaney's and had a man-to-man talk with Carlos. What Carlos Chaney lacked in warmth, affection and words, he made up for in action.

• • • • •

This evening, the belt did not seem appropriate. Carlos went back to their room with determination in his voice said, "Boys, something is going to change. This messing around has got to stop." Without another word or action, he turned, and went back to his room to sleep on it. His hope was that an idea would come to him that would help him to discipline his boys so their restless energy would have a more productive and less frustrating outlet.

At work the next morning, during break time, he said to his buddies as he was pouring coffee from his thermos, "I've got to give my boys something to do to get them to quit fighting and picking on each other. Any of you guys have an idea?"

"Sign 'em up for baseball Chaney! Kids love it and they learn a lot of good lessons plus they get tired and go to sleep when their heads hit the pillow. But don't wait. Tonight is the sign-up for the Hessville Little League."

"Great idea, Frankie! I'll do that."

Immediately after work, Carlos headed to Montgomery Ward and bought each of the boys their first baseball glove. When he got home, his steps had determination, and he had a confident, "I-think-I- got- this-figured- out" smile on his face.

"Boys, come here. I've got something for you."

"What have you got Dad?" Darrel's question was hopeful but had some trepidation. There was unfinished business from last night and Dad's steps sounded serious when he walked in the back door.

"Baseball gloves. You boys are going to play ball and tonight we are going to get in the car and drive down to the Caldwell Complex and get you signed up."

"Gee Dad, that's great," Larry said.

Darrel said, "Sure is. I thought we were in trouble."

"Well, I hope you will use up all your energy learning to play ball so you will behave better around the house."

Early that evening, they were signed up for Hessville Little League and so was Carlos. In a twist of fate, the beginning of playing ball for his boys was the beginning of coaching for a dad who never had a dad that played ball with him. How did he know the finer points of baseball and fatherhood when he did not have anyone teach him or have an example to draw on? Maybe it came from a deep longing in his heart for what he did not have, that helped him be what he would be to his sons.

• • • • •

Little league is where baseball first becomes official for a boy. It is played on a real field with a pitcher's mound, base lines, base pads, and grass in the outfield. Home runs were counted because they went over a wooden fence littered with logos and mottos of local sponsors, and wild pitches were rescued by a chain link backstop. The loud and rowdy boys got to chew their bubble gum, spit on the ground, and sit on a bench in a real dugout, just like their Big League counterparts. Every team had a manager and coaches. Each game had real umpires to oversee the proceedings. Spectators consisted of parents, siblings, and other family members and friends who cheered from the bleachers. For many 8 to 12-year-old-boys, the experience rivaled all the drama of the Big Leagues, nerves and all.

Most importantly, there were uniforms. No other suit of clothes was like it and nothing could mimic a real baseball uniform with matching cap and an individual number. For boys in the 50's and 60's, the shoes were not cleats, just sneakers. The socks had stirrups that went below the arch of the foot, with the tube of the sock, the color of the team's cap and two or three white stripes, stretching around the calf all the way to the knee, above where the elastic of the pants bunched.

When Darrel put on his uniform with the #15, and took the Hessville field, in his imagination, he was no less than Ernie Banks himself. He fell in love with the game from the instant he put on that Montgomery Ward baseball mitt. His dad showed him where to spit in the pocket and form it to the right shape to catch and hold a ball. It felt like a perfect fit over his little hand and skinny 8-year-old arm.

The uniform may have stirred his imagination and the glove may have sparked his passion, but it didn't play the game. Darrel had to learn to catch, throw, hit, and run. Practice was as important as playing the game and his dad, ever the disciplinarian, knew that perspiration preceded performance. Threading 6-inch stainless steel pipe with hand-turned dies and fitting them with elbows, flanges, and couplings, was hard, dirty work for Darrel's dad. Carlos performed these muscular and intricate tasks dutifully for 36 years and he had the calluses, soaked black by lubricating oil, covering his palms and fingers to prove it. Just about all of his clothes smelled like a mixture of sweat, metal, and oil.

At the end of his 7-to-3 shift, he would drive home and park the used, semi-late-model family car in the driveway next to the house. He always entered the kitchen through the back screen door and without fanfare, headed to the bathroom. Shedding his dirty clothes, he quickly took a shower before allowing himself a brief rest before dinner was served. After the meat and potatoes were served, with Dad and Mom at each end of the table, Mary Kay on one side with her brothers sitting side by side on the other side of the Formica-top kitchen table, the boys washed and dried the dishes, alternating between them who did what each night. Whatever the case, they both knew that when they were finished, out came the ball and gloves for an hour or more of catch, depending on how quickly they finished their chores.

Outside in front of their modest 900 square-foot house, a typical 1960's house for Hammond, father and sons would loosen up their arms with short, easy throws. Dad would throw to Darrel, who'd throw back to Dad. Dad would then throw to Larry, who'd then throw it back to Dad. And so it went, every night for at least an hour, throwing the ball back and forth. For boys 8 and 10 years old, the Chaney brothers had good arms. Each time one threw back to his dad, they took a step back and their throws would have more zip. No rainbows here as the ball smacked with a loud snap when it hit Dad's glove. The only time that play was delayed was when a car passed on the gravel street. "Car!" Dad would holler. When it passed, he would resume, but this time throwing grounders which his little guys scooped up, set their feet, and fired back quicker than any hitter could run to first base. This was their daily routine, interrupted only by games and team practices.

You could always count on the Chaneys to be the first to arrive at every practice and game. As soon as they got there, they would grab the equipment bag and the bucket of baseballs and get out on the field to start throwing. Every spring, all the Little League Baseball teams wanted the Chaneys. Larry was a power hitter, Darrel could pitch and field. Carlos was always there to coach and sometimes, Ellie would take on the responsibility of being the Team Mom.

As the years passed, Darrel added more sports with more games, more workouts, and more practices. Things just intensified. Babe Ruth baseball followed Little League and, after that, there was American Legion. Football season followed baseball, and basketball season came after football. All these experiences served to fan the flames for the Big Leagues for this kid from Hammond, Indiana.

All the while, Darrel's Dad was there. In his youth, Carlos was a track star. He taught Darrel the crossover step and how to steal a base. He certainly didn't have to teach Darrel how to hustle or work hard as he let nothing discourage him from lifting weights and doing pushups, not even blisters that Darrel got from playing basketball, which made his feet raw. He simply taped them up and kept playing.

Hammond, Indiana in the turbulent 60's, and his father's non-verbal style didn't seem like the ideal chemistry to fan a Big League dream. Carlos would rarely compliment Darrel directly but his presence communicated enough for Darrel, who paid careful attention to every expression of approval. During Darrel's senior year, he quarterbacked Hammond High School to a win in the State AAAA Football Championship. His Dad still set curfew at 11:30, which Darrel broke by an hour because of celebrating with his buddies. This earned an immediate grounding. The next morning his hunger for Dad's approval was satisfied when he overheard his Dad, with unmistakable pride in his voice, recount to his Mom, "Darrel was really good last night."

Darrel was really good and others were beginning to take notice. Darrel was awarded Parade Magazine's High School All-American Quarterback. Universities from across the nation recruited Darrel to come and play football for them: Purdue, Indiana, Illinois, Ohio State, and Iowa, to name a few. All expressed an interest in him on the gridiron. Ball State University in Muncie, Indiana, was the only school that was going to allow Darrel to play both baseball and football. "You play with us and the scouts will find you," Ray Louthan, Ball State's Athletic Director told Darrel. The challenge of being a two-sport athlete greatly appealed to Darrel. He even accepted an invitation to visit the campus. As he was readying himself that weekend, Ara Parseghian, head football coach of Notre Dame, also extended an invitation for Darrel to come to South Bend.

Call it naiveté or just being faithful to his prior commitment, Darrel expressed his apologies. "Mr. Parseghian, I am honored to be asked to come and visit Notre Dame but I have already accepted an invitation to visit Ball State University for that weekend, so I won't be able to come at that time. If you can, please invite me for another weekend."

That was the last Darrel ever heard from Notre Dame.

It was looking like his immediate future was accepting the scholarship offer to Ball State University when Tony Robello from the Cincinnati Reds called and asked to meet with him. He brought along Dale McReynolds, the scout who spotted Darrel. They met with the Chaney's at their little house in Hammond. Each took a seat in the now crowded living room to sit down and talk about the possibility of Darrel becoming a prospect for the Big League club. If Carlos was impressed that a Major League Baseball scout and recruiter were in his living room offering his son a chance to play in the Big Leagues, he disguised it well. He wanted the best for his son, so he acted as Darrel's agent. The recruiter was very direct. "We would like for Darrel to become a part of the Cincinnati Reds organization and I am prepared to offer him an $8,000 contract to become a prospect and begin playing in our minor league system."

"Mr. Robello my son is a darn good player. A lot of colleges want him to come and play football and they are willing to offer him a full-ride scholarship with a good education." To prove this point, he walked into the kitchen and came out with the folder containing over 25 letters they had been saving from schools which had expressed an interest in Darrel. It was an impressive collection. He placed the folder in front of Tony. "The Reds need to know how in-demand my son is."

The Reds knew Darrel was good (he was batting .462 in American Legion). They also knew he had other options. They wanted him but there were other good, young ball players out there willing to accept their terms. Time was limited, so the Reds were not going to budge with their contract.

"I'll tell you what, Mr. Chaney. Your boy can play football with one of those universities or he can play baseball with us but I need to know when I leave here tonight. The offer stands. You decide which it is going to be."

"Excuse us," Carlos said, taking Darrel a few feet into the kitchen.

"What do you want to do?" he whispered, almost loud enough to be heard back in the living room.

"I want to play ball. I want to make it to the Big Leagues." Darrel responded excitedly.

"OK, son. This is it. This is a big decision that will greatly affect your future. Your mom and I are behind you."

Father and son looked each other in the eye and without any more words, turned and walked back into the living room.

Carlos stuck out his hand. Tony Robello stood and extended his hand. "So we have a deal?" he asked rhetorically.

"Yes sir!" Darrel exclaimed. "I'm excited to become a part of the Red's organization and become a professional baseball player. This is a dream come true!"

The paperwork was spread out on the coffee table and Carlos pulled a pen from the selection in his shirt pocket. He always had a plastic pocket protector that he used at the refinery with more than one pen. There might not have been any more important use for one of them than to sign Darrel's first contract with a Big League baseball team. And to think that it started that fateful night when a Dad decided that he had had enough of his sons fighting, bought a couple of Montgomery Ward baseball gloves, and signed up an 8 year-old for Little League.

That was part of a grander plan because God put the desire in Darrel's heart which gave direction and momentum to his life, making His Big League dream grow up.

Bottom of the First

GOD PLANTS A DREAM
IN EVERY MAN

*"Being confident of this, that he who began a good work in you
will carry it on to completion until the day of Christ Jesus."*
Philippians 1:6

*"Your time is limited, so don't waste it living someone else's life.
Don't be trapped by dogma – which is living
with the results of other people's thinking.
Don't let the noise of other's opinions drown out your own inner voice.
And most important, have the courage to follow your heart and intuition.
They somehow already know what you truly want to become.
Everything else is secondary."*
Steve Jobs

Boys are supposed to have Big League dreams. They are planted in their hearts by God. Tirelessly, God will work on and in and through him every day, and in every circumstance of his life, to see that his dream becomes his purpose, and that it is fulfilled.

Many boys dream about baseball but there are other dreams outside of sports that motivate guys to find and fulfill God's purpose for their lives. Men should not be embarrassed by their boyhood dreams or minimize their importance and discard their heroic hopes because they were wild, adventuresome or unrealistic. In <u>Wild at Heart</u>, John Eldredge invites men to explore the masculine heart that God put in them from the day they were born; actually as they were being knit together in their mother's womb. It is God's design and part of the DNA of a man.

"Capes and swords, camouflage, bandanas and six-shooters, these are the uniforms of boyhood. Little boys yearn to know they are powerful, they are dangerous, they are someone to be reckoned with. How many parents have tried in vain to prevent little Timmy from playing with guns? Give it up. If you do not supply a boy with weapons, he will make them from whatever materials are at hand. My boys chew their graham crackers into the shape of handguns at the breakfast table. Every stick or fallen branch is a spear, or, better, a bazooka. Despite what many modern educators would say, this is not a psychological disturbance brought on by violent television or chemical imbalance. Aggression is part of the masculine design, we are hardwired for it. If we believe that man is made in the image of God, then we would do well to remember that "the Lord is a warrior; the LORD is his name' (Ex. 15.3).

Little girls do not invent games where large numbers of people die, where bloodshed is a prerequisite for having fun. Hockey, for example, was not a feminine creation. Nor was boxing. A boy wants to attack something—and so does a man, even if it's only a little white ball on a tee. He wants to whack it into kingdom come. On the other hand, my boys do not sit down to tea parties. They do not call their friends on the phone to talk about relationships. They grow bored of games that have no element of danger or competition or bloodshed. Cooperative games based on 'relational interdependence' are complete nonsense. 'No one is killed?' they ask, incredulous. 'No one wins? What's the point?' The universal nature of this ought to have convinced us by now; the boy is a warrior/ the boy is his name. And those are not boyish antics he is doing. When boys play at war, they are rehearsing their part in a much bigger drama. One day, you just might need that boy to defend you." (Taken from, Wild at Heart, by John Eldredge, Thomas Nelson Publishers, pp 10, 11)

Darrel's boyhood dream to be a Big Leaguer was about more than baseball. His ability to achieve his hero status of being a Big League shortstop was where he expected to find his significance on the stage that meant the most to him—a Big League ball field. If he could do that, he would be able to do anything. Nothing more needed to be done. From that position, he was powerful, influential, and significant.

From the moment he watched his first Cubs' game on TV, he had the dream. From the day he put on that Montgomery Ward baseball glove, he believed he had the ability. When he donned his Little League uniform, the dream had focus. Having his Dad coach and participate fueled the dream.

Go back into your boyhood and remember what dream you had?

Did you assemble model cars and dream of driving in NASCAR? When you built Lagos, did you build tall skyscrapers? Did you take things apart and put them back together, or just tear them apart, because you liked working with your hands and enjoyed figuring out how things operated? Did you like music and dream of performing before great audiences, or composing concertos that symphonies would perform? Could you doodle, draw, paint and see things that were not yet on a canvas? Maybe you saw suffering and dreamed that one day, you would discover a cure for cancer; or you saw wrong and wanted to rescue the victims, beat the bad guys and make the world a safer place to live?

I've heard of boys and girls as young as four years old feeling a call to ministry or the mission field. They would hear a speech, see a slide show, or read an article in National Geographic that would stir a yearning in that direction. Their fondest imaginations would be enduring tropical heat, eating exotic foods, surviving dangerous animal encounters and meeting people who spoke different languages, wore strange clothes, and had differently-colored skin.

Inside those games and imaginations lie the key to boys growing up into what they were placed on earth for. In the fulfillment of that dream, a man would feel fully alive, worthwhile and vital.

There are a few vivid memories from my boyhood dreams.

Greatness on the baseball field, in Little League and beyond was in my dreams. During summer vacation, which lasted from the first week in June until the Wednesday after Labor Day, we played sandlot baseball every day. If we were not playing a game—3 against 3, with right field as an out—we were playing catch. Until we got a little bigger, our house served as a back stop. It was no use replacing the storm door window so my Dad inserted a piece of Masonite that looked pretty good when it was painted the same color as the house. The small basement window was usually covered with plastic. Needless to say, there were a lot of wild pitches and passed balls. Dad was patient with the broken windows and the bare spots in the yard, worn where the bases and pitcher's mound were.

His motto: "I'm not growing grass. I'm growing boys."

Growing up, our yard was the perfect shape for our baseball diamond—the lattice separating our back yard from my grandfather's made for a perfect home-run fence. Many years later, when I would take my boys to visit their Grandma and Grandpap, they were able to play on it; it became one of their first ball fields.

That was certainly the case for my younger brother and me, in our boyhood, although my younger brother seemed to excel more than I did. He became an all-star and was the ace of his team's pitching staff. One of my boyhood disappointments was that I was good, but not good enough to be an all-star, which was what it took to earn the red and blue cap with the white HL for Hepburn Lycoming Little League.

Maybe I couldn't make the all-star team but when I was in my own little world of building model cars, I would dream of having the coolest car around and winning on the half-mile dirt oval. I loved putting model cars together. I didn't follow the directions and rarely used the decals that were included. I knocked out one side of a wood box measuring 12 x 12 x 12 inches and it became my spray paint booth where my AMT, 1:25 scale plastic cars were transformed into my vision: rarely like the one on the box, always souped up, fast and colorful, like the semi-late models I saw race on the half-mile dirt track at Selinsgrove.

The money to buy the models came from my paper route. For 5-½ years, 6 days a week from 3:30-5:00 in the afternoon, I delivered 77 newspapers in my neighborhood. I walked door-to-door, carrying the papers in a big orange Williamsport Sun-Gazette sack that hung over my shoulder. When I started, I was so small in stature that we had to fold the shoulder strap and pin it with a huge safety pin so the sack would not drag on the ground. This was one of the few jobs available for a kid in those days, except for mowing lawns and shoveling snow, which I also did, using the built-in network from my paper route. I was the only kid with money but the greatest long-term benefit was that I learned to talk to adults.

Another of my boyhood passions was hunting with my Dad. Fall in central Pennsylvania meant beautiful foliage, Penn State football, and hunting. First was small game season and then, deer season. There were two weeks for hunting bucks. If you didn't get your buck (only one deer per hunter and the vast majority did not get anything), there were two days to try and get a doe. For many boys like me, this was the passage to manhood. Learning to shoot, being tough enough to endure the cold fall and winter in the Pennsylvania woods, and experiencing the success of bringing home some game to eat and brag about made a boy proud enough to feel like a man. While I had a few successful hunts, I never killed a buck, which was the goal of every white-tailed deer hunter. It still makes me cringe to think of the one year on the first day of buck season, when I missed a buck, THREE times, just ten minutes into the season. He was lucky enough to show up on the left side of this left-handed shooter and I wasn't deft enough to take the shot right-handed. So I awkwardly pointed, fired, and missed. And again! Then I missed again! He finally took off, leaving me with a jaw that was sore from the recoil of the 30/30 and a seriously-bruised boyhood ego. The dream of bagging a trophy buck would have to find fulfillment in another way.

Life is hard on dreams. Sometimes recalling deferred dreams is painful, as they are reminders of what did not happen, what went wrong and personal weakness. This pain lingers.

Years later, when I would hit a bump in the road wherein a critic focused on a perceived weakness of mine; endured a rejection from a colleague who said, "Thanks, but no thanks"; experienced a setback in which the ministry did not turn out as I had hoped or imagined, in the resultant pain, I recognized some haunting memories that again, said "good, but not good enough." Missed opportunities felt like the three errant shots on the first day of buck season, but these opportunities were more important.

Maybe you dreamed of playing in the Big Leagues but you were not coordinated and couldn't play ball. You never made the all-star team and when little league was over, your baseball career was finished. Recreational softball with guys from work or church is the fullest use of your skills—a lot of fun but not the glory that was your dream.

A lot of boys don't have dads to fuel the fire. They go to school, try to get on a team but never seem to find anything they are good at. Conversely, there are the boys whose dads demand they be what the dads never became but always aspired to become. A lack of skills and interest frustrates the dad and exasperates the son.

Sometimes it is the cost: opportunities to pursue your passion and skills were too expensive for your family's budget. Growing up in a single-parent home in a bad neighborhood with little potential for escape eventually extinguished the flame inside your heart because you always heard, "We can't afford that."

Maybe your dream was considered a childish fantasy which you would outgrow when you grew up and encountered "real life." At least that was your perception because it was the way everyone in your life treated you. It is tough when a dream is misunderstood.

Darrel made it to the Big Leagues, once being a part of the World Series winning team. There were a lot of battles along his journey which caused him to feel that the Big Leagues did not produce the significance he expected.

The gauntlet of setbacks may be the world's attempt to extinguish your dream but it is God's plan to focus, purify and maximize your dream.

Joseph was a character in the Bible with a God-given dream. His dream came true when he interpreted the dream of the Pharaoh. Way back in Genesis, even before Moses lived, this story reveals the profile of a dream (Genesis 37-42). First, discovering a dream stirs optimistic excitement. Then it is quickly misunderstood, bitterly resented, and dramatically resisted. A change of setting proves equally frustrating and nobody seems interested in helping. The drama of Joseph's life drove his dream underground for 40 years, before it became a reality.

He dreamed that he would be in a unique position that would give him authority over his eleven older brothers. Naive enthusiasm got him thrown into a pit and sold into slavery. About the time things started looking up for Joseph, he resisted the inappropriate advances of his boss's wife, who, now scorned, framed him. He was sent back to the dungeons and when it appeared as though things couldn't get much worse, he was forgotten.

Still, the One who gave him the dream had not forgotten him. God weaved all of Joseph's experiences into a fulfillment beyond anything that Joseph could have asked for or even imagined.

Where is your dream?

Even when life is hard on dreams, God has a dream for your life. You can be confident, your dream matters and God will work on it until it is completed.

A lot of my dreams were fulfilled in different ways than I had imagined. They guided my steps, shaped my character and the efforts and relationships I had encountered produced results beyond measure.

I never made it to the Big Leagues but I did learn to enjoy the game. I played baseball with my boys, and we created a lot of great memories. By writing about a Big Leaguer, in my own way I have made it to the Big Leagues of baseball. The victories keep coming. Writing takes imagination that was cultivated in part by building model race cars. Delivering newspapers provided the time to fantasize about my dreams. Communicating with people of all ages and at every opportunity, honed the skill that filled every encounter with eternal potential.

Antlers from a prize buck do not decorate my wall but exploring the beauty of the outdoors cultivated an adventuresome spirit in me. I have hiked and camped a couple hundred miles of the Appalachian Trail and summitted over twenty of Colorado's highest peaks. The magnificence of creation is reward enough but beyond the expansion of my soul, my vision for ministry and life is wild and outside of the box. I often go the hard way but as I look back at the journey, it has been rich, full, and rewarding, even when it means surviving the mistakes and the failures. A vivid imagination, full of ideas and high hopes, helps all of my relationships and situations be filled with potential and pleasure.

The setbacks, detours, delays and failures are woven together to produce results beyond every man's wildest imagination. Opportunities that are different from those dreamed of, do exist. The measurement of results looks different than the ones pictured in the boyhood years. This way is best because in the achievement of the dream, the process has matured the dream and the dreamer, producing an understanding of who he is, not just what he does. The design and purpose of his life, the presence of God who is working in, on, and through his life even when he is unaware, are being revealed. His life matters. His impact is beyond measure. He is powerful and significant.

He has made it to the Big Leagues.

What's the Score at the End of the First Inning?

You start the game on defense. Here you are fielding what life hits to you.

- What dreams can you remember from your childhood?
- Who was in your life that fueled your dreams? Who fought your dreams?
- How did you handle your dreams?

When you are up to bat in the bottom of the inning, what are you going to do?

- Pray for God to reveal His dream for you.
- Identify dreams you had and still have.
- What will you do today that is connected to your dream?

The Second Inning

Heroes

Ernie Banks is still Darrel's hero.

Top of the Second

DARREL'S BIG LEAGUE HERO

"As iron sharpens iron, so one person sharpens another."
Proverbs 27:17

"A hero is someone right who doesn't change."
George Foreman

Darrel met his hero in 1969, Darrel's rookie year in the Big Leagues.

Darrel and the Reds didn't have much to celebrate as they neared the halfway point of the season with a weekend series against the Chicago Cubs and Darrel's hero, Ernie Banks. Cincinnati sat in third place in the NL West, 2.5 games behind the division leading Atlanta Braves but playing just five games above .500. The Cubs, conversely, were in first place in NL East, 8 games ahead of the New York Mets. They displayed their first place prowess in the opening game, beating the Reds 14-8, with Darrel going 0-2.

Darrel's failure to reach first base kept him from experiencing the fulfillment of a dream that started nine years earlier.

• • • • •

On a beautiful spring afternoon in Hammond, Indiana, kids piled off the school bus at Delaware Ave. Girls in dresses cradled their books in their arms as if trying to protect themselves from the boys who teased them as they horsed around—running, hollering, and burning off the energy built up from a day of classes at Our Lady of Perpetual Health Catholic School. It was also known as OLPH, which the public school kids teasingly referred to as "Old Ladies Pool Hall."

Darrel had better things to do and without turning to the left or the right, he ran straight home. With his books tucked under one arm and his jacket slung over his shoulder, he cleared all the front porch steps in one jump and crashed through the front door. "Hi, Mom, I'm home!" He threw his books onto the living room sofa and turned on the TV for his favorite afternoon activity, watching the Cubs play baseball.

In 1956 almost all Major League Baseball games were played during the daytime. The Cubs, however, didn't begin playing night games until 1988, so every home game was played under the sun, which was fine for Darrel. For an eager boy it was a long time to wait for the black-and-white TV to warm up. He could hear the voice of the Cubs' play-by play announcers, Jack Brickhouse and Lou Boudreau on WGN, Channel 9, before the picture came into focus, and it only increased the anticipation.

Darrel loved baseball! It didn't matter to the young fan that the Cubs were not very good in 1956. That April, they had only won three games. In May, they "improved," with one more win. But seven wins in two months was simply dreadful! By the end of the season, they would finish 33 games behind the Brooklyn Dodgers, who had won 93 games, about as many as the 94 the Cubs lost. The Dodgers would go on to lose the World Series to the Yankees in a seven-game classic. For young Darrel baseball was baseball, especially in April, where hope sprung eternal. In the age before ESPN and superstations with just about every game being televised, it was just great to be a Cubs fan and get to watch them on TV.

The fire of Darrel's love for baseball and watching the Cubs, was fanned by the young shortstop, "Mr. Cub," Ernie Banks. Entering his fourth season in 1956, he was coming off an All-Star season as the starting shortstop for the National League, when he hit almost .300 while slugging 44 home runs. He finished third in the MVP voting, behind Roy Campanella and Duke Snyder but ahead of Willie Mays. Darrel was in awe of Ernie, who could do everything on the baseball field: hit for power, run the bases with speed, play with a great glove at shortstop and throw like a shot out of a gun. As a Little Leaguer, to the best of his ability, Darrel tried to copy every move and technique of his hero. Darrel couldn't get enough of the Cubs, Ernie Banks, or baseball. "I want to make it to the Big Leagues and be a short stop like Ernie banks," he declared to himself and to anyone else who would listen.

He watched every game on TV and would scan the sports page of the newspaper the next day to check the standings and read about his team and his hero. He cut out pictures and put them on the wall of his room. Being a Big Leaguer was all he talked about, so much so, that Carlos and Ellie, his parents, Larry his brother, Mary Kay his sister and all of his friends began to notice how much this meant to Darrel.

It was easy for Darrel's dad to encourage his son's admiration for Ernie. He knew that there were a lot of little boys who wanted to be like Ernie Banks when they got older and a lot of men wished they could play ball as well as Ernie Banks. Beyond baseball, Ernie was a man worth emulating. His attitude was unfailingly positive, no matter how abysmal a season his team was having. His demeanor and smile were contagious and his character, noble. Kids absolutely loved him because he always took time with them, looking each in the eye and asking them questions as he signed autographs.

Over the next four years while playing Little League, Darrel watched as many Cubs games as he could and applied all he learned from watching Ernie to his playing. It was a good time for both players. Darrel grew exponentially in his skills as a shortstop, pitcher and hitter. Ernie Banks was becoming one of the Major Leagues' major stars, posting impressive numbers. In 1957, he was second in home runs behind Willie Mays. In 1958, he led the Majors by hitting 47, which was five more than Mickey Mantle, and then was named National League MVP. In 1959, he duplicated the feat. The Cubs were still a sub .500 team but Ernie's unwavering commitment and consistent performances gave Chicagoans something to cheer about and young admirers, a lot to look up to.

To everyone's great pleasure, Ernie accepted the invitation to speak to the Hessville Little League at their awards banquet on August 25, 1960, in Hammond at St. Michael's Hall. Carlos' involvement, Darrel's leading role on his team, and the league all-stars helped the Chaney family get seats at a table near the platform for Ernie's speech. "I've waited all my life for this. Tonight I'm going to get Ernie's autograph." After what seemed like a lifetime, even though it was only about four years, and watching all those games on TV and a few at the stadium, Carlos' strategy and Darrel's dream seemed to be coming true.

Ernie managed to find time for these kids and their families in his Big League schedule. After the game at Wrigley that hot August day, Ernie drove to Hammond to keep his appointment with the Hessville Little Leaguers and their families. The speech was scheduled after dinner but the empty seat beside the podium kept the eager boys, especially Darrel, too nervous to enjoy their meal.

From the back of the banquet hall, when everyone was enjoying their dessert, a raucous of nervous excitement broke out. There, bigger than life, wearing a gray suit, white shirt and tie, and flashing that amazing smile, was Ernie Banks in person. Darrel stood at his table to get a better look, but his dad grabbed his arm and told him to sit down and mind his manners.

"This is all wrong, Dad. Those guys in the back are getting his autograph, and I'll never get to talk to him." A mob of worshipping kids surrounded Ernie. He signed a bunch of programs and laughed as he maneuvered his way to the platform. The parents managed to get the boys back in their seats as Ernie passed. Darrel tried to be happy to see Ernie but couldn't believe he would get this close and not be able to meet him or get an autograph. "Be patient, Darrel. We'll try to get it after Ernie speaks and before he leaves," Carlos told Darrel, trying to save the evening so Darrel could enjoy the speech.

Darrel was on the edge of his seat, right in front of the podium. Ernie did not waste the opportunity to be a positive influence on this crowd. "When you go to play, play hard. When you go to work, work hard. And when you go to pray, pray hard. And learn to tell the truth and you will never have to remember what you said."

As Ernie wrapped up he said, "Before I go, I want you all to know I realize I'm a role model for a lot of your kids. I understand what that means. I understand there is someone here who pitched a no-hitter this year." Darrel, thought, "I pitched a no hitter." "And there is a young man here who is an all-star short stop and wants to be one like I am." Again, Darrel thought, "That sounds like me." "I also understand there's a young man in the audience who wants to be a Big Leaguer like me." "I want to. He must be talking about me." "I would like to meet that young man. So, Darrel Chaney, would you please come up here." Darrel, with his mouth wide open in awe, looked at his dad and then his mom and was getting out of his seat and squeezing his way between the backs of chairs as he made his way toward the platform. Carlos handed Darrel a program and pulled a pen from his pocket. "While you're up there, get that autograph!"

Carlos knew what he was doing when he arranged for that front table. The applause died down as Darrel approached his hero at the podium. Ernie put his arm around him and said, "Now Darrel, tell the audience the truth. What do you really want to be when you grow up?" He said, "Mr. Banks, all I ever want to be is a Major League Baseball Player, just like you!" Ernie took the program and signed it and said to him in front of 1,000 kids, moms and dads, "I'll see you in the Big Leagues!"

Darrel took the autographed program home and hung it next to the crucifix above his bed. Ernie's words settled in his mind, heart and soul, and they were lived out in his actions. He played hard, worked hard, prayed hard and told the truth, so he could make it to the Big Leagues.

For the next three years, Darrel played with the Tigers in the Hessville Babe Ruth League. There were no dugouts, fences or sponsors for the boys who wanted to play at the next level. They sat on a solitary bench when they were not in the field and a few parents watched from a six-step set of wood bleachers behind them. The boy who could hit a ball into the patch of woods beyond left field was awarded a home run. Darrel, a natural lefty, learned to switch-hit with the supervision and permission of his manager, his dad. It worked. He hit home runs and batted from both sides of the plate for the rest of his baseball career.

Next was Hessville Post 232 of the American Legion, which sponsored the team for 16, 17 and 18-year-olds who played their home games at Hessville Park. At this age, the team experienced road games, playing other American Legion teams in nearby towns. Mr. Hankins managed Darrel's team effectively, and with only one arm. In an accident at the manufacturing plant of American Can Company, he lost his left arm. He could still hit grounders for infield practice by throwing the ball up and grabbing the bat from under his right arm with the same hand, then swing it in time to hit hard grounders to the infielders as well as high-pops to the outfielders.

Dale McReynolds, a scout for the Reds, saw Darrel tear it up in American Legion with a .462 batting average. The day after that meeting in the living room when Darrel signed with the Reds, Mr. Hankins announced to the team and to the parents, "It is with sadness and pride that I tell you, tonight will be Darrel's last game with us. He's signed with the Cincinnati Reds and will be leaving tomorrow for the minor leagues."

The Reds drafted Darrel in the second round of the Rookie Draft, the same draft in which the Athletics took Reggie Jackson in the first round, and the Twins got Steve Garvey in the third round. Twenty two of the sixty in that draft made it to the Big Leagues.

After he signed with the Reds in the living room of his home surrounded by his family, Darrel only had one day to say his good-byes. The next day at

7:00 in the morning, Dale McReynolds picked him up and put him on a plane at O'Hare airport for a flight to Sioux Falls, SD. Darrel had become a member of the Reds' Class A Rookie League team, the Packers. He only batted .206 on a team whose average was .177 but playing at the next level was a huge step toward his dream.

His first summer as a pro wrapped up in early September. After a couple weeks at home, Darrel headed to the Instructional League in Clearwater, Florida, where the Astros and Reds took their high picks, the players with the most potential, to develop their skills. Hard work and a lot of practice didn't bother Darrel because he had a great work ethic and, after all, it was all going to help him make it to the Big Leagues. At times, Darrel would get to play with Big Leaguers because they would come down to the Instructional League to work on their timing, get some more at-bats and find a way to fit some more baseball into their year.

In 1966 baseball was not a lucrative career. The dream was to play the game, travel to America's great cities, win, and have your name included with your hero's on scoreboards, in newspapers and on baseball cards. During the off-season, Darrel would get a job at home, in the city of Hammond. Even though he was thankful for a little money, the job only made him dream about baseball as he drove up and down the alleys of Hammond making sure people put their trash cans where they were supposed to after garbage pick-up.

Darrel had a successful spring and jumped up to the AA Knoxville Smokies to play ball under manager, Don Zimmer. But his baseball season was cut short so he could serve his country in the Army Reserves. His Big League toughness and skills were developed in others ways; through basic training at Ft. Campbell, Kentucky and Advanced Individual Training at Ft. Sill, in Lawton, OK. Six months of mandatory active duty had to be completed before he could return to baseball.

On Christmas day, 1967, Cindy Pajak, Darrel's childhood sweetheart and square dancing partner, all the way back to ten years of age, agreed to marry Darrel. Their marriage in February of '68 began in the uncertain world of the professional baseball player. Even after missing a year of baseball, Darrel was invited to Spring training in Clearwater, Florida. When the season started, he played for the Asheville, North Carolina Tourists AA Team, managed by Sparky Anderson.

In all he did Darrel's focus remained clear. Along the journey the words of Ernie Banks connected with his commitment to work hard, play hard, pray hard and tell the truth, in order to make it to the Big Leagues. After three years in the Minors and at the end of Spring training, the suspense increased. What was the next step? Did he have what was required? Were the right people making note of his progress and, if so, would he find favor in their eyes? Was it going to be another year in the Minors? Would he go up a notch, or down? Would he even be released, return to Hammond with his new bride, and get a permanent job with the city of Hammond?

On the last day of 1969 Spring Training, Darrel still did not know what was next. Manager Davey Bristol of the Big League Club scheduled meetings with Clyde Mayshore and Darrel. One more spot was available. The rest of the team already knew that they had made it, were heading for the Minors, or worse, going home. In the locker room, for Darrel and Clyde, the mood was tense. They knew that one would experience the thrill of making it to the Big Leagues and the other's dream would be deferred. Today, one player would take the giant leap closer to his dream and the other would step back into the Minors and, perhaps, closer to the biggest disappointment of his young life.

Clyde's appointment was first. Darrel sat nervously in the locker room, with sweaty palms, dry mouth and butterflies in his stomach wondering what was going on behind closed doors.

The door opened and Clyde came out crying. He tried to hide his emotions and profound disappointment. Clyde quickly made the painful walk to his locker where he packed his belongings and headed out to another season of trying to prove himself. He would not be part of a team which was getting ready to begin a Big League season filled with hope and potential.

Darrel was pretty sure he made the team and his meeting with Davey was brief and to the point. Yet, it was not until he heard the words from Dave's mouth that he could really breathe again. "Congratulations Darrel, you made the club."

On April 11th, Darrel's first game experience was to pinch-run for Fred Whitefield in the top of the ninth inning in the Reds' 6-4 loss to Atlanta.

On April 19th, the eighth game of the 1969 season, Darrel took the field as a Big Leaguer for the first time. Bob Aspromonte hit a grounder to Darrel who threw him out at first for his first big league defensive play. Darrel went 0 for 3 that day but he was not alone in a low performance. The Reds were shut out.

Darrel's first time with the Reds playing the Cubs was a three-game series early in June. Every game mattered but this game was at Wrigley Field. Darrel would not be in the stands watching as Big Leaguers played America's favorite past time. Instead of sitting on the couch in his living room watching other guys on TV, he was on the field, in the game and the TV announcer was calling his name.

As Cubs' fans were arriving, Ernie Banks was down the third base line as always, spending time with the kids and giving autographs. Darrel was on the field running his warm-up sprints, hitting batting practice and getting ready to take the field, but part of his attention was still focused on Ernie Banks.

Ernie's influence had been a presence in Darrel's life in his formative years and his climb to the Big Leagues. He looked at the autograph on his Hessville Little League program countless times, "I'll see you in the Big Leagues." The words and even his voice from the Little League banquet often rang in Darrel's ears and thoughts. "When you work, work hard and when you play, play hard and when you pray, pray hard. And always tell the truth and you won't have to remember what you say." Darrel knew that Ernie had a significant part in his success and it felt as though he had been there through it all.

It matters what people think about you, especially if it is someone you consider to be significant. Darrel wanted to find a way to let Ernie know that he made it to the Big Leagues. If Ernie could only know a fraction of how much he meant to Darrel or as Darrel hoped, remember the words he wrote to Darrel, "I'll see you in the Big Leagues". Darrel was only a kid then, one of a countless number of fans whom Ernie met over those nine years, one of thousands to whom he gave an autograph. Even though Ernie cared, he could not possibly remember the kid from Hammond.

Players from the opposing teams did not fraternize in 1969. Darrel was going to have to meet Ernie on the field during the game but it would have to be natural, a perfect series of events. Darrel was nervous and excited at the thought of playing on the same field as Ernie. He was also a Big Leaguer now and he wanted Ernie to see that he not only made it, but that he also deserved to be there.

On Friday afternoon, Darrel came to bat at the top of the second inning with two outs and nobody on base. He took one more swing with two bats, tossed one bat down and made his way to the plate. Ernie was just 90 feet away. With his heart beating so hard he could feel it, he stepped in the batter's box for his first at-bat at Wrigley Field. He managed to contain his nerves and lay off the first pitch. With a 1 and 0 count, he jumped on the next pitch and hit a grounder which was caught on the second bounce by Nate Oliver, who then fired it to first for the third out of the inning.

Tommy Helms drew a walk to open the fifth inning. Darrel took the plate, only a little less nervous but no less determined to reach first. With the count, two balls and two strikes, he went down swinging. In the sixth inning Jim Beauchamp pinch-hit for Darrel who would come out of the game. He would not get to first this game but he used his glove for four putouts in the field: a high pop-hit by Willie Smith, a line drive by Ron Santo, a double play on a grounder from Don Kessinger and a pop-fly by Billy Williams. The Cubs won 14 to 8.

Saturday afternoon was a great day for a ball game. The crowd was full of excited people off for the weekend, out with family and friends, and excited to watch their first-place Cubs play baseball. Everybody around Darrel knew he was the most excited one at the ball park. Even the press knew Darrel wanted to meet Ernie. The human interest story of the kid who made it to the "Bigs" and got to play with his hero, made the sports page. But, once again, Darrel's dream would be deferred when he led off the third inning with a ground-out to the short stop. In the top of the fifth, he missed Ernie again but he let him know he could hit when he lined a double in the gap to right field.

In the top of the seventh, Darrel came up after Johnny Bench grounded out and Tommy Helms doubled to center field. In the on-deck circle, Darrel cast a glance at his proud parents who were sitting near the field on the visitors' side. Darrel gave them the tickets he was allotted as a player and Carlos had the day off from Sinclair. His eyes filled with tears as he saw his son batting in a Big League ball game.

Darrel dug in at the plate, cocked his bat and locked on Bill Hands for his wind up. His first pitch was a curve ball. Darrel hit it on the end of the bat and it was a bouncer to second. Tommy who was running was safe at third and Darrel, with good speed, in a bang-bang play, stretched to beat the throw at first.

"Safe," the umpire yelled and spread his arms out with palms down. It took Darrel ten steps to slow down and he turned into foul territory and walked back to the bag. With his left foot on first and his hands on his knees he glanced at his parents and bowed his head for a quick and simple prayer, "Thank you God for getting me here." An arm reached around his shoulder and he looked over to see the hand that grabbed him. He thought it was the first base coach giving him instructions on what to do with runners on the corners and one out, but it was a large black hand. Darrel snapped straight up and looked his hero right in the eyes from just inches away.

"Darrel Chaney. I knew you'd make it! Welcome to the Big Leagues!!"

Then in front of 36,000 people Ernie Banks gave the kid from Hammond a Big League hug.

Did Ernie remember Darrel? Did he read it in the paper or did someone tell him the story? Who cares? It didn't matter.

It was a defining moment for both of them. Ernie received the reward of living the life of a role model. Darrel experienced affirmation from his hero and the realization that he had made it to the Big Leagues.

Bottom of the Second

EVERY MAN NEEDS A HERO — EVERY MAN NEEDS TO BE A HERO

"Even when I am old and gray, do not forsake me,
my God, till I declare your power to the next generation,
your mighty acts to all who are to come."
Psalm 71:18

"The world's battlefields have been in the heart chiefly;
more heroism has been displayed in the household and the closet,
than on the most memorable battlefields in history."
Henry Ward Beecher (1813-1887) American politician.

We need heroes.

Having a hero expands our world. It connects the dream God gave us using a real person that inspires each of us to believe that we have both purpose and potential. That purpose and potential becomes strength and determination when attempting difficult challenges, taking high risks, and achieving monumental results.

Laura Boswell, Editor of *Healthy Kids Magazine***,** wrote, "From Amelia Earhart to modern-day heroes, we all need role models to look up to—people who inspire us to new heights. For children, too, heroes are important in that they help kids overcome fears, set personal goals and accept challenges."

"It's important that kids have these kinds of heroes as they demonstrate a way of making the impossible attainable; it gives children something to stretch for," said **Rebecca Elder, Ph.D., St. Louis Children's Hospital.**

Ernie Banks was a sports hero that made a difference in Darrel's life.

I am old enough now, to look back over my life and identify a few men who measured up to the level of hero in my life. It was not in sports and, at the time, I did not recognize their hero qualities. Yet, I recognized their attributes as mentors or encouragers in the struggles of ministry and everyday life.

My Dad rises to the top of a small list of my heroes. Grief jolted me in my approach to the first anniversary of his death. A big part of grief work is learning to live with a piece of you missing. I did not realize how big of a piece of my life he was. It is too often true that you don't know what you have until you don't have it anymore.

We had a genuine, respectful and strong relationship even though it was long distance. The only thing that separated us was miles. As an adult I never lived closer than a couple hundred miles from where I grew up. College took me seven states away from home and my ministry opportunities never brought me much closer. Opportunities scattered around the country had the most appeal to me.

Dad did not like to travel. Most of the times I saw him, it was on our annual vacation back home. Maybe he blamed me for moving away but I only thought it made sense to expand my world and pursue opportunities of ministry in exciting places. Occasionally in the early years, he and Mom would visit us but he was not comfortable being away from home and he always had a reason to hurry back. My kids knew their grandfather and what he stood for but they did not get to have many conversations or enjoy hanging out with him.

The bigness of his life existed in his unwavering commitments to God and His church, to our great country and to his family. He lived beneath his means, spent less than he earned, saved a little, gave at least his 10% tithe and, beyond that, was generous to those in need.

He epitomized the greatest generation—what he did in WW II was heroic. And he has the medals to prove it. He never talked about them or showed them to me but after he died, I was reading his discharge papers and learned that he earned battle medals with clusters for service "above and beyond the normal call of duty."

Normal duty was as a machine gunner on a B-17 named "Lassie Come Home". On June 7th, 1943, Dad was in the belly of the plane for his 28th bombing mission. This time, he and the crew of 10 were loaded up for a bombing raid over Germany, headed for Berlin.

Grandma's battle was fought through prayer. She devoted every Wednesday to prayer. For hours at a time, she would remember, by name, missionaries, pastors, churches, the sick, neighbors and families in need asking God to bless, protect and care for them and be glorified by their lives. Dad credits his survival to his mother's prayers.

Resistance was tough on the flight that Wednesday in June 1944. There was flak and fighter fire. Debriefing reports revealed that his plane was hit by fire from a diving fighter. When Dad saw the wing on fire he knew they were going down. He immediately unmanned his 50 Caliber machine gun, ripped off his oxygen mask, and turned for the door at the back of the fuselage where he was going to bail out at 25,000 feet. It would be his first jump. Before he got to the door, the many sounds of war—racing engines, guns firing, men screaming and the burning plane with the g-forces throwing him beyond his control—crescendoed into a fiery explosion and the debris of "Lassie Come Home" fell to earth. The sound of the wind from a free fall was all he could hear but he did not remember how he got out of the plane nor did he remember pulling the rip cord to deploy his parachute. He knew that he must have because he remembered reaching the ground, the throbs of a severely sprained ankle greeting him, along with a handful of German farmers with pitchforks, shovels, and a shotgun. There was no time to find his missing chute. He was carted off, put in a cell with stone walls in the back corner of the local jail until German soldiers came and took him. He was made an official Prisoner of War for the next 11 months, housed in one of Germany's five major Stalags for U.S. and Allied Forces prisoners. Five of his crew never saw another day.

Maybe that had something to do with why he did not like to travel. When he got stateside, he built the life he fought for and his buddies died for. He did not drink or go to parties in college—college was for education. His social life was simple. He would go hunting and fishing with Jack Connelly, Uncle Stuart and his buddies. He met his Geri Young at church. They were married, lived in a little upstairs apartment of his parents' house until he built his own on an adjoining lot. During the booming 50's, that is what a man did, and my Dad did it with faith and devotion. He kept his job at Lycoming for more than forty years. It is a plant where small airplane engines are still manufactured.

He avoided the vices of smoking and drinking—he saw enough of that during the war and did not believe it pleased God.

For many years, he taught Sunday School classes to young boys, sent many of them to Susque Boys Camp and, beyond his expectations, became a hero of at least one of those boys. I know, because in an amazing twist of fate, I met him 45 years and 1,600 miles away from that class. When I met Bob Newton in Colorado at my church, he asked me if I was from Williamsport, Pennsylvania and if Bob Hettinger was my dad. After my affirmative answer he said, "He was my Sunday School teacher when I was a boy and, when I went to college and they asked, 'What man in your life do you most want to emulate,' I said, your Dad."

Dad cared for his parents and when my widowed Grandfather could not live alone anymore, he and Mom took him in. One momentous day, my 97-year-old grandfather told my Dad something that was long overdue. He called him to his side in the bedroom where he was living. My dad sat beside his wheelchair. Grandpap placed his still strong and impressive hand on my Dad's leg and said, "You are a good son. I love you and I bless you."

My Dad, in his late 70's, did not seem to need anything but he was waiting a lifetime to hear those words. In the late years of his life, they meant everything to him and he did not want my brother and me to have to wait as long. While he was not frequent in telling us that he loved us, he did. It was not a routine expression at the end of a phone call or the appropriate thing to say when we left Pennsylvania at the end of one of our rare visits. He really meant it when he said it but he wanted us to have even more.

The feeling of completion and strength that he received when my Grandfather blessed him was a Biblical reality that he would give to my brother and me. I admit it felt awkward to sit with him standing beside me, his hand on my head as he prayed God's blessing over and into my life—maybe it was because my wife and kids were watching. The unfamiliarity of it was uncomfortable but beneath that self-consciousness was an undeniable feeling that this was right. It was strengthening my soul and would transcend all of my circumstances.

Dad never departed from those values and commitments through his life and he finished the way he lived. He followed the example of his mother and intensely prayed for my brother and me, our wives and our kids, until the day he died. In the wee hours of the morning, the week before he died of acute leukemia, his pain was out of control. I was afraid he was going to die with just the two of us there as he cried out in pain. There was the hope that he was going to Heaven but he wanted, one more time, to pray for each of his family by name and ask God to care for and bless his wife, his sons, their wives and each of his grandchildren. The pain meds began to do their work and he was able to go to sleep, but his hero status was forever engrained in my mind.

Ernie Banks had talents and opportunities that gave him a platform to be a hero to many adoring fans. He worked hard to be the best shortstop he could be and he played the game with intensity and excellence. He also used those opportunities to make a difference in the life of someone as impressionable as Darrel.

Bob Hettinger also had a platform that came from being a dad, a WW II veteran, a hard-working man who built a house and made it a home for his family. He used his platform to make a difference in the lives of his sons, and, at least for me, in ways that were not always understood or esteemed with the value he and his actions deserved.

As different as Ernie and Dad were in their platforms, talents, and lifestyles, they were alike in embodying the traits of true heroes.

They both lived life as though it mattered.

I wonder what Ernie thought after his speaking engagement with the Hessville Little League. Did he really expect to see the 12-year-old Darrel in the Big Leagues? If he is like most public speakers, on his ride home, he was thinking about what he should have said and did not, what he did not say and should have, and already planning to do better on his next speech. He was probably not so full of his own importance that he thought, "I said what I should have, the way I wanted to, and the kids listened attentively and received just what they needed so I am sure their lives will be changed because of their encounter with me tonight."

When I called my Dad and told him I met one of his students from a class he taught many years earlier, he quickly remembered the boy in his class, Bob Newton. When I told him how much Bob admired him, my Dad was shocked to think that his meager efforts at his first teaching opportunity to that small class on Sunday afternoons, made a life-long impact on one of his students. I also doubt he realized how much I admired him and the way he lived his life, as well as the magnitude of his influence on me.

For both Ernie and Dad the results were immeasurable. There was a conviction that you do what is right because it matters, even if nobody is looking and you cannot see an immediate result. There is meaning to our lives that is bigger than we are. We are given a life to live in a way that we can make a difference. God will work in and through our lives to accomplish something too big to measure. Whatever they did, they did it as though it mattered. And it did.

They took time to give attention to others.

Big Leaguers do not need to speak to Little Leaguers—not at banquets nor for autographs before or after games.

Dads have their own interests and problems. How can a young man find time to teach a bunch of boys who really do not want to be in a class on a Sunday afternoon? Why would a dad, who was getting old, spend the time to think about the need to bless his sons and how he was going to do it?

Taking time for others costs something and heroes are willing to pay that cost. They know their life is expanded in what they give to others. Their satisfaction comes in giving themselves away.

They gave hope and vision to someone's future.

An experience in the 12-year-old Darrel's distant future was established when Ernie blessed Darrel with the words, "I will see you in the Big Leagues." For the next nine years, there was a vision in Darrel's heart and mind of an encounter on a Big League field in a Big League game.

Bob Newton taught kids in my church 45 years after being in my Dad's class. It was not his first time to lead a children's ministry. He saw in Dad something that he liked and he saw it in a way that made him think, "I want to do that. I can do that." And throughout his adult life, he did just that.

Ministry has been very different than I dreamed it would be when I was in Bible College learning Theology and taking Preaching Classes. My naiveté had visions of grandeur with little cost, no conflict or suffering.

But, in spite of my immersion into the harsh realities of leading people, even after many years with many struggles and disappointments, my energy and hope for life and ministry continues to grow. I realize that God gave me the hope of a future, the trust for results from the example and blessing of my Dad. It is not the results that I see that count, but the confidence in knowing that my life matters to God and is producing fruit even when I do not see it. I know my life matters because it did to my Dad, who assured me that my life and my work matter to God, as well. I can expect greater things in the future because he put his hand on my head and spoke blessing into my life and into my future.

In the book, <u>Letters From Dad</u>, Greg Vaughn, describes three types of blessings.

"First are General Blessings."

"Second are Blessings from God to Christians."

"Third are the Blessings we can give to each other." (From the book, <u>Letters From Dad</u>, by Greg Vaughn, Grace Products Corporation)

Blessings are spoken into our lives like Ernie did to Darrel or in a formal ceremony, like my Dad prayed over me. Every man longs for a Blessing. We have the power to speak blessing into another's life.

We value words of appreciation and positive affirmation. They are not mentioned often enough in the course of everyday life and we long to hear them. Just a word can fuel a man's motivation and energy. It can be the blessing that a young boy or another man is looking for.

Words can give a future to hope in, to strive toward and to work for.

The person who means the most to us is the one who has listened to our dreams and observed our talents and determination; one who has given us a vision for our future and, actually, gave us a future to live for. Perspiration, sacrifice, and struggles will not stop us in our pursuit of it because we are filled with strength of purpose and character. Whatever the endeavor, there is the assurance we have made it to the Big Leagues.

They recognized someone's accomplishment and conferred honor on the one who achieved it.

When Ernie greeted Darrel at first base with the words, "I knew you'd make it, welcome to the Big Leagues" and, with the physical touch of his arm around the shoulder and the hug in front of the 36,000 fans and fellow Big Leaguers, his recognition honored Darrel and conferred upon him the reality that Darrel was a Big Leaguer. The road ahead would not be easy. That reality would be tested with a year back in the Minors, time on the bench, boos from the fans, difficulty with the bat and drama in his personal life with moves, finances, and the death of his mother.

Experiences of affirmation, similar to the one Ernie gave to Darrel, do not happen every day—they are rare. But if we experience just a couple of them in our lives, they become defining moments that last throughout a career or maybe a lifetime. One of my Dad's proudest moments was the day of my ordination. He travelled to see that ceremony. He even stayed for the reception afterwards and celebrated at our house in Ohio. A few times over the years, especially after a difficult battle or in the middle of a painful struggle, he would remind me that I was in something much bigger than I could see. This was God's work— it was the Big Leagues. It was for Him, it would be by Him, and the results were up to Him.

A lot of men have never heard anyone say, in any way, shape, or form, I am proud of you; you have made it; you are a man; your life matters; you are in the Big Leagues.

Without even realizing it, men's spirits are thirsty for this blessing and confirmation.

If a man has not received this type of confirmation from a significant man in his life—a hero—then he needs to pray for and look for a man who will pronounce this significance and blessing into his life.

This reality also empowers each man to become a hero.

John Trent instructs fathers on how to be heroes by pronouncing a blessing to their children in the classic book, The Blessing. Through meaningful touch, spoken words, expression of high value, a vision of a special future, and an active commitment, all of the ingredients of an effective game plan are in the playbook. (From the book, The Blessing by John Trent, Pocket Books)

If baseball teams have scouts for skills and talents who recruit, sign, coach and train, then certainly pastors, churches and men of God can also produce the environment where every man can hear the words, "I will see you in the Big Leagues" and then some day celebrate the reality, "I knew you'd make it. Welcome to the Big Leagues."

What's the Score at the
End of the Second Inning?

What has been hit to you?

- Who is your hero?
- Has any significant man blessed your life? Told you that you matter? Affirmed your skills and talents? Cared about your dreams? Given you hope for a bright future?

When you are up to bat, what are you going to do?

- Pray for God to bring admirable men into your life?
- Who, in your life, needs a hero?
- What can you do to bless him?

The Middle Innings

Facing the Competition

The Third Inning

Resilience

Big League Rookie

Top of the Third

SURVIVING AN AMBUSH ON "DARREL CHANEY DAY"

"What then, shall we say in response to these things?
If God is for us, who can be against us?"
Romans 8:31

"The greatest of human freedom is my right to
choose my attitude in any given situation."
Victor Frankl

Every man who wants to play in the Big Leagues had better be ready to face the competition.

Competition from the other team is an expected source of resistance. It is intense, planned and focused so the other guy, whether friend or foe, attempts to defeat you and put you in the loser's bracket.

Sometimes a man is his own greatest competition. The struggle comes from within. Doubts, fears and wounds that he did not know existed rise up to compete against him when he is making decisions. His performance, even his ability to dream or hope is weakened. They will provoke him to defeat himself if he does not defeat them first.

Just living life with changes, injuries, sickness and forces beyond anyone's control produce challenging competition that bring drama, sometimes trauma, to every area of life. It feels like life is going uphill and into the wind. Strength, determination, endurance and some outside help are requirements to persevere in life's storms.

These experiences, some deep and dark, can come in unexpected ways, at times when a man least expects them and from surprising sources.

The next five chapters address battles that threaten the dream in every man's life. However, he is created to win these battles in his effort to make it in the Big Leagues and God reveals a game plan for every opponent, distraction or force that comes against him.

• • • • •

Hammond, Indiana—-July 22, 1970. Of all the people who woke up that warm spring morning, for at least three of them, it was going to be a memorable day.

Bruce Pardoe woke up with a manic exuberance that made the clock seem as though it were standing still. The 11-year-old's normal high energy was turbo-charged because the avowed baseball lover was going to watch a game at historic Wrigley Field. He, along with approximately 2,000 others in Hammond, was going to make the short trip to Chicago to watch one of their own play baseball on the hallowed grounds. It was Darrel Chaney Day at Wrigley Field!

"Mom!" Bruce practically screamed as he entered the kitchen. "When do we leave for the buses?"

"Dad!" He asked hastily, not waiting for an answer, "have you got the tickets?"

Bruce sat down at the table and poured himself a bowl of Post Raisin Bran cereal—2 scoops of healthy goodness but, more importantly, the best source of cereal-box baseball cards. His well-worn Spalding glove—a Willie Mays signature series, was lying on the table, underneath his Little League baseball cap with an Astro's logo, the team for which Bruce played while in the Hessville Little League. Not that many years ago, Darrel had played in the same league, which served as another reason for Bruce's excitement as he wolfed down his breakfast manically. Wiping the last vestiges of a milk-mustache off with his sleeve, Bruce grabbed his glove, placed his cap onto his unkempt red hair and bolted out the door, heading straight to his teammate and best friend, Davey Cole's house.

It was going to be an extra-special day!

• • • • •

Darrel awoke that morning with the same type of excitement, somewhat refined by age but not much. Always the clown, he skipped into the kitchen to his Mom's famous bacon and eggs, singing, to the tune of "Happy Birthday", "Happy Darrel Chaney day to me, happy Darrel Chaney Day to you, Happy Darrel Chaney Day to everybody, today is MY day!"

Mom just rolled her eyes.

"Just sit down and eat your eggs," said his dad, matter-of-factly, "Save the celebration for the ball park."

The previous night, Hammond's finest turned out to recognize Darrel's newly-found success, with a banquet in his honor. Among those in attendance were some of Darrel's Reds' teammates: Pete Rose, Tony Cloninger, Pat Corrales, Jim Merrit and Woody Woodward (Darrel's road trip roomie). He even repeated a joke Pete Rose had told when he addressed the assembled crowd. In trying to put a pretty face on an ugly rookie year which saw Darrel bat an anemic .191, he proclaimed that he was going to turn things around and be comeback player of the year. When the seasoned Rose heard that, he retorted good-humouredly, yet painfully honest, "You can't be a comeback player because you haven't been there yet!"

Everyone laughed and no one's spirit was dampened by Darrel's struggles at the plate. He was a Big League baseball player, playing for the mighty Cincinnati Reds and that mustered the hope of everyone in his hometown. Sitting at the same table where he ate his breakfast when the Big Leagues were still just a dream, Darrel relished the reality that his dream had come true. Since Hammond was close to Chicago, Darrel was allowed to stay at home with his family instead of at the hotel with the team. A home-cooked meal seemed a fitting way to begin such a special day but his mother was beginning to show a bit of her own nervous excitement even before Darrel finished his bacon and eggs. "Darrel, hurry up!" She hollered with a sense of urgency. "You don't want to be late for your own day!"

"No problem, mom." Darrel replied, "I've got plenty of time." Deep down, he, too, was nervous. Enough so, that he left Hammond early and was the first player at the field that day.

· · · · ·

In stark contrast to little Bruce and the second-year Big-Leaguer-Darrel, a bitter soul also arose to face the day. He, too, would be a part of the 2,000 from Hammond who were going to Chicago.

Let's call him Scrooge.

Scrooge was as angry as everyone else was excited. He was also a star athlete growing up in Hammond and was, in fact, a competitor of Darrel's in high school. The AAAA State Football Championship newspaper clippings were still plastered on the wall of his room. But he was not the big star that Darrel was and thus, had to live in Darrel's shadow. He was not a Parade High School All-American quarterback who got 25 college scholarship offers nor did he get any offers from a Major League Baseball team. Perhaps it was the pictures that stirred this bitterness, this jealousy, serving as a painful reminder of what, in his mind, should have been.

Breakfast was quiet as Scrooge stared into his cereal bowl. His dad and mom were divorced, leaving just Scrooge and his mom. "Aren't you and a few buddies going to the ball game today?" she asked, breaking the silence.

"Yeah," he mumbled, "we're goin'."

"You ought to be happy, son," she said, encouragingly, as any mom does who wants to see her son happy but hasn't a clue where to start. "You'll probably see your old friend Darrel, play. You should be proud to have known a guy who made it to the Big leagues."

"Yeah, right, that'll be great!" Scrooge snarled sarcastically. "It'd be better if I was playing and Darrel was coming to watch me."

No, instead of wanting to celebrate his friend's success, Scrooge had something else in mind for Darrel Chaney Day.

· · · · ·

A crowd was beginning to assemble at St. Michael's Ukrainian Hall. Nearly 30 buses were formed in the parking lot as people began to climb aboard. The characteristic idling of the diesel engines and the smell of exhaust fumes permeated the normally quiet location. Bruce Pardoe's parents, particularly his mom tried in vain, to keep him close so as not to get lost among the throng. Every time she grabbed for his arm, Bruce was like that fly who kept getting away—right there but just out of reach. "Bruce!" she scolded, "don't get lost. We've all got to keep together."

"But Mom," Bruce whined back, "can I please sit with Davie? We want to trade baseball cards."

Without further incident, they boarded the same bus as the Cole's and the two eagerly found their seats. They made quite the pair, with matching sweat-stained baseball caps pulled down to their ears and the visors bent at a precise angle, not so much to keep the sun out of their eyes but to signify that they were ballplayers. Indeed, they looked like they were ready to play in a game themselves, wearing their Astros Little League jerseys, dirt-covered PF Flyers and baseball gloves big enough to cover their skinny pre-adolescent arms. As the bus began the relatively short trek to Chicago, Bruce and Davie were lost in their own worlds, sharing their cache of baseball cards.

Scrooge and his buddies were older than Bruce and Davie. They were Darrel's age, in their early 20's, and were too cool to act excited. They slumped into their seats in the back of a different bus, rough-housing and joking with each other in ways which separated them from the rest of the crowd. They were trying to conceal a banner that Scrooge had made with much thought and skill at home, and were laughing while thinking about their plans of displaying it at the game.

The "Darrel Chaney Day" banners, the presence of Mayor Joseph Klen, Darrel's high school baseball coaches, Greg Jancich and Jack Georgas, his Little League coach, George Wimmer, and other local dignitaries left this bunch unimpressed, at least, they behaved that way. Scrooge seemed to resent it.

It took an hour and a half to get to Chicago. Mom and Dad enjoyed a few quiet moments of reflection and pride. They were as proud as any human could be. "Imagine, our son made it to the Big Leagues and all our friends and neighbors are celebrating with us."

Mayor Klen shook more hands that day than he had all year. The kids kept the noise level up on the busses with their chatter. The roar of the wind through the open windows blew girls' hair, occasionally ruffled a newspaper or tried to steal a baseball card out of the window to the screams of the boy who was about to lose it and flailed his arms to knock it down to safety.

Earlier, Darrel had kissed his Mom good-bye and told his Dad, sister and brother, "I'll see you at the ball park."

The excitement of driving to Wrigley Field, to park in the player's parking lot, dress in the locker room and actually set foot on the field was almost too much to comprehend.

Even more today, Darrel pondered, "My name will be flashed on the scoreboard. Ernie Banks and the Mayor will have a ceremony at home plate; 32,000 people will recognize my achievement, especially the great folks from Hammond. It is too good to be true." Darrel saw it more as the fulfillment of a dream than the celebration of accomplishment. He knew he was blessed.

The magnitude of the moment almost took the joy away and replaced the excitement with nervousness. Alone in his car, with the window rolled down and the wind blowing through his hair, he thought how blessed he was. "For all the kids who play Little League, the hundreds of thousands, and for the thousands who play in Minor League, less than a thousand each summer play in the Big Leagues—thank you, God! Thank you, Mom and Dad! Thanks Coach Jancich and Coach Georgas! Thank you, thank you, thank you everyone!"

The long caravan of buses rumbled and roared toward the city, creating a scene which drew the attention of those not fortunate enough to be part of this fun, huge excursion of happy and excited passengers.

The scenery changed as the buses headed across the Calumet Bridge to Lake Shore Drive and then in to the city. Passengers craned their necks to catch the sight of the magnificence of the tall buildings in Chicago. The bus engines roared as the drivers down-shifted, then slowed and merged with the city traffic on their approach to Wrigley Field. The engines slowed to a more quiet idle, the air-brakes hissed and people began to move about and grab their belongings as the buses stopped at the curb. The doors opened and the built-up anticipation was about to be released.

Families regrouped, distributed the tickets and proceeded to the turnstiles. Bruce and Davie were overcome by the awesomeness of the moment and feared they might get lost. This was the big city and a Big League ballpark, almost bigger than life itself!!

"Programs, get your programs! Programs, get your programs here; thirty five cents!" filled their ears. The smell of hotdogs and popcorn stirred their olfactory senses; the hustle and bustle of the crowd; people talking as they walked; checking tickets; ushers helping people locate their seats, all of which produced the environment unique to a baseball stadium. After all this fun, the best was yet to come because they still had a ball game to watch and their favorite players from both teams, Pete, Johnny, Ernie and Darrel, would be there. Just attending a game at Wrigley Field was a special event.

Darrel parked in the players' parking lot; he was the first player to arrive. Most of the Cubs parked there, but the Reds arrived on the team bus. He may not have become famous yet, but his 6'1" athletic frame, suit, and sunglasses revealed that he was not just one of the fans. Here was a Big Leaguer!!

Darrel arrived at the players' entrance and found his locker. For a moment, he looked around at the empty locker room and savored that he was part of this Big League team. Rose, Bench, Morgan, and Anderson were the names on the jerseys. Chaney was also on a jersey, above the #12, and ready for Darrel to dress and head out for pre-game warm ups.

Scrooge and his cronies made it to their seats with feelings of excitement overshadowed by jealousy and the dastardly deed they were about to perform. They were scoping out the best place to display their banner where Darrel would be sure to see it. They sat in the upper level above first base, with the rest of the Hammond fans. It was sad that in the reality of percentages where less than 2% of baseball players made it to the Big Leagues, and that one of their peers had beat the odds, resentment, rather than celebration, had dominated their souls.

Bruce and Davie closely followed their parents through the crowd, trying to take in the sights and sounds of the vendors and booths. "Mom, can I have some cotton candy." "Not yet, Bruce." "Get me a souvenir bat, those little ones that say Cubs on it, Dad." "Later, Davie."

Dad looked down at his ticket. Bruce and Davie had been squeezing theirs as though their lives depended on it. Aisle 323, Row 24, Seat, 9. Now the rest of the family looked for their seats, same aisle and row but seats 6, 7 and 8. Davie's family was in a different row but with a little juggling and a patient usher, Davie and Bruce managed to sit together.

As they headed through the entrance to the aisle into the bright sunlight, a vista opened into the grandest, most spectacular sight their young eyes had ever beheld. Some older eyes still think it is the most awesome sight of their lifetime.

Below them was an expanse of green grass, big and broad enough to symbolize eternity. It ended only by the famous ivy fence which stopped the defense but not the hitters who could earn a trip around the bases and all the way home if they could hit a ball over it. Seats for 32,000 people and the skyline in the background had Bruce's and Davie's eyes the size of saucers and their mouths hanging open with a wordless expression of amazement, "Awwww."

And there, down on the field they were. The Big Leaguers, in real life. This was not TV. They were in person doing their pre-game warm-ups. Some were having batting practice, others were shagging flies or scooping up grounders. They were getting their muscles loose by throwing with each other or running their sprints from the base lines.

Everyone's eyes searched out all the sights but especially tried to see their baseball hero. Hey, there is Ernie Banks! I see Pete Rose. But, then, the excitement of the Hammond people took on an added excitement as they saw someone they knew and someone who knew them. "Darrel! It's Darrel!! #12. Running his sprints from first baseline." They hollered, "Hey Darrel!! Yeah Chaney!!!"

Darrel's eyes searched the stands for his family and friends. Earlier, he had come out and, as was his custom, did a "reverse blimp." Blimps looked down on the field from up high. Darrel would lay down on his back behind second base, look up and drink it in just as a thirsty cowboy gulps fresh water. He'd just lay there and, with the smell of popcorn and hotdogs which he remembered from his trips as a kid, he would pray, "Thank you, God, for putting me here."

On one of his sprints, he caught the glimpse of a large, well-done banner which was held up by Scrooge and his cronies. This banner took some thought and preparation. It was intentional and designed to have an impact.

Their first banner said, "Who is Darrel Chaney?"

"Pretty cool," Darrel thought, "after all, it is my day!" He noticed, but tried to act the Big Leaguer and not pay much attention.

A few sprints later, another banner was hung by the same conniving bunch. The "Who is Darrel Chaney?" banner was replaced by a new banner which exposed the intentions of the displayers.

It read, "Who cares?"

The expectation is for the opposing team and their fans to root against you; that is normal in competition. But, on "your day," to have someone from "your town" intentionally try to "rain on your parade" and steal your joy, is an emotional ambush in an unguarded moment. It is an unexpected way from an unexpected source that inflicts pain that hurts for years.

Prior to the national anthem, a ceremony was held at home plate where the mayor of Hammond handed Darrel the keys to a brand-new 1970 Pontiac Catalina, which he drove until the wheels fell off.

Darrel's hero, Ernie Banks, who was a part of the ceremony, joked with Darrel, "If you had played better last year, they might have given you a Cadillac."

Darrel didn't get to play much that game. The Cubs were beating the Reds, 10 to 2 by the sixth inning. Sparky Anderson wanted to get Darrel in the game and, in the eighth inning, he used him as a left-handed pinch-hitter against the right-handed pitcher, Bill Hands. Darrel grounded out and then played third, in place of Tony Perez, for the final inning.

The day was filled with many happy memories, especially for Bruce and Davie. Scrooge probably felt a sick sense of satisfaction. Darrel was conflicted—on one hand, grateful and as exhilarated as any 21-year-old experiencing celebrity status could be, but challenged with the reality that not everyone celebrated his success.

That ambush with the arrow of rejection struck his soul. It was not a defining event for his life, career, or even the day. But it lodged itself in his memory and worked, in combination with other arrows, to challenge his confidence and threaten his sense of significance and what it meant to be in the Big Leagues.

Bottom of the Third

EVERY MAN GETS AMBUSHED AND NEEDS A SURVIVAL STRATEGY

*"Do not repay anyone evil for evil. Be careful
to do what is right in the eyes of everyone.
Do not be overcome by evil, but overcome evil with good."*
Romans 12:17, 21

"Nobody can make me feel inferior…without my permission."
Eleanor Roosevelt

Darrel got ambushed on his own day—"Darrel Chaney Day" at Wrigley Field in Chicago. Every man, at some time in his life, experiences an ambush.

The element of surprise is what makes the ambush so dangerous. The victim is unprepared so he cannot properly respond to, or process the crisis. As he dusts himself off and assesses his injuries and losses, the wounds are often hard to detect. Physical wounds are easier to diagnose and treat than mental, emotional and spiritual injuries.

The effect is subtle and a man might not even recognize it but he has changed and the change is not for the better. Doubts and fears have been planted. Their effect is not immediate but future events contain an element of dread. He does not know where it comes from but instead of enthusiasm, vision, and courage, his new normal is to live with the nagging feeling that something is going to go wrong. Suspicion infiltrates relationships.

This is dangerous because expecting the worst usually produces that result.

And it is common. Every man gets ambushed.

A friend and ministry colleague, Kevin, moved to the South with his family from Detroit to begin the difficult work of planting a church. The fledging group met in a theater and then a Jazzercise room. Each week they had to set up and take down chairs and other worship furniture and, if the work was not demanding enough, maintaining the focus of the ministry strained many relationships. The risk was often rewarded by disappointment of people who grew weary of the task, or grew critical of Kevin and his leadership style.

Kevin clung to God for strength so that he could be faithful to the vision. The church made incremental steps of success. The first building project gave the church credibility and it began to expand. One success led to another and soon, a 20-acre parcel of land was donated to the church. It became the new location of a sanctuary which strengthened and expanded the ministry of the church to the explosively-growing community. Bureaucratic zoning hassles, financial sacrifices, long hours of building and architectural meetings, fund-raising and the sacrifices of many people resulted in the completion of this project wherein the sanctuary hosted the community for worship, instruction and personal growth.

The Sunday for the first worship service arrived. Extra hours of preparation ironed out the logistics. Local and denominational dignitaries were invited. The event was advertised. Church members invited their friends and neighbors and the community turned out in the thousands. The excitement was contagious. The risk, sacrifices, and hard work had paid off and it was certain that this church was going to impact its community.

As Pastor Kevin was greeting the worshippers after the service, he was basking in God's blessings and the congratulations of his excited congregation. But there is always at least one.

"Well, I hope you are happy now!" she sarcastically said to Kevin. "Now you have your mega-church!" The words spewed accusation of improper motives and selfishness at Kevin. In a time of celebration, he was ambushed by a person threatened by his success.

There are a lot of ways a man can get ambushed.

Arriving at home with the announcement of a promotion and raise he is greeted, not with excitement or congratulations, but the accusing question, "Now, how much are you going to be away?"

At the office the salesman is working his territory in a fragile economy and is pleased each quarter to meet his quota and even exceed the company's goals, only to discover that there are budget cuts leading to reorganization and his territory has been eliminated.

There are many pastors, teachers, trainers, managers and coaches who have worked hard on a presentation, sermon, lesson or game plan. He did his best and knows it was a good job. A lot of people responded positively but there was one malcontent whose agenda, conscious or unconscious, was to oppose him. This guy rejected the content or style, and reports that he's quitting and taking his business elsewhere. Surprised by his words and the loss of a client, parishioner or friend an emotional injury occurs. Lying dormant for a season or masked by busyness or denial, it waits until a later time to emerge. Then, the victim will not even know why the anger, doubt or fear surfaces the way that it does.

A lot of men have experienced the most damaging ambush that takes place before the boy became a man. Dads that only correct with a pointing finger of blame, or worse, a clenched fist or a loud, stern voice cause a boy to accept negative emotions, a poor self image and meager aspirations as a normal state of existence.

Darrel learned how to face the fast balls of Big League pitching but he also had to learn to face the competition that was covert when it attacked his confidence and significance. In the "Darrel Chaney Day" ambush and in all the other crises Darrel would face, there were spiritual forces at work. "Steal, kill and destroy," was the enemy's goal. (John 10:10)

Every man must learn how to face this competition.

He should know the other team's strategy, tactics and personnel. The competition may not be who he thinks it is. Every battle has a spiritual component. A common mistake is to believe that the enemy is the person who spoke against him, the words or actions that hurt him, or even himself for getting in harm's way.

At every ambush in life, there are forces of evil at work. "For our struggle is not against flesh and blood, but against the rulers, against the authorities, against the powers of this dark world and the spiritual forces of evil in the heavenly realms. In addition to all of this, take up the shield of faith, with which you can extinguish all the flaming arrows of the evil one." (Ephesians 6: 12, 16) This world is in spiritual conflict and every man is in direct line of "flaming arrows". Satan aims them at him. Spiritual warfare should not surprise him; he should learn how to resist it, fight it and recover from his wounds.

When a man is unaware that there is an enemy, it makes him an easy target for an ambush. And, if he does not know about the Shield of Faith or have the skill to use it, he is defenseless. Under those circumstances, wounds are guaranteed. If we could see with our physical eyes, the mental, emotional and spiritually wounded men, I believe we would see a battlefield scene that resembles Gettysburg. Symptoms are not limited to depression, apathy, anger, selfishness, insecurity, immorality and hopelessness, but that ugly list covers a lot of territory. He might not know why his struggle with pornography is so strong—it is more than a sex thing, it is a compulsion. The outbursts of anger, he thinks, are inherited from his dad or his Scotch-Irish red hair. Fear of money, avoidance of corrective confrontation, procrastination in submitting the proposal or inaction to attempt a bold and creative venture are all signs of wounds from his past that affect a man in the present.

A man can do more than lick his wounds. More than likely, he has forgotten the initial injury. Good news. He probably doesn't need to spend hours, days, weeks or months talking about it or analyzing himself. He can do this by himself, or in the presence of a friend or men's group where Godly men minister to each other. Praying this simple prayer can begin the healing process; *"Dear Lord, Jesus, by the power of your passion on the cross where you crushed the head of the serpent, Satan, I ask you to reveal to me where I have been injured in this area of my life. Show me where the fiery arrows have struck me. I pray in Jesus name. Amen".* Then quietly listen as God begins to reveal things. Perhaps it will be a simple thought or an event from the past or a feeling of shame, fear, anger, hate or doubt. Identify it. That is the arrow and the source of the wound. It is where the "fiery arrow" is doing its damage.

For Darrel, the prayer was, *"Lord, I recognize the arrow of accusation that my success is not real and that I am not a legitimate Big-Leaguer. I remove the arrow as I renounce that lie of Satan by the power of the passion of your blood which was shed on the cross. I receive your healing touch into that injured area of my life. Where the arrow pierced me and burned for years has been a stronghold of Satan's causing doubt and pain in my life. I ask that you fill that space with your Spirit so that I will be strong and victorious where I have been hurt and vulnerable. I pray in the grace and power of Jesus Christ. Amen."*

Not every problem in a man's life is solved that way but every man has struggles which are only solved in that way. Spiritual injuries require spiritual remedies.

Once a man experiences that kind of victory, he never wants his injuries to hinder him again. His significance is secure because he sees himself for who he really is. There is new energy and victory that enables him to face the future with vision, courage and conviction.

But as surely as a terrorist will try to attack democracy and freedom, a man's freedom will be attacked. When the flaming arrows are shot at him, he can take his Shield of Faith and defend himself. The flaming arrows will be extinguished and will fall harmlessly to the ground.

The Shield of Faith is the expressed affirmation of what the believing man has been given by God through Jesus' work on the cross. It produces a new identity. From this new place his significance is secure and he can face any challenge. Failures are merely interruptions on the road to meaningful accomplishments. Purpose guides his efforts. Adequacy is only a prayer away. Strength and courage become the new normal.

So who do the scriptures say the believing man is?

The list below answers that question. I first saw this combined set of promises and affirmations in Neil Anderson's works (From The Bondage Break, by Neil T. Anderson, Harvest House Publishers, pp 213, 214). Every man should affirm his belief in these facts by reading them out loud.

I am God's child.
I am Christ's friend.
I have been justified.
I am united with the Lord and I am one Spirit with Him.
I have been bought with a price.
I belong to God.
I am a member of Christ's body.
I am a saint, a holy one.
I have been adopted as God's child.
I have direct access to God through the Holy Spirit.
I have been redeemed and forgiven of all my sins.
I am complete in Christ.

These will become his "Shield of Faith". These truths protect every man who uses them. They repel the fiery arrows which are aimed at his soul. The ambush will come, but he will be victorious. The injuries from past ambushes will be healed and he can live with vision, strength, and the companionship of God. He will experience his God-given significance.

• • • • •

I had a dark sense of dread as I was driving to a dinner meeting. It did not make sense. The people I was meeting with were friends who had partnered with me in an exciting new venture of planting a church. We were in agreement about our challenges but I felt the desire to run in the opposite direction. I was the leader. Running away was not an option but going forward, weakened by a burden of dread that weighed me down was also not a good choice.

So, I prayed. "Lord, please show me what is bothering me. What is hindering me?" It was a simple prayer.

Alone in my Jeep I listened and it did not take long for an answer to come.

Seven years earlier, I was in different meeting, in a different location with a different group of men. It was a season of ministry and a meeting that I wanted to forget. I thought I had forgotten it but the wounds of that painful night were never healed and the memory came back with vivid clarity.

I had been enjoying a happy and growing ministry in a church where I was the founding pastor. We had grown from nothing to a couple of hundred people, met in a variety of settings and were settling into our own newly built church home. My desire for small groups and one-to-one discipleship did not match the desires of some of the new people that had come into the church. They began to oppose my leadership and solicited the support of others in the congregation which led to this meeting.

My board members met without me so they could freely discuss the direction of the church and all that was involved. With the help of my critics they compiled a list of things they did not like about my leadership style or vision for ministry.

Their first criticism was that I preferred the book Megatrends over the Holy Bible. The last criticism was that I was spiritually immature. The others on the list supported their accusation that I was doing a bad job. I knew there was disagreement over ministry direction but I was not prepared for this list. It was an ambush that injured me deeply and sent me into an emotional tailspin. With some anger, but mostly doubt and fear I tried figure out how to respond and what my next steps should be.

The worst kind of criticism, according to Ed Silvoso in his book, That None Should Perish, is criticism that holds some truth, but lacks grace. (From That None Should Perish, by Ed Silvoso, Regal Books, pp. 123, 124) I did not feel grace in that list, but recognized some truth. The criticisms were more painful than they were constructive.

The Holy Bible was my foundation for faith and instruction and I certainly did not prefer Megatrends to Scripture, but I did read Megatrends and noted changes in our culture so we could focus our ministry to the changes of our community. Ministry styles were changing at that time and I was working in a denomination that emphasized cultural relevance, without changing our message, in missionary efforts. I was not sure if I was wrong or where I went wrong or what to do.

Evidently all of those in the meeting thought they were more mature in their relationship with God than I was. Undoubtedly I did need to grow. The words of the Apostle Paul applied to me then, and still do. "Not that I have already attained all of this or have achieved my goal, but I press on to take hold of that for which Christ Jesus took hold of me."(Philippians 3:11-13) How does somebody respond to a criticism like that? What was the measurement for maturity?

A few painful months later that block of people headed for greener pastures. Part of me was relieved to be free from the constant scrutiny and criticism of people who disapproved of me or my approach to ministry. All of me was shell shocked at the losses of friendships, the setbacks in the ministry and the confusion of what to do next. All I knew to do was keep working and hope I would learn some valuable lessons. I believed the lie, "Time heals all wounds" so with the mask of optimism I put as many experiences and efforts as quickly as I could between me and that miserable experience.

So, seven years later, when this memory surfaced during my prayer, I knew what I had to do. The wounds were never treated. I learned some lessons and sought to apply them, but the spiritual wounds were never spiritually addressed. The rejection I felt had festered into a fear that I would be rejected again and the criticism caused me to doubt my dream for ministry, my unique personality and the interests and vision God had given me.

My healing prayer as I drove down the highway was, *"Lord Jesus, I recognize the pain and accusation I heard that night and during that season of my life. I renounce the arrows of accusation that say I am unfit to minister* (whether or not they were the words of my critics, that is what I heard) *and the fear that my friends will reject me in the same way, and that I will not survive. I ask you to heal me in this aching part of my soul and redeem the results of that ugly meeting, in my life and all affected. In Jesus, I pray! Amen!"*

Immediately the mood lifted. The dinner meeting that I was driving to resulted in positive decisions that strengthened our plan moving our new ministry in a healthy and productive direction

• • • • •

Since then, I have encountered critics and made mistakes worthy of criticism, but when the cancer of anger, doubt and fear recurred in my mind and emotions, I found strength in God's promises regarding my identity in Christ and the significance He has given me.

Ambushes will occur. Every man will be wounded and carry battle scars. But he can be healed from those wounds and be even stronger than before. Toughness and resilience will characterize the way he lives. His significance will survive every attack and he will know, he has made it to the Big Leagues.

What's the Score at the End of the Third Inning?

What has been hit to you?
- Describe an ambush you experienced?
- What were your feelings?
- What were your thoughts?
- How did your respond?

When you are up to bat, what are you going to do?
- How can you prepare for a future ambush?
- Where do you find safety and a shelter?
- Who can help you experience healing from past ambushes?
- Who can be a friend to you when you go through an ambush?

The Fourth Inning

Perseverance

He put a good swing on that one.

Top of the Fourth

DARREL'S BIG LEAGUE SETBACK

"Consider it pure joy, my brothers and sisters, whenever you face trials of many kinds, because you know that the testing of your faith produces perseverance. Let perseverance finish its work so that you may be mature and complete, not lacking anything."
James 1:2-4

"The longer I live the more I realize the impact of attitudes on life. Attitude to me is more important than facts. It is more important than the past, than education, than money, than circumstances, than failures, than success, than what other people think or say or do. It is more important than appearance, giftedness or skill... The remarkable thing is we have a choice every day regarding the attitude we will embrace for the day."
Chuck Swindoll

On the last day of Spring training, Sparky Anderson called Darrel into the dugout to give him the news no Big Leaguer wanted to hear.

Darrel and the Reds had good reason for high hopes for the upcoming '71 season. They were coming off a year with 102 regular season victories, a sweep of the Pittsburgh Pirates (a team with baseball greats, Matty Alou, Roberto Clemente, Willie Stargell, Manny Sanguillen, Al Oliver and Bill Mazeroski) in the National League Championship Series, resulting in an appearance in the World Series.

The loss to the Baltimore Orioles in five games of the World Series had the Reds hungry to win it all this year. Darrel played in three of those games. In his one at bat, he was the third Red to strike out in the top of the 7th inning but the strike outs followed a three-run-homer by Lee May, which put the Reds ahead 6 to 5. He had the best angle on a ball hit by Davey Johnson behind third base. Darrel called off Tony Perez and made the catch in foul territory getting the first out in the bottom of the 9th inning. It was his only put-out in the Series. In that game, the Reds' lead held for their only win in that World Series.

Darrel did not see a lot of action as a player in the Post Season but, in only his second season, he had post season and World Series experience—a lofty accomplishment. His hero, Ernie Banks, never did and neither did Sammy Sosa, Ken Griffey Jr., Rod Carew, Gaylord Perry or Phil Neikro. And they represented some of the best players the game had ever seen. Batting titles, home-run championships, Cy Young awards and Gold Gloves constituted the awards the members of that group held. "Second baseman Rod Carew made the ALCS four times—twice with the Twins and twice with the Angels—but never played in the World Series." (Rick Bause, Sportlifer Blog, October 4, 2010)

But that was last year. New decisions had to be made to fill out the roster and start a new season. Management assembled the team they thought would win another pennant and do better in the World Series. Putting a winning machine together meant developing talent and depth at all the positions. Improving each player was part of the club's strategy. Darrel's batting average was .191 in 93 games in 1969. Through the 57 games he played in 1970, it increased to .232. The young hitter needed more at-bats to become more than a good glove at short stop.

Cindy, Darrel's wife, and one-year old son, Keith, were already on their way from Tampa to Cincinnati. It did not quite feel like home yet but after having lived in four different towns in the two years before Cincinnati, it felt good to return to a familiar place.

"Hey Darrel, come here. I need to talk to you." Sparky Anderson did not wait to get in the locker room or to the office but met Darrel in the dugout. Just the two of them were left on the field. "We are going to send you down this year. We want you to get some more at-bats. I think I am gonna be doin' you a favor."

Disappointment, shock, fear and confusion swept over Darrel. He was torn away from his teammates and the glory, pride and hope of the Big Leagues. How would he tell Cindy and his parents? What would the press say and the people in Hammond think? Failure was a real possibility—did he just wake up from a dream that came true only to have it over in two years? He felt like he was kicked in the stomach and he could not hold back the tears.

Cindy was with their son, Keith, and her parents, who were helping her make the move to find another temporary home in Cincinnati. They were driving the "Darrel Chaney Day" Pontiac and towing a U-haul with everything the young family owned. Cindy called Darrel from her hotel in Knoxville.

"Hi, honey! We're halfway there. We stopped in Knoxville."

The tone of his voice reeked with disappointment. Used to the normally enthusiastic Darrel, Cindy knew something terrible had happened. "Honey, what's wrong?"

"Don't stop in Cincinnati. I didn't make the team. They are sending me to Indianapolis."

They were both silent. Darrel couldn't even talk.

Cindy choked back the tears because she did not want to make Darrel more upset but her parents saw everyone's excitement crashing down. Her mom sat next to her on the bed, holding Keith. Her dad sat directly across from her and faced her from the other queen-size bed. Smiles of anticipation where replaced by questions, worry and dread.

"What's wrong?" Cindy's mother silently mouthed. Cindy could read her lips but just shook her head and waved off the distraction. Her quiet

Polish Catholic father reached out and put his hand on her knee. She was holding the phone with both hands hoping the right words would come.

After what seemed like minutes, she broke the silence, "What does this mean? What are you going to do?"

"I don't know. I'm going to take a couple days and think about it. Maybe I don't have what it takes. I guess they think I'm not good enough."

Setbacks like this are confusing, especially when you are only 23 years old. Darrel's dream for the Big Leagues, plans for success and hopes of greatness did not include backward steps or inglorious learning experiences.

"Doesn't this sort of thing happen to a lot of guys?"

"Not the good guys."

"Hang in there. Don't do anything quickly—something will work out. I will go stay with my parents in Hammond until you decide. I am sorry for you but maybe this is for the best, somehow. Remember, if you do not play in the minors, you don't play at all. I will be praying. I love you—I'll talk to you when we get to Hammond." A change of destination required a quick adjustment of plans.

Always efficient, Cindy's mind was already beginning to figure how they were going to adjust to the pay cut from the $11,000 minimum Big League pay to $800-per-month for at least the four months of the minor league season. She needed to cancel the reservation for the apartment in Cincinnati. Friendships were beginning to form with the wives on the Reds and now she would have to start all over, with a new town, a new apartment and with new friends. Watching the husbands play ball in the dimly-lit and uncrowded Owen J. Bush stadium in Indianapolis only 113 miles away, was a world away from the glory of family seats in the Big League Riverfront Ball Park, watching the Big Red Machine emerge into greatness and savoring all the prestige and excitement of a pennant race, playoffs, and a World Series.

Darrel's parents did not handle the news as well. His mom cried and his dad exploded with as strong of words as he would use. "Crimeny sakes! He's a darn good shortstop and nobody works harder than he does! If he would only play more—you can't get your average up by sitting on the bench. He is so close. I hope he will get back up but I'm afraid they'll be so busy winning, they'll just forget about him."

Darrel's next call was from Vern Rapp, the manager for the Indianapolis Indians, Cincinnati's AAA team. "Darrel, I know this is tough but you are going to be my everyday shortstop. I need you to sign that contract and get back to camp." If Darrel did not accept the offer, he was finished in baseball.

The Big League team was on its way to opening the season with a two-game home-stand with the Atlanta Braves before its first road trip to New York to play the Mets. Instead, Darrel had a couple more weeks of practice with the Indians of Indianapolis before their first game on April 16th against the Iowa Oaks, the Oakland Athletics farm team.

Licking his wounds, the optioned-out Darrel accepted his one-and-only choice to play professional baseball—but it was in the Minors, not in the Big Leagues.

Back on the field, the mood was different from a pennant-chasing Big League team. While these guys were good ball players, they were under scrutiny to be good enough—good enough to be noticed, and good enough to do better than another player on the majors. Darrel's challenge was to earn a spot on a solid, defensive infield with Lee May, Tommy Helms, and Tony Perez.

A hitting slump, a couple of errors, or a performance that is anything less-than-stellar could be fatal to a baseball career. More than a team trying to win, these individuals needed a performance to showcase their skills. Team victory was secondary. Vern, a strict disciplinarian, had his work cut out; his goal was to get these guys to play together and to care about more than themselves.

The next two weeks of extended spring training were grueling for Darrel. He could not get as excited about playing with Ray Borowicz, Al Crawford, and Bill Ferguson – all of whom never played in the Big Leagues. Future Hall of Famers, Sparky Anderson, Johnny Bench, Tony Perez, and Skills-Worthy-Hall-of-Famer, Pete Rose, were the guys Darrel wanted to build a career with. No one on the Indianapolis Indians was a sure thing.

Cindy and one year old, Keith, were living in an upstairs bedroom of her parent's house in Hammond until Darrel got to Indianapolis. Darrel hitched a ride with Greg Slape and the teammates road-tripped the 990 miles to Indy.

The players and the wives had at least two common denominators—they were from somewhere else and lived with an uncertain future. There was a decent apartment complex that would give leases as short as six months so most of them settled there. A two-bedroom and one-bath apartment was going for $160.00 a month. Darrel and Cindy would gladly give up their deposit if they left early to go the Big Leagues.

The only Indianapolis sightseeing that interested Greg and Darrel was getting a look at the Owen J. "Donie" Bush stadium.

"It looks so big," Darrel said as he stood on second base and did a slow 360.

Greg was kicking the dirt on the pitcher's mound. "It's probably because there is so much sky without the upper deck and no stands in the outfield."

"I like the Ivy on the fence. Kinda looks like Wrigley." Darrel hollered over his shoulder when his 360 paused to study the outfield fence. "I've got a few good memories there. Hope I get back."

The new home stadium opened for baseball in 1931. It was built at a cost of $500,000 and could seat 15,000 fans. The Ivy on the fence was part of the effort to look like a smaller version of Wrigley Field. Unlike Wrigley, it had lights but about half as many towers as a Big League ball park. The Indians began playing in 1903 and, as soon as it opened, they made Bush stadium their home and stayed there until 1997, except for seven years during the 60's.

In the 50's it was also the home field for the Indianapolis Clowns. "Better known for their colorful antics, the Clowns were also a sound baseball team. In 1952, they won the Negro American League championship with a young cross-handed slugger from Mobile, Ala., named Hank Aaron." (From the Negro Leagues web site, http://www.nlbpa.com/indianapolis_clowns.html)

Would more baseball greatness grow out of Bush stadium? Greg and Darrel sure hoped so.

Opening day finally came; it was a night game. The guys came from their hotel rooms and got dressed in the old locker room. It had the smell of new paint but there is a limit to what fresh paint can do to a 40-year-old building. Wooden lockers, tile floor, old plumbing with a trough-style urinal, toilets that barely flushed, and showers that hardly produced enough lukewarm water to get a man wet, were added reasons not to stay in AAA.

But they were guys and they were there to play ball, not hang around the locker room.

They had taken a few hours of practice during the day. When they took the field for the warm-ups, it was darker than they expected, even with all the lights on. The stands were beginning to collect the night's crowd and had a few hundred fans an hour before game-time. Don McLean's "American Pie," "Take Me Home, Country Roads" by John Denver, and other 70's hits were being played over the public-address system.

"There aren't many people here, Darrel," his new buddy, Tony Muser, complained. "Just wait, we might get 5,000," Darrel responded without hiding his sarcasm. "I do hope they get the infield smoothed out. I was getting bad hops in practice."

In this line up, Darrel was batting second in the order.

"Playing every day and batting in the front of the order— this might not be too bad."

On his first trip to the plate, he dug in, took a couple of practice swings and watched the first pitch. "Wow, it's dark here. They need more lights. I can hardly see the ball."

But his young eyes adjusted and with the next pitch, he ripped the cover off the ball on a hard single to left field. The whole first game was a good one. He went three for four, had six put-outs at shortstop and was involved in two double plays.

"How'd that feel, Darrel," Vern Rapp asked him in the locker room.

"Great! Can't wait to get back tomorrow."

Darrel was not the rookie on this team or the least of the greats. He had more major league experience than anybody else and was the only one to play in a World Series. His confidence soared. It was time to play ball but also to be a leader among the team. He knew from the first game it was going to be a growing and improving place and, as always, his intensity level was high and his attitude was willing. After the first game, his emotions were beginning to feel positive again and he was excited to be in Indianapolis.

He and Cindy talked on the phone only once a week, trying to keep their long distance phone bill down. She had the number of the pay phone outside the locker room so Darrel would not have to reverse the charges and have them pay more.

"Honey, I think this might be a good thing. It really felt good tonight."

"Great. I had a feeling this was going to be for the better. God has a plan. Hey, do you have any news about housing in Indianapolis?"

"Good news there, too. There are some apartments where the other married players and their wives live. I've even seen a couple of kids who are Keith's age."

"How soon can I get there? If you get us a place I can drive over with Dad and Mom. It's only a couple hundred miles."

"We have a road trip to Evansville and Iowa coming up. I'll be gone 9 days, beginning Friday."

"Can you get us a place that I can move into while you are away?"

"I think they have apartments available. Tomorrow I will check and, if I can, I will. Then you can check in with the manager when you get here. I can't wait to see you and Keith. If I played this well without you, just think how well I will do with you in the stands—oh, and, you won't have a hard time finding a seat or getting close to the field."

"That's okay, you won't be there for long. We will make it a great summer."

"Call me at the same number tomorrow and I'll try to have an answer for you. I love you."

"I love you, too, Honey. Show them how good you are. Bye."

The next night was just as good—well, almost. Darrel went two for four but one of those hits was a double and drove in two runs. He was flawless in the field and short-stop continued to be a hot spot. His pitchers were producing grounders and, the more action Darrel got, the better he felt.

"Darrel, you are doing real good but you are trying to be a power hitter. You are not a power hitter. Getting on base is what matters. I know home runs are fun but I want you to shorten your stoke and go for base hits." Vern worked to develop and maximize the talent of each player.

The Minor Leagues developed talent but they also sifted a population of "wannabe" Big Leaguers. Those who lacked the skills were exposed quickly and the meticulous statistics proved the point. But there were a lot of guys that got stuck in the minors and not because of their baseball skills or athleticism. They had a great swing, their arms were strong, and they were fast runners. The problem was they resented the process of getting to the Big Leagues or staying there. They resisted the advice of the non-glamorous Minor League manager. Patience was lacking and so was adjustment that came from constructive criticism.

Not everyone appreciated the scrutiny and some mistook correction as disapproval. Athletes who reach this level usually have large egos. They want somebody to recognize how good they are, not to tell them how to play ball. At times, they don't even respect the manager. They question his decisions, his knowledge and his experience.

"Who is Vern Rapp? What did he do in the Big Leagues? Did he ever manage in a Big League team that won? If he didn't make it, how will he help me make it?"

Some guys do not realize that the best manager is often the guy who has made the effort and knows the struggle but has not achieved at the highest level. He can identify with the pressures and failures of the younger guys. He is a better manager than the superstar who is impatient with a rookie who needs to make adjustments, increase his confidence and learn baseball strategy. A new player is going to make mistakes and a guy like Vern can help him work through it. Inevitably, he will do better next time.

Vern put a lot of time in the minors; first, as a player and then as a manager. He knew everything about the Minor Leagues and about the young guys, the skills they needed, their fears, their insecurities, their dreams, and their egos.

Darrel possessed an eager attitude, an open heart, a humble spirit and an appetite to improve. Like his hero, Ernie Banks, he always gave his best effort, learned and improved, regardless of his circumstances. It started with the healthy relationship he enjoyed with his dad. He believed he could learn something from high school coaches, Babe Ruth, American Legion managers, Instructional League coaches and teammates.

Darrel was a pleasure to coach because he was eager to play and teachable. He followed the rules, showed respect, listened to instruction and was a student of the game in skills and strategies. He was looking for anything that could help him achieve his dream and get back to the majors.

"Shorten my stroke. Go for base hits. No problem."

The adjustment paid off immediately. He was never content but he got comfortable in the Minor League process as soon as he saw the results.

· · · · ·

The guys were in Evansville playing the Triplets, the Milwaukee Brewers farm team, on their first road trip. Cindy, with son, Keith, and a packed-to-the-gills, non air-conditioned Pontiac, drove the 159 miles almost due-south from Hammond to Indianapolis. Her dad's car was also packed. The mattresses were strapped to the roof in anticipation of getting settled in a cozy little apartment.

They arrived at the apartment complex, one in front of the other, and pulled up to the empty parking places in front of the sign that read, "Office."

Cindy parked and got Keith out of his car seat. It was a hot summer day, so everyone was wearing shorts and enjoying the sunshine as well as the feel of summertime.

The door was unlocked so Cindy walked into the office. It was quiet and no one was there so she rang the little bell on the counter. From the adjacent apartment came a middle-aged man, not overly friendly, but helpful enough. "Can I help you?"

"I'm Cindy Chaney. My husband reserved an apartment for us and I am here to get the key and move in."

"Ah, yes. A ball player's wife and son." Looking at a sweaty, little red-faced Keith, "Are you gonna play ball someday, like your dad?" Keith had been sitting long enough in the car and did not want to be still any longer so Cindy put him on the floor to toddle around. She tried to neaten his hair which had a Dennis-the-menace cowlick and then tucked the little terry cloth tank top into his matching green shorts. "We have several of the Indian players' families here. Your husband signed everything so I will just have to see some ID and then I will take you to your apartment and give you your key. Your husband already has his. I believe he has put a few of his things in it already."

Keeping one eye on Keith, she rooted through her purse to find her wallet in order to display her driver's license. Not too worried that this woman and child with an older man in the car in the parking lot fit the profile of imposters, he performed his due diligence by glancing at her picture and her name on the driver's license. In just a short walk around a small yard, Cindy got to enter her new home. The manager unlocked the door and let her in. Underwhelmed but satisfied, Cindy stepped in and took the tour which only took a minute. "This will be fine. Thank you."

She packed and moved only the essentials, hoping this would be a brief stop in their lives. At least, they would be together soon. They had been apart almost a month. Cindy had missed her husband and Keith wanted to play with his dad. A faithful family man, Darrel was tired of hotel life and having to eat every meal in a restaurant. Road trips were bad enough for that—he wanted a family-oriented life.

After just a few trips from the cars to the apartment, everything was unpacked. "Dad, I think I can handle it now. We don't have that much. I just need to make the beds, set up the kitchen and put Keith down for a nap."

"OK, but I am going to get you a few things from the grocery store to hold you over until Darrel gets back in a couple of days; then I'll head back to Hammond."

Even before Pop could get back from the store, Cindy made her first new friend. Nancy Muser and her little boy, Tony Jr., showed up at the apartment. The door was ajar to get some air moving through the hot apartment. "Knock, knock. Cindy? Anybody home?"

Cindy was laying Keith down for his nap in the little bed her dad had assembled. It felt good to hear someone call her name, especially this quickly. She didn't even have time to get homesick or be alone. With a big smile and a cheerful expression, Cindy brushed her hair back. "Hi. I'm Cindy. Excuse my appearance. We just got here and the drive was hot—I just got the car unpacked. "

"I'm Nancy Muser. Darrel said you were coming. Tony, my husband is on the team, too. I don't mean to interrupt—I can come back later."

"Oh, no problem. I'm glad to meet you. Do you like it here?"

"It's okay for a temporary stop. Hopefully, it won't be too long for any of us. But we will make the most of it. There are some more girls like us here. I'll introduce you when you are ready."

Keith went out like a light and didn't get to meet his new friend. Nancy and Cindy talked about Indianapolis, what it was like to live with their husbands away so often, and living with potential and hope in an uncertain future. Tony Jr. played with a few of Keith's toys that were out on the living room floor. Nancy and Cindy were finally done chit-chatting so Nancy returned to her apartment with plans to come back later when the boys could keep each other company.

· · · · ·

Everything related to playing baseball was going well on the road trip. The Indians took two out of three from the Triplets and swept the Iowa Oaks in Des Moines. Morale was high. Vern did a good job focusing the guys on baseball and playing as a team. Cheers, high fives and attaboys went from manager to players, and from player to player.

Bus rides instead of airplanes, cheap hotels, smaller, dimly-lit ball parks and a couple thousand fans in the stands were all constant reminders this was the Minor Leagues but they were small prices to pay because there was a purpose to each play.

The fans were into the games. Kids wanted autographs and old-timers in bunches coached and umpired from the stands. It could have been a lot worse for these guys who did not have to work a 9-5 job, but got paid to get better at the game they loved, hoping to earn a spot in the Big Leagues.

Playing in every game, even though it was only nine games so far, felt good to Darrel. His mental and emotional focus increased just knowing he would be in the line-up every day. The 120 games in which he played almost equaled the total for the previous two years in Cincinnati. The only reason he missed 20 games was because of his mandatory Army Reserve meetings.

His batting average stayed in the high .200's, even reaching .300 for a few days. At Mile High Stadium, against the first-place Denver Bears, Darrel went 5 for 5 in a mid season game — one single, two doubles and two triples. One almost got out of the park. If it had, Darrel would have hit for the cycle. Darrel was named to the American Association All Star team (they did not have an All Star Game) and the Indians won their division championship. They celebrated like the Big Leagues with cigars, beer and champagne.

Cindy and Nancy attended every home game with Keith and Jr. in tow, always carrying their plastic wiffle-ball bats — the official toy for these boys in the summer of '71.

Disappointment defined the Reds sub-500 and fourth-place finish that season. Even their attendance was seventh out of the twelve National League teams. But in September, Darrel and Cindy were excited to give their notice to their apartment complex, sacrifice their deposit, and head back to Cincinnati for the rest of the season in the Big Leagues.

After Darrel was called up from Indianapolis, he only played in ten games for the Reds in 1971 but he was back in the Big Leagues and he was there to stay.

Bottom of the Fourth

EVERY MAN NEEDS TO PERSEVERE THROUGH HIS SETBACKS

"In his heart a man plans his course, but the Lord establishes his steps."
Proverbs 16:9

"Experience, the most brutal of teachers.
But you learn, my God do you learn."
C.S. Lewis

A boy dreams of success but not the process of getting there. A man makes plans for his future but not his setbacks.

Setbacks happen for a lot of different reasons; some from good intentions, others from circumstances gone wrong. Some are catastrophic and change life permanently. Other times a man can ride out the storm or work through the crisis.

A trip back to the Minors may not seem like a big deal to the fan rooting for the team, but for the player who is being sent back, it is a difficult setback, full of confusion, difficulty, stress and fear. Baseball players get sent down to the minors but each man has a setback of his own.

Joseph, referred to in the Bottom Half of the First Inning, experienced severe setbacks over and over again. He was not alone. There is not a character in the Bible who did not experience setbacks.

Moses wanted to set his people free. He started with a 40-year setback which caused him to live in exile in the desert. After he finally freed his people, there was another 40-year setback. This time a million freed people wandered in the desert before entering the Promised Land. During that journey, there were many setbacks: lack of food, water, disease, low morale, lack of leadership, and enemies that sought to destroy them.

David, an anointed king of Israel, overcame some giant obstacles similar to Goliath, yet he suffered setbacks from the reigning king of Israel, Saul. David dodged a spear which Saul threw at him. David went into hiding in caves throughout the rugged countryside with his army of renegades. Once he became King, he brought shame upon himself in a moral failure with Bathsheba. That was followed later in life with a heartbreaking setback with his headstrong son, Absalom, and all the politics, wars, and bloodshed that a coup can bring.

There is a figure in the Bible of whom nothing negative is written. Still, he had setbacks. Daniel served from a position of captivity, earned the favor of his captives but, at the same time, was a threat to his peers. So they set a trap for Daniel. Yet he survived his time in the lions' den—and they were hungry lions.

The disciples were thrilled to find a Messiah who was going to fix all their problems and restore the injustices of an unwelcome Roman occupation. They had Pharisee setbacks who opposed Jesus' feeding the hungry. The One the disciples followed gave them setbacks to their own agenda. When He told them His ways were higher than their ways: "Love your enemies; blessed are the persecuted; blessed are the peacemakers." He surrendered Himself to a death that was shameful—personally, politically, and practically, and they were confused and devastated by this unimaginable setback.

These beautiful Bible stories of resilience and deliverance always inspired me but until I had to experience the pain of my own broken-world setback, I did not understand the complexity and vulnerability of a man who is being "sent down."

• • • • •

I did not know how bad things could get in ministry and what people who called themselves "men of God" could do.

My dream was not focused, my purpose unknown when I was young and feeling the need for direction in my life. During my junior year of high school, through a conversation with my father, I experienced a call to ministry. I stood at the end of my Dad's bed, after flipping through some college catalogs, to hear him say, "Have you considered the ministry?"

"No," I replied, "I have never felt a call."

"What do you think 'a call' is? You won't see it written in the clouds."

Something happened inside of me at that moment. I did not hear any voices other than my Dad's, and there were no flashing lights. The earth did not move but my life changed. There was a feeling in my chest that this was right and, for the first time in my life, I had a focus. I did not know my next step or how everything would turn out but I knew the direction my life was going to take.

I was blessed to be in a family and have a church community that welcomed and encouraged this type of decision. A large secular high school in the late 60's was a place where this kind of decision was not only misunderstood, it was also unpopular. So I only told a few friends and managed to graduate without any serious opposition.

My college education was at Toccoa Falls Bible College, later to be called Toccoa Falls College, where men and women trained for ministry. I was attending classes with roommates and friends who were going in the same direction and we were instructed by professors who were on the same team. If there was any opposition, it was only to correct mistakes and to develop my potential. The bad guys of the world were out there somewhere but they were not in my camp.

I was young, naïve, optimistic, inexperienced and in a position of trust. Trouble and disagreements were minor. My education and preparation for ministry included learning theology, some church organization and preaching skills, but nothing about leadership dynamics, personalities in ministry, conflict management or conflict resolution. So when I graduated from college, I was prepared to preach sermons but not deal with confrontation. Besides, from my perspective, the villains were not in the church but outside and somewhere else.

I managed to get through almost eight years of ministry relatively unscathed in Warren, Ohio, as a Youth Pastor, and in Delray Beach, Florida, in my first pastorate of a small church. There were bumps in the road but I was able to speed over them as I grew personally, and climbed the ministry ladder to loftier goals and positions in ministry.

So when I was invited to join the staff of one of the fastest growing new churches in my denomination, I was ready to go.

As an added enticement, it was located in the esteemed town of Princeton, New Jersey. Princeton is a place of influence and affluence, between New York City and Philadelphia. People of prominence from all walks of life have come to these hallowed grounds to visit the town regularly. It is common to see nationally and internationally prominent people while having breakfast at PJ's Pancake House, or lunch at the Nassau Inn, or even coming out of church.

As I was leaving church one Sunday morning, I saw George Gallup getting in his car on Nassau St. That day he was driving an old station wagon which had a missing headlight. I was infatuated with the prestige of Princeton, the magnitude of the northeast corridor, and the success of a rapidly-growing church, especially with such a dynamic and appealing congregation.

The Senior Pastor was a man my own age. I got to know him when we were doing our ordination work. His energy level was off the chart and I enjoyed being around a guy who could make things happen. His skill set and style converged with the fast-moving pace and high expectations of the northeast, and the church rapidly grew under his magnetic leadership.

Of course, I would not look for anything to go wrong in such a magnificent setting. I could only see the potential and what was right. The things that were about to happen, I would not have understood if someone told me because I have never experienced anything like it nor would I have expected anyone to do such hurtful things.

I knew a little about baseball but I knew nothing about "hard ball" until I was a victim.

In all of my stations of ministry, my longevity was at least a few years, but we were only in this assignment for eleven months. My mentor, Al Broom, of Church Dynamics International, coached me in parts of my job related to starting small groups, developing a ministry strategy, establishing it on a strategy-board and providing one-to-one discipleship for personal growth and development of individuals. These were all initiatives to assimilate the people of a fast-growing congregation. They were a welcome addition to the pastoral team of this congregation who loved the frenetic energy of the founding pastor but was looking for a system and order that would be sustainable.

My wife picked up on the warning signs even when I was totally blind to the dangers. If I saw them, I chose to overlook them. In our home, he would come in and we were told to turn off lights to save the church money. He was the most aggressive driver I ever encountered but I thought it was just the wild side of a highly talented, wild man who could get a lot done. Like the saying goes, "sit down, shut up and hang on", that was the only way to ride and, since I liked excitement, I could endure this foolishness even though my wife was terrified and saw it as unnecessary, careless aggressiveness.

Every day, he would call me, early in the morning before we got to the office and, again, late at night when we were at home. It seemed like a close relationship at first. I thought he needed fellowship or really enjoyed working with me. My discomfort, while growing, was small enough to sweep under the rug and ignore it. The controlling nature was new to me and I did not recognize it as dysfunctional or realize how stifling it would become.

I seldom felt the freedom to take a day off or have undisturbed times and, when I did, he would always let me know how much harder he was working and usually find a reason to call me. It did not take long before I began to feel as though I had no life outside the church or apart from him. It seemed as if I would've let him, he would've taken every part of me and built a wall between me and those I loved. Throughout our brief time together, we had a couple of heart-to-heart conversations and one unique characteristic of our agreed-upon solutions was, "Let's keep this between us." This kept me from building strong bonds with anyone else and if I ever would have said anything to anyone I would have been guilty of breaking our confidentiality agreement.

This relationship was beginning to suffocate me. I did not know how I would ever experience freedom or ministry in a positive way. It would have been insubordinate to go to any authorities about my feelings because I was sworn to secrecy. At that time, I did not know nor understand what was taking place; I could not have articulated it as clearly as I can now, with 20/20 hindsight.

The idea came to me that perhaps I too, could plant a church. Someday I would like to do what he did and having seen the beauty of a new church, I thought this was something I would like to have in my future.

I told him this during one of our meetings which was designed for me to share my goals and desires for the future. In retrospect, I believe the meeting was really a loyalty check and my desire for anything else was considered disloyal. By the end of that day, it was evident that my days were numbered in this ministry, and that they were few. With a vision for anything else, I was considered "dead-wood." So plans for my departure began immediately and it would be only a couple of weeks away.

I was hoping that I would find an ally when we met with the denominational leaders. When we sat down to lunch, the leader from our denomination, sat to my right and without asking any questions, he looked straight at me and said, "I am really upset because you have not done what we asked you to do." It was a new experience for me to be rejected so completely. The vows of secrecy, it appeared, were to keep me from the authorities because my colleague was talking to them and putting me in an unfavorable light.

When we announced my resignation to the congregation, they were stunned. Susan was seven months pregnant with our second child. We had no place to go and no other plans. It would have been irresponsible to abruptly move under those circumstances and everyone knew it. I was under pressure, especially from the denominational leader, to cause no problems. If he had truly known me, he would have known that I would not have caused problems under any circumstance. In my final sermon to that congregation, I preached from the story of David, the King-to-be, during one of his setbacks when he had the character not to harm his pursuer, Saul, even though he had the opportunity. He said, "I will not harm God's anointed." It would have been wrong for me to speak against the number one man, even though I believed he was wrong in so many ways.

After our final Sunday service and an appropriate farewell from a perplexed congregation, we went home, packed the moving truck with the help of a few friends and headed out, sad, confused and scared, to my in-laws' house in North Carolina. After eight years of ministry, I was homeless, jobless, and fearful of the damage to my reputation. I had no idea how I was going to find a home and care for my family, let alone find another place in ministry.

But beyond what I could see, God was already working on my next step. Before we left Princeton, a kind and helpful woman who consulted people in the preparation of their resumes, helped me find effective verbiage that would be compelling and translate my ministry skills into more common uses, such as planning, organizing groups of people, communication, public speaking, etc. She also told me of a couple of friends who lived in Atlanta, in case we ended up there. We previously had some interest in that area and the denomination wanted a new church in the northern suburban county of Gwinnett. It was my job to trust God more than I ever had, and let him lead me forward to places I did not know and to learn new lessons.

As soon as I got to Atlanta, I contacted her friends, Jay and Liz who were hospitable to me—they opened a room for me while I was doing the initial scouting for the potential of starting a new church. Susan and our firstborn, Danny, were living with her family, in North Carolina. All of our belongings were stored from floor-to-ceiling on one side of their double garage. About a month after we had moved into this temporary location, I rushed back to North Carolina from Georgia, barely in time for Andrew's birth, which was three weeks ahead of the due date. He has been full of surprises from day one.

One day, Jay invited me to join him at an executive men's Bible study at a nice restaurant in the midtown section of Atlanta. I was introduced to the guy sitting next to me. He was Darrel Chaney. I do not remember how many times I attended that group but I know it was the time I met Darrel.

Darrel and I crossed paths a few years later. Our new church was up-and-running and I was involved in the community. It was my pleasure to offer the invocation at the Gwinnett County Chamber of Commerce breakfast. This day, it was in the large conference room of the Falcon Inn, the hotel on the headquarters and practice field of the Atlanta Falcons football team.

"Hey, Darrel, remember me? How would you like to get a men's group started here in Gwinnett?"

"Sure, I remember you. I have been wanting to do something like that. Do you have a card? Here is mine. Call me and we will get together and see what we can do." We started two groups and went through years of meaningful studies, developed new and lasting friendships in weekly early morning meetings at Applebee's and County Seat Café. Before either restaurant opened for the day's business, in their hospitality, they allowed us to use their empty dining room to host our group. June Jones, the Atlanta Falcons coach at the time, shared his story with about 70 men on one of those great days.

Leaving Princeton was a severe setback filled with the drama of a major move, inadequate resources and relational intrigue. There were plenty of reasons to throw in the towel, but God walked with us one step at a time. He kept my attitude positive and eager for the new things He had for us. A strong foundation of faith that God is present in the hard times and a family that encouraged me with that truth, got us through the setback. Our character was tested and strengthened, and our vision for the future was brought into a clearer focus. He brought promise and purpose out of that painful setback.

• • • • •

"Dan, did you hear what is going on in Princeton?" Five years after I left Princeton, I got that call from a person in my congregation who had family in the Princeton church. My former colleague was leaving under unpleasant circumstances.

A couple of years after his sad departure, we experienced vindication and healing from some of our deepest wounds, when Susan and I were invited back for the church's tenth anniversary. I was the keynote speaker for the Sunday worship services. Old relationships were renewed. We all learned a lot of life's hardest lessons, but, perhaps, the greatest lesson was that God is present in the setbacks and He used them to teach us to put our trust in Him. He will help us survive our setbacks and grow stronger because of them. They test our commitment and refine our character.

My setback was very different than Darrel's, and yours may be different than mine, but there are some things that setbacks have in common. There are things that every man needs to do to make it to the Big Leagues.

Setbacks will happen.

Maybe you are experiencing a setback. You are normal. This is part of every man's journey to the Big Leagues.

Layoffs, pay cuts, bankruptcies, foreclosures, divorces, accidents and sickness comprise only a partial list of events that can happen to a man. You may have deserved the promotion but someone else got it. You have the best product with the best proposal but the CEO might be afraid to make a decision and you don't get the deal. You lost a big account because a cranky customer complained and the complaint was inaccurate.

Working through setbacks rather than avoiding them is mandatory on the road to the Big Leagues. You will not have to pursue them—believe me, you would not want to—they will find you, but neither do you have to fear them. Setbacks are a normal part of every man's life.

In his book, Epic, John Eldredge points out that every life is a story that unfolds like a drama and contains all sorts of characters and settings. It does not come to us like a math problem. (From Epic, by John Eldredge, Nelson Books a Division of Thomas Nelson Publishers, p. 2) And, every good story has a villain.

Interesting stories have drama and trauma; heroes endure the pain, discover solutions, survive attacks and thrive in the process, especially if they know God is writing the story. God does not write boring stories.

Darrel never went back to the Minor Leagues but he had more setbacks. I survived my first broken world setback and planted another church. I also experienced setbacks there but through it all God was present. His presence is enough. He instructs, sustains, strengthens and guides.

Attitude makes the difference.

It really does not matter what the cause of the setback is. Maybe somebody did you wrong or you were a victim of a difficult economy. It is your attitude that makes the difference.

A lot of men give up on their dream. Others listen to the voices of self-doubt. Still others, with anger and vengeance, waste their energy on the villain.

Darrel signed his contract, moved to Indianapolis, and suited up every day.

I decided to continue in ministry and venture into church-planting. Forgiveness was necessary and was more than a feeling or a one-time decision. Each time ugly thoughts and feelings surfaced, I had to make the correct choice.

What is a good attitude?

It is the commitment to make the right decisions, over and over again.

Like the stages of grief, there will be denial, confusion, anger, and bargaining before a man comes to understanding and acceptance. These are normal feelings and, as the situations arise, there are many opportunities to make choices.

You will know the right one — the one that leads to the Big Leagues.

Accept Responsibility.

"Shorten your swing." Darrel knew his batting average was low. The Minor Leagues might not have been the only option for Sparky Anderson and the Reds organization but it was a valid one. If Darrel had been hitting .300, they would not have had to make a decision. He did need more at-bats.

Had I been more mature in my ability to confront mistakes, resolve and manage conflict, and stand up for myself, I might have been able to stay in Princeton and possibly even help refine a very talented colleague. I will never know but the event revealed my weaknesses as much as the villain in my story.

This is often a painful but always a necessary step to maximizing personal growth and learning.

Learn as much as you can.

The emergency of a setback requires a thorough assessment of the situation. Amped-up emotions open our eyes to see what we might normally overlook and tune our ears to hear what we otherwise would not listen to.

Learning is about desire more than intelligence. Not everybody can master an academic subject but every man who is hungry can ask questions, listen to advice, and gain more experience.

Be still and process your new information and seek God's revelation. Maybe it will be a few minutes in a coffee shop with your Bible and journal. Fear wakes a lot of men up in the early morning hours. The family is sleeping making this a perfect time to pray, read and spiritually listen. Writing your thoughts and plans protects your mind from endlessly rolling thoughts and "what-if" scenarios. If you hike or camp, make sure to take with you something you can use to write or record you new insights. When God gives you a breakthrough of revelation, write it down.

Give it 110%.

Intensity develops during a setback. Focused thought strengthens every man for intense action; he becomes stronger and wiser than before the setback. Focusing the intensity produces Big League results.

A man makes plans but the Lord determines his steps. Setbacks seem like a step in the wrong direction, but the way forward is not always up. You know you are in the Big Leagues when you survive your setbacks.

What's the Score at the End of the Fourth Inning?

What has been hit to you?
- Describe your worst setback.
- List the ways this setback affected your life (i.e. financially, relationally, emotionally, etc.).

When you are up to bat, what are you going to do?
- How do you accept responsibility in the setback?
- Why did the setback happen?
- What do you need to maximize your learning ability?
- What did you learn?
- When will you be able to continue at 110%?

The Fifth Inning

Worth

Getting a hit against the Braves.

Top of the Fifth

ANOTHER ONE-YEAR CONTRACT CHALLENGES DARREL'S BIG LEAGUE WORTH

"And my God will meet all your needs according to the riches of his glory in Christ Jesus."
Philippians 4:19

"Gimme a blank contract. I'll sign it, and you fill in the figures."
Red Sox pitcher **Lefty Grove,** to owner
Tom Yawkey sometime in the 1930's

The only way to play in the Big Leagues is to have a contract.

A contract is an agreement between the player and the ownership. Darrel's contracts were a lot different than those we hear about today but there has always been competition and drama in getting and signing a contract.

Contracts were required to be postmarked by midnight on December 20th. The four-page legal document would arrive in the mail a day or two before Christmas, if it arrived at all. Every day Darrel would check the mail. "Nothing on the 21st. Of course not. It probably was not mailed until yesterday but, maybe it was mailed earlier or maybe I am not getting one", Darrel wondered aloud to himself.

After the season was over and the World Series was played, great strategy sessions took place by the front office and by management of every Big League team. All the information was put on the table. Scouts reported new and upcoming young players. The development of the talents in the Minor Leagues with all of the statistics was brought to light by their managers. All of the trade possibilities were scrutinized. What do we need? Who can we get? Who do we have to give? Every player's performance from the previous years was analyzed. From this vetting process, a list was formulated of who would be invited to spring training.

December 22nd. Darrel watched for the mailman who usually came by 11:00 a.m. Darrel made at least two trips to the mail box prior to that time and also at 11:00. Still no mail.

"The mail man is late today. It must be the Christmas volume. I wish he would get here," Darrel agonized.

It was noon.

"Darrel, I see the mailman coming down the street." Cindy's future was involved in this, too. The excitement of Christmas was overshadowed by the tension of worrying about the future. It became an annual event because for each of the seven years in which Darrel would play with the Reds, he would receive a one-year-contract and he would be more eager to get his contract than any little boy or girl would be for Santa to arrive on Christmas Eve.

Darrel walked out to meet the mailman. He knew him personally because delivering the mail was one of Darrel's off-season jobs. In today's world of big, Big League salaries, it is hard to imagine a Big League ball player as a mailman but for three years, Darrel was just that. One year he worked the midnight shift, loading boxes for Parcel Post. These were pretty good jobs compared to the year he tried sales. Cindy was the only one to buy a Holiday Cheese-Plate from Darrel. The commission did not make up for the cost.

"Sorry Darrel, not today." The mail-carrier handed the rest of the mail to Darrel. "Maybe tomorrow."

Cindy could tell by Darrel's hesitant pace, there was still no contract. She greeted him at the door with a hug and a sigh. "We'll wait until tomorrow."

Darrel turned down the invitations to play college football and consequently the training for a professional career outside of sports. Other than baseball, he did not have any good options and, if the contract did not come, his temporary jobs would become his new lifestyle. There is nothing wrong with working for the city of Hammond as a garbage can inspector, as a mail carrier or holiday-cheese-plate salesman but these were not in Darrel's dream for his future.

It was Wednesday, December 23rd. Darrel interrupted his morning appointments to come home and check the mail. The contract had to be mailed on the 20th, so if it was not in the mail, Darrel was going start worrying.

The players did not know the cards that were in the deck when management was having its winter strategy meeting; they might not agree if they did. Those meetings were full of opinions from which gut-feeling decisions were made. Each name was discussed and for guys who were on the bubble, the risks were high.

Among the usual bills and the seasonal Christmas cards, there was a thick envelope with the return address of the Cincinnati Reds. Darrel held the bills and cards in his left hand and waved at Cindy, who was looking out the kitchen window, with the contract envelope in his right hand. His pace was eager and nervous.

As much as they cared about the Christmas greetings from family and friends, the cards and the bills were cast aside while Darrel and Cindy sat on the edges of their chairs, facing each other, elbows on the table,

Cindy's chin in her hands, while the envelope sat on the corner of the kitchen table.

"Well, here it is. Are you ready?"

"Yes," and Cindy motioned with her hand, "open it!"

Darrel tore open the envelope and unfolded the cover letter to make sure it is what they expected. Speed-reading, he mumbled, "Dear Darrel, We are pleased to offer your contract for the 1973 season. Please sign it and return it at soon as possible. We look forward to seeing you at Spring Training. Your reporting date is February 16, 1973. Sincerely, Sheldon Bender."

The cover letter was put behind the five pages in Darrel's hand. He quickly shuffled page one, then two, then three, to the back of the stack. He and Cindy always skipped over the legalese and clauses, which were usually straight forward, and even though they were nervous to look at it, went directly to the compensation paragraph. There it was—the Reds were offering Darrel another year at $18,000.00.

"A nickel ain't worth a dime anymore," Yankees catcher, Yogi Berra, said years earlier. If that made any sense, it might apply here.

This was the bottom of the 1973 Big League salary. Taking into account the bigger salaries, the average was $36,566.00 which, according to Michael J. Haupert of EH.net, was worth $147,506 in 2002. So $18,000 was not good but it was livable. The fact that it was only for one year challenged this young couple to stretch it as far as they could.

"We can make it on that," Cindy said with thankfulness in her voice.

"And the extra $18,000 for our share of playing in the 1972 World Series was also a big help. Hopefully, we will do that again. It's more than I make in a year of loading trucks at night for Parcel Post."

"Yep. And you are getting paid to play ball."

This was before arbitration was a factor in resolving salary disputes. When arbitration figured into contracts, a player who had six years with his team and didn't think he was getting paid enough could bring his case to an objective source. The team would show why he was or was not worth it and the arbitrator would decide.

It was obviously before the years of big salaries, so Darrel would not approach his salary the way Mike Norris did. After losing in salary arbitration, he said, "No problem, I was either going to wake up rich or richer."

Darrel only negotiated one salary three years earlier when Keith was born. He was making $10,000, the minimum Big League salary. Then, a new family man with another mouth to feed, Darrel asked Chief, Sheldon Bender's nick name, for a $1000 raise.

"Darrel, here is what I will do. I won't give you anything but I'll give your wife $500 and your son $500. How's that?"

"That'll do, Chief. Thanks!"

Darrel's contract with the Reds was always handled by Chief, who was the director of the Reds' farm teams. Chief took care of the one-year contracts as well as the salaries of the lower-echelon players. General Manager Bob Howsam, took care of Bench, Rose, Morgan, and the high-dollar, multi-year and big-name contracts.

The clauses in the contract included the player's commitment to not play for anybody else or ride a motorcycle. However, a player was obliged to make two charity appearances on behalf of the team during events designated by the front office.

Following Spring Training and once the player made the team, the team owner's commitment was to pay the agreed-upon salary. If Darrel had a bad Spring and the team wanted to send him down, his contract would be void. He would get a minor league contract with corresponding wages which he would either accept or would be finished.

There were no guarantees.

It felt good to be a Big Leaguer as long as it lasted. But the pressure was always on to make it last. Every year Darrel had to earn his position for the ensuing year. Every game and every at-bat had significance beyond the impact of the game.

Cindy felt it too. "We enjoyed the day because there might not be a tomorrow in baseball."

Darrel did not get a multi-year contract until his second year after he was traded to the Atlanta Braves. His three-year contract guaranteed his income for those years but not his making the team. While it would benefit the team owners financially to keep him, they could release him if his performance was inadequate or if new players emerged who were better. It was all about who would most likely help the team win.

Darrel got his Big League contract. Seven times with the Reds and once with the Braves he got one year at a time and, one time, he got a three-year contract with the Braves. Each time he waited for someone else to decide if he was worthy to be part of their team.

Bottom of the Fifth

EVERY MAN'S WORTH IS REVEALED IN A COVENANT

*"Then he took a cup, and when he had given
thanks, he gave it to them, saying,
'Drink from it, all of you. This is my blood of the covenant,
which is poured out for many for the forgiveness of sins.'"*
Matthew 26:27, 28

"Money doesn't talk, it swears."
Bob Dylan

Every man needs to know he is worth something. He would like to find it in a lucrative contract.

Darrel's contract indicated the Reds still wanted him on their team for the next season and he had some guaranteed income for another year. He would take what he could get.

The modern Big Leaguer who got a one-year contract at the minimum wage could still buy a house for cash, cars for both he and his wife, and pay off his college loans—$486,000.00 is the Big League minimum salary in 2012. At $3,444,000.00 the average player's salary, he can buy a bigger house, buy me a house, and, if he invests properly, can spend the rest of his life sleeping-in and playing with the kids every day. Thirty-four players have multiple-year contracts worth between $100,000,000.00 and $275,000,000.00. I can only imagine what one person would do with that amount of money.

"I love being the highest paid player in the game," Alex Rodriguez, the Yankees' Third Baseman once said, hiding any embarrassment, if he had any, for making that much money.

Baseball is more profitable these days than it was in Darrel's day. TV revenues and product sponsorships produce great wealth for the owners and for the players. After several baseball strikes, both sides found better ways of spreading the wealth.

What man would not want to be in a successful enterprise which offered a lucrative, multi-year contract?

Letters which verified the agreed-upon amount of income as well as a welcome to my new set of responsibilities was the closest thing I ever got to a contract in my over thirty five years of employment. That's the way it is for a lot of men.

After our premature exit from Princeton, I applied to start a church from scratch in Gwinnett County, an area of metro-Atlanta which was exploding with growth. Leaving without a plan and living with my in-laws left me in a weak bargaining position. I went to the denomination with "my hat in my hand." In addition, I was worried about the political fallout from a denominational figure who never heard my side of the story.

"We would love to have you plant a church in our district," the church-planting director for the District enthusiastically declared.

I needed to hear that and I was eager for my attention to turn away from the hurt of the past and the confusion of the present. I wanted to start planning and look toward the future. The hunt to find a new place to live and minister was necessary but now it had become an adventure. The scouting and exploring was fun.

"There is an area around Lawrenceville, GA, which I would like you to examine. We will pay for your travel there and your hotel for a week. Check it out. If you are interested, we will meet and discuss the terms." That was his way of saying, sort of, "We'll offer you a contract."

Lawrenceville, the County Seat of Gwinnett County, was a strained blend of the old and the new. The two did not easily mix. On the surface, there was the feel of southern hospitality. I thought I would fit in when the Huddle House waitress told me, "You aren't a damn-Yankee, yur jest a Yankee." That seemed to be a good thing except I planned on staying. That's what a "damn-Yankee" does. A Yankee is a northerner who visits, spends his money and then goes home where he belongs. I suppose I was too desperate to see the darker side.

The beautiful colors of Fall and warm temperatures welcomed me which made me glad to be out of the Northeast that difficult October.

Gwinnett County was filling up with young professionals from all over the country—the South, the Midwest, and the Northeast. They were coming from everywhere, even internationally, and it was the fastest-growing county in the United States. Beautiful swim and tennis subdivisions were being built everywhere. They were filled with lovely homes that had professionally landscaped lots with sod lawns, Dogwoods, Bradford Pear trees, forsythia and azaleas. Jobs were abundant, the pay was good and the livin' was easy. It was the most exciting place for a church-planter to be. Any denomination worth its "weight in salt" would want to find an eager, energetic and talented guy like me (at least, I thought so), and support him well to launch a church with their name on it.

Everywhere I went, I saw this unique blend of established South, which I liked from my college days in Toccoa, Georgia. My wife, a Savannah native, felt at home. After the turmoil of Princeton, the feel of the South with its warm weather and southern accents provided a welcome comfort.

All of the potential excited me and made me eager to accept this job. Plus, I needed one. I was now a young father with a precious wife and two little boys. I knew we needed a house and an income. There is a difference between living "by faith" and living "on faith." The latter is impossible—you can't eat faith or put faith into your car's gas tank. I know God has, can, and does perform miracles but, usually He leads His followers to live by faith, trusting Him to adequately be there and lead to sources of provisions.

The church-planting director came for a visit. We met at the Cracker Barrel on Jimmy Carter Boulevard. We then took a drive around Gwinnett and discussed some of my observations.

I was trying to appear more interested in what I was going to do for the District, the people of Gwinnett County, and the "Glory of God" than what I was going to be paid, but my heart was beating with anticipation and my mouth was anxiously dry, waiting to hear what they were going to offer me to launch a ministry in this white-collar community. Not only did I need a salary to meet my needs but also to cover the expenses for an office, mailings, supplies, advertisements and rental for a building that will house worship services. Surely they knew that and starting new churches was a denominational commitment. After all, I was new to this community and didn't know anyone yet and no one was waiting to support this venture.

I pulled my 1979 Volvo up to the north-bound entrance ramp to I-85 when the director, riding shotgun, verbally offered me "my contract." This was the moment I had been waiting for.

"Dan, we are going to do more for you than we have done for anyone else," he announced.

I liked the sound of that. Sort of like Alex Rodriquez, I did not mind being the highest paid church planter in that District.

"We are going to pull all the stops."

Keep talking.

"No holds barred."

Okay, I'm ready. Give it to me. Numbers began to formulate as I thought he must be talking $40,000, $50,000 or more for a couple of years, plus some ministry expense support. Even that wouldn't be enough because the median income was above that in Gwinnett County in 1985, especially in the growing Lawrenceville area, but it would be a great start.

"We are going to give you $ 2,000 a month for a year, plus health insurance."

I did not know what to say. Inside, I was about to panic. I wanted to scream, "How in the world do you expect me to live on a piddly $2,000 a month and launch a church?"

Outwardly, my response was more noble and godly-sounding than I was feeling. "Well, I appreciate the support, especially since it is a higher level of support than normal, but I will have to find an additional job to supplement it during the early stages and, when I get a core group together, we will see what we can come up with."

Whether you're a baseball player, church-planter, executive, engineer, chemist, doctor, or a salesman, every man is looking for some security in his contract or employment agreement. If he is an entrepreneur, he is looking for the sales agreement in response to his proposal. The contract means he is worth something. For a man to feel like he is in the Big Leagues, he needs to know somebody sees value in him, that he has a job to do, that there is a reason to get up in the morning, go to work and, hopefully, make a difference.

My contract was not enough but within the effort to fill the additional need I discovered a higher covenant that every man wants. It is better than a contract, will suffice even if there is no contract and, if there is, puts it in the proper perspective.

After the church-planting director went home, I returned to North Carolina to visit my wife and sons at the Chapman house—Susan's parents. We did not know that cancer was growing inside Susan's mother. She had not been well for a while, but we thought she was just fighting colds, fatigue, or something else that was much less serious. They knew we were in a desperate place so, in spite of Susan's mother feeling badly, they extended us hospitality. I told them about our contract, such as it was. We were thankful that we had a new direction—a future and a ministry that fit with our passion and calling—but our sighs were heavy with uncertainty.

"What are you going to do?" Susan's dad, Don, asked.

He was a pastor and a church-planter. Even though he was my father-in-law, I had always felt a collegial connection with him because we were in a unique fraternity of pastors. I respected what he accomplished in Hendersonville, NC. At the age of 38, he left a comfortable position with C&S Bank in Savannah to move his family to Toccoa Falls College and prepare for a new career in ministry. He knew what it was to risk it all and to see God open doors and provide.

Susan held our newborn, Andrew, in her arms while our four-year-old son Danny, admired his new Atlanta Falcons cap which I bought for him at the Falcon Inn. She was listening as her dad and I were talking, and she was agreeing with the new direction for our lives. She was living as much by faith as I was, maybe more. While I was running back and forth to Atlanta and trying to get something started, Susan had to do the hard work of waiting for the contract to come together while I attempted to find a home and a way to get things started.

"You are not working for man, you are working for God and He will make a way," Don assured me. I knew it was true. Don walked his talk. "He did it for me; He will do it for you."

Advice means more when it comes from someone who has lived it.

It also matched what my Dad was telling me.

Over the next month, I met more people, attended a few more Bible studies with my host, Jay. I knocked on every door I could. I used the professionally prepared resume' that I received before I left Princeton. Another of my preparer's friends was a VP of Human Resources at Coca Cola's World Headquarters, across North Avenue from Georgia Tech. Her connection helped me get an interview at Coke, but no job resulted and I was not really surprised. I did not know what I was applying for because my heart was not to work at Coke. I was only trying to find a place to supplement my income so I could plant a church. This was a frighteningly defining moment: I was not qualified to do anything other than work in a church. The church I would work in, did not exist.

I was desperate.

The Atlanta Journal and Constitution became my breakfast partner at the Waffle House many mornings as I poured over the "help wanted" ads. Nobody was looking for a guy with a degree in Theology who liked people and wanted to help others part-time for a few months or a year. In one pathetic attempt, I showed up at a casting-type meeting for a group that, allegedly, was finding people to do infomercials and small spots in TV and movies. That is what their classified ad said. I sat in the makeshift warehouse lobby, in my suit, white shirt and tie, looking around at young people who were hoping to be discovered. The girls were there with their mothers and armloads of different outfits, paying for the photo sessions that the group was selling so they could put their portfolio together. There was no opportunity there for me and probably not for them either. It was just a group selling expensive photo sessions to exploit people with fantasies.

Atlanta has always had huge conventions and visitors' businesses, so I thought I would try to get a job in one of the magnificent hotels which hosted people from around the world. I am a people-person–I hoped I could get a job as a bellman, or concierge or as a desk clerk.

The Waverly Hotel, a beautiful and expansive hotel on the west side of Atlanta, at the junction of I-75 and I-285 was where I was headed. I got in the car and was driving there to see what I could find but being new to Atlanta, I got confused and took the wrong exit off of the Perimeter. Maybe it was because Peachtree was in the name of the exit but as soon as I exited Old Peachtree, I knew this access road was not the exit I needed. I was stuck in the left-turn lane so I had to head up Old Peachtree road to find a place to turn around. Just past the BP Gas Station, there was a parking lot. On the building was the sign, Walk Thru the Bible Ministries.

"Walk Thru the Bible?" I thought. "I think I have heard of them. They have a curriculum for reading through the Bible. I wonder if they are hiring."

My high-powered resume' which resulted in nothing at Coke, was in my pocket. I didn't leave home without it. Besides, I was hoping to give it to someone at the Waverly.

Tammy, Walk Thru's very friendly receptionist, greeted me.

"Hi. Do you hire?" I asked. I thought it might be the type of ministry where people raised their support to work there. I really knew nothing about the organization but I had interviewed at Coke, read the paper, tried to be "discovered" for TV and was heading for a hotel job. Why not ask?

"Yes, we hire employees. I don't know if we are looking now, but you can leave a resume'."

"That would be great. I wasn't expecting to be here so I don't have a cover letter or an envelope."

"No problem. I'll type a cover letter for you and give you an envelope. Then I'll give it to our HR people and we will see what happens."

Tammy's words were like a cold drink to a thirsty, parched man. The drama that brought me to Walk Thru made me appreciate my $2,000 a month contract even more. I began to see what I believed and what Susan's dad said, "God would make a way." I wrote my cover letter in the lobby of Walk Thru The Bible. Tammy typed it and I trusted her to get it to the right people. I left, filled with hope.

"Susan, I found Walk Thru the Bible Ministries today and left a resume'." I was always enthusiastic, animated and verbose. I wanted her to jump up and down and shout with glee when I called her, but she quietly said, "That's good. What's next?"

"Well, I know I did not get the job yet and still need an interview but this is the first step. I think it might be what I'm looking for."

"It is good news. We will pray."

I left my hosts' home phone number with my resume' because this was ten years before I had a cell phone. Each day, when I came home from my networking and scouting in Lawrenceville, I would check messages.

After a week, when my enthusiasm was fading into deep concern, the call finally came. I arrived at the house after they had gone to bed. On the kitchen table was a note: "Fred Phanco from Walk Thru called for an interview. You need to call him back if you are interested. Here is his number."

Getting up the next day was easy because the first thing I did was call Walk Thru. I reached Fred's secretary and scheduled an appointment.

It was nice to see Tammy again in the lobby of Walk Thru. "Thanks for your help with the letter and the resume'. I have an appointment with Fred Phanco at 3:00 for an interview."

"That's great. I'll let him know you are here."

In just a few minutes he came out and greeted me with a smile, a handshake and a professional persona that exceeded what I expected from a ministry. I went back to his office and told him my story, what I was looking for and why I only needed a job for a few months: the support was coming in from the fledgling group that was beginning to come together. Because it was toward the end of the year, Walk Thru was trying to sell the Daily Walk, Family Walk and Closer Walk to churches and ministries in advance of the New Year. They needed someone, preferably a pastor, who could talk to other pastors in an effort to sell the magazines over the phone.

This was perfect, better than I could have asked for or even imagined. And I was just right for the job. My experiences in ministry, even back to when I was a paperboy learning to meet people and carry on a conversation, converged into a winning combination.

"Dan, I am pleased to offer you this job and welcome you to Walk Thru the Bible. Let's go back to Human Resources and meet Doug Russ who will formally give you your contract and collect your personal information for withholding and payroll."

I could not have been happier. The supplement that I needed was provided for me in a way so accidental I had to see that my steps were directed by God who had a plan for me and a commitment to working in my life.

"Where are you staying now, Dan?" Doug asked. He needed my current mailing address and he was interested interest in my saga.

"I am staying with a very nice and hospitable couple who opened a room to me. There is only one problem," I said with a smile. "They are Georgia Bulldog fans and I am a loyal Penn State fan, so that causes obvious problems." Penn State beat Georgia in the Sugar Bowl for the National Championship just three years earlier.

Their jaws dropped. Fred looked at Doug. Doug looked at Fred. "It is a confirmation!!!" Doug proclaimed. "We are both Penn State alumni." He pointed to the Nittany Lion on his book shelf and lifted the mat with the logo that he kept behind his desk. We laughed in disbelief. In Atlanta, God not only provided me a job but helped me find it where I wasn't even looking. And He gave it to me with a twist that made me feel His favor. I believe there were four of us laughing in that moment of praise and pleasure.

God had worked in my life many times before but never had I felt His work like I did in the combination of those two contracts.

For most men, there is a lot of stress in getting an acceptable contract but many times there is even more stress after signing the contract because that is when the work begins. A contract is "*a*: a binding agreement between two or more persons or parties, *especially,* one legally enforceable; *b*: a business arrangement for the supply of goods and/or services at a fixed price." (Merriam-Webster Online, M-W.com).

What every man is really looking for in a contract are terms he can live with—the better the terms, the more secure he feels. He hopes he will get what he is worth and that he will be able to produce what is required of him.

Every man would love to get a lucrative contract but most never will, which usually results in him feeling as though he either never made it to the Big Leagues or would not be there for long.

There is a much better offer.

It produces great security and reveals that every man has great personal worth.

It is guaranteed — paid in blood and sealed by the Spirit.

And it is offered to every man.

There is a part of God's character and nature that is often overlooked. I know for most of my Christian life I missed it. It is a truth that connects Biblical doctrines and events so they make more sense as a whole and are individually richer and fuller. When a man connects the lesson to his personal life he discovers an ongoing relationship with God who is involved in all of the events in his life and the outcome of all of his experiences.

This part of God's character and involvement in a man's life is revealed in this name for God, Elohim. Our English translations of the Bible hide the meanings in His names, just as a baseball manager's signs keep the opposition from knowing he is putting on the hit-and-run. His hand motions which scratch his nose, brush his face and adjust his cap mean something and even if you know the code you better be paying attention or you will watch a pitch when you're supposed to swing, or stand still when you should have run.

It is a good idea to learn the code that God uses to help us know Him and we better pay attention, too:

"God" = Elohim
"LORD" = Jehovah
"Almighty" = El Shaddai
"Most High" = El Elyon
"Lord" = Adonai
"The Everlasting God" = El Olam
"Lord of Hosts" = Jehovah Sabaoth

Each one means something special which helps us to know God better and enjoy Him more. I recommend a study that explores each one. (From *"The Names of God"* by Andrew Jukes, Kregel Publications)

The name that applies here is Elohim, the Covenant Making and Covenant Keeping God.

A covenant is similar to a contract because it is a binding commitment, but it surpasses anything that a contract can offer. Within it is a sacred oath made by God Himself, to His creation and all who exist in it, that He will restore everything into a perfect relationship with Him and with each other.

The first time God is revealed in the Holy Scriptures, the name Elohim is used–the Covenant-Making and Covenant-Keeping God. He created the heavens and the earth but "Now the earth was formless and empty, darkness was over the surface of the deep, and Spirit of God (Elohim) was hovering over the waters" (Genesis 1:2). It makes sense to me and many other believers and scholars, that between verses one and two, the catastrophic fall occurred when Satan and one-third of the angels were thrown out of Heaven and the creation was profoundly damaged. As God was hovering, he was brooding with deep emotion and determination to restore all that was lost.

"Under this name, we see God, according to His own will, working on a dark and ruined creature until, by His Word, all is set in order and made 'very good.' This is the name which we need to know before all others. This, therefore, is the first revealed in Holy Scripture; for it shows us One, who, when all is lost in darkness and confusion, brings back, first His light and life, and then His image into the creature and so makes all things new and very good." (ibid. p. 15)

This is not the only time we find this name used. Over 2000 times it is used in the Old Testament to reveal the tireless and stubborn commitment of God to work on, and in and through His creation and creatures.

"We have first the view of 'Elohim,' who, in virtue of His Being, in the might of love in virtue of relationship, cares for and works on His fallen creature, lost and fallen as it is, because it is His creature, and He is Love, and, therefore, He can never leave it nor forsake it. This is the view of God so fully shown us in the first chapter of the Bible and recognized and illustrated wherever we read of 'Elohim' and his doings." (ibid. p 37)

Throughout the Old Testament, God honors His covenant with His people, the Israelites. In spite of their rebellion and disregard, He works to help them understand, repent and return to Him so they will find the benefits of an unhindered intimacy with God. Kind David understood, as evidenced by these words showing security, rest, and trust.

"Whoever dwells in the shelter of the Most High
will rest in the shadow of the Almighty. I will say of the LORD,
'He is my refuge and my fortress,
my God, in whom I trust.'"
Psalm 91:1, 2

For the thousands of years of the Old Testament, through patriarchs, prophets, priests, and kings, God offered and worked His covenant. In the white space between the Testaments, it was still in effect but a new covenant was coming wherein the blood of animals was not the guarantee. It would be the very blood of Jesus, the Son, on the cross of sacrifice and shame that would seal this new covenant.

"20 Now may the God of peace, who through the blood
of the eternal covenant brought back from the dead our
Lord Jesus, that great Shepherd of the sheep,
21equip you with everything good for doing his will,
and may he work in us what is pleasing to him, through
Jesus Christ, to whom be glory forever and ever. Amen."
Hebrews 13:20,21

The gospel of the covenant is presented by God to man, not as a point to begin negotiations but a complete offer to a man that exceeds his wildest imagination. The deal is on the table and a man can reject it, ignore it, consider it or accept it by faith.

The worth every man is looking for is found through Elohim, the covenant-making and covenant- keeping God. Man does not need to anxiously wait by the mail box for any part of this contract. Instead there is a standing offer made by Elohim from the time of creation until every man is invited, through the Spirit, to accept it by faith and discover new benefits and significance every day.

Human contracts demand as much as they offer. A player can be released or placed on waivers, ending the relationship and the opportunity to continue a career with the team who offered the contract. Sure, he will get a temporary income but when the money is paid, it is all over. Maybe another team will pick him up or make another offer but the next contract will be equally demanding and limited in time. When the contract expires or the player is released, he may be a member of the Major League Alumni Association but he is no longer a Big Leaguer.

The man who accepts the offer of God's covenant will experience the benefits of God's covenant commitment to him. When he reads the Bible and understands that he has been "discussed" in the mind of God ("You have searched me, Lord, and you know me", Psalm 139:1) and God wants him on His team, he will know he is in the Big Leagues. Man does not need to worry about the pay because in this covenant, God promises "to meet all your needs according to his glory in Christ Jesus." (Philippians 4:19) God will stay on the job because man is His "workmanship" (Ephesians 2:10) and He promises "Never will I leave you; never will I forsake you." (Hebrews 13:5)

Darrel's contract mattered to God because Darrel mattered to God. God was already deeply committed to Darrel's life and was working to complete His work in and through Darrel. Eagerness and curiosity in what God would do next could have replaced the anxiety in the drama of waiting for the contract to arrive in the mail.

Looking back on my contracts in the church planting adventure reveals that God was involved and working His plan in my life. My circumstances felt desperate but I could have confidently rested in the dramatic situation, enjoyed the surprises and felt stronger if I had only been more fully aware of the extent of the covenant that was offered to me.

Every man's vast worth is contained in this amazing covenant. The man who receives it and lives in it knows he is in the Big Leagues, whatever his game and whatever his circumstances.

What's the Score at the End of the Fifth Inning?

How are you catching what life hits to you?

- How do you measure your worth?
- When have you felt most worthwhile?
- What sustains your feeling of worth?
- What threatens it?

When you are up to bat, what are you going to do?

- Will you accept the terms of God's covenant?

A prayer of faith... "*Lord God. Thank you for thinking I am worth something to you. Thank you for planning and working to forgive my sins, redeem my worth and give me a future and a hope. I receive all you have for me. Help me grow in it and learn more. In Jesus name I pray. Amen.*"

- What can you do to explore the terms of this covenant?
- How can you apply the benefits of this contract to a specific situation in your life right now?

The Sixth Inning

Perspective

Top of the Sixth

DARREL'S COMPETITION
WITH HIMSELF

"'For I know the plans I have for you,' declares the LORD,
'plans to prosper you and not to harm you, plans to give you hope and a
future."
Jeremiah 29:11

"Failures are the finger posts on the road to achievement."
C.S. Lewis

Very few players get to bat in the bottom of the ninth inning of a decisive League Championship game with one out and the potential pennant-winning run on third base.

It was a great game—an instant classic.

Rain could not dampen the spirits or quiet the crowd. The one and a half hour delay caused by the rain provided more time to talk about the see-saw Series between the "Lumber Company" and the "Big Red Machine."

The Pirates convincingly won Game 1, 5-1 and didn't allow a Reds' run after the first inning.

The first inning was a big one for the Reds in Game 2, but after four runs they were held scoreless until the eighth inning when they scored one more run. Those five were enough to beat the Pirates at home who scratched out three one run innings in the fourth, fifth and sixth.

When the Series moved to Cincinnati, the Pirates took the lead with a close 3-2 game, but the Reds would not let them take the next game. The Machine scored seven runs. Pittsburgh's bats were quiet as they could only muster one run.

With the best of five series tied at two games each, the whole city of Cincinnati was ready to unseat the Pirates, the reigning world Champions. In 1970 the Baltimore Orioles beat the Reds in five games of the World Series, but the next year the Pirates won the Series in seven games. Both teams wanted back into the Fall Classic to face either Detroit or Oakland.

October 11, 1972 was one of those days in baseball. Over in the American League, the Oakland Athletics were trying to finish off the Detroit Tigers and head into the World Series. In an afternoon game, they were tied in a pitcher's duel. Catfish Hunter, for the A's gave up only one run in seven and a third innings and the Tigers' Mickey Lolich allowed just one run in nine innings. In the top of the tenth, it looked like the A's were going to win the American League pennant. They scored two runs in the extra inning and if their pitchers could keep the Tigers from scoring more than one run, they were in the World Series. But a wild bottom of the inning that included a wild pitch with runners aboard, a fielder's choice and a walk, the Tigers scored three runs for a walk-off win that sent the ALCS to a fifth game. The A's had to wait until Game 5 to advance to play the Cincinnati-Pittsburgh winner in the National League.

The Pirates jumped out to a two to nothing lead in the second inning on a single, double and single by Sanguillen, Hebner and Cash, the first three batters. In the top of the fourth, the same three batters would put another run on the scoreboard with three consecutive singles.

Darrel led off in the bottom of the third. He got behind in the count 0-2, to the 19-game winner, Steve Blass, who came after Darrel with a fast ball and a curve ball, both called strikes. The next pitch was a fast ball outside but Darrel was patient and let it go by. Blass came after Darrel with the slow curve again and Darrel was ready for it. He hung back and lined a single to right field stopped by Roberto Clemente on one hop. So Darrel led off the inning and got the first hit for the Reds. Don Gullet, the Reds' pitcher, was the next batter and he bunted the first pitch down the first base line for a successful sacrifice as Darrel moved to second.

Pete Rose came to the plate with Darrel on second and one out. He was the leading hitter for either team in the NLCS, batting .471 with eight hits in seventeen at bats. He took the first ball and then on the second pitch hit a routine ground ball toward Willie Stargell at first base. But the ball hit the artificial surface cut-out in front of the dirt base area and bounced straight up. Stargell got a glove on it, but couldn't control it and the ball went into the outfield. Always hustling, Rose stretched it into a double and Darrel, on the move, scored the Red's first run.

The 27-year-old Al Michaels and veteran broadcaster Joe Nuxhall were calling the game on the radio. Curt Gowdy and Tony Kubeck were calling it on TV. Joe's matter-of-fact call was drowned out by the roar of the crowd and a very excited and loud Al Michaels made the call on the radio.

That was the only run the Red's would score until the fifth inning when Cesar Geronimo led off the inning with a solo home run to come back within one run of the Pirates, and that would be all until the ninth inning.

The Reds, behind 3 to 2, were down to their last three outs.

This great and hard fought season and the winner of the League Championship Series was about to be decided. Either the Pirates or the Reds were soon going to be celebrating. The home team fans were trying to make something happen and, as Al Michaels announced with his clear and intense, high- pitched voice, "The noise is deafening!"

The Pirates closer with just a 1.93 ERA came in to finish off the Reds and, hopefully, take the Pennant back to Pittsburgh. Dave Giusti had 54 appearances and 22 saves. Johnny Bench was the first batter he would face. Baseball fans live for innings like this.

Joe Nuxhall had headed down to the locker room to get ready for the post-game interviews. Al Michaels was doing the play by play. Michaels, who would get to call the Miracle on Ice in the 1980 Olympics, was getting the opportunity to call a great Big League game early in his career. He and Joe were the regular announcers for the Cincinnati network and in a few moments he would apologize to the national audience for his inability to hide his excitement for the Reds in this very tense game, as they were down to their last three outs.

Ever since the rain delay almost four hours earlier, the tension was building with hopes for home team victory in a fantastic finish. "This place will go bananas because the Reds are coming to bat in the bottom of the ninth with the Pirates leading the Red's three runs to two," Al said with as much excitement in his voice as the fans had in their cheers.

Coming to the plate was Johnny Bench. He was one for three in the game and five for seventeen in the Series. The first pitch was a slider—0 and 1. He watched a slider outside for the next pitch and the count was 1 and 1. The count changed to 1 and 2 as Johnny swung and missed.

The call came from Al Michaels this way: "Johnny swings and hit this one a mile. Johnny had all of that one, but foul, all the way to the Red seats in the upper deck. The count, 1 and 2. Here's the pitch, a change-up, Bench hits it, (volume increasing) back goes Clemente! (pitch of voice goes higher), at the fence!" and with a crowd whose hopes for the future have just been fulfilled, everyone is screaming so loud that Al's voice is barely detectable, "He's done it!" Al let the crowd's roar say it all as Johnny made his way around the bases. The score is now tied 3-3.

While Al was broadcasting the excitement to everyone listening on their radios, Curt Gowdy and Tony Kubek were bringing the drama to millions watching TV in their homes. None of the 41,867 had left the stadium and each and every one was standing, cheering and doing whatever they could to help their team pull out one of baseball's most dramatic victories on a crazy day in October.

In the dugouts the adrenalin was flowing. After Johnny's home run, Darrel realized, "If this thing continues, I might get to bat." Bench was the clean-up hitter so if even one of the next hitters reached safely and the Reds avoided a double play, Darrel would come to the plate.

Nobody could sit down and the cheering from Bench's homer had not stopped when Tony Perez got a single on the first pitch. It was the perfect situation for a home team broadcaster as the excitement grew to even higher levels. "Here comes Perez. Base hit to center field. The Pennant is at first base with nobody out. Denis Menke comes up to the plate."

"It's deafening in here….Everyone is standing! Everyone!!" Probably Al was too, if he could lift his microphone off the table.

In the dugout, Darrel took his bat out of the rack, put his helmet on his head and moved to the end of the dugout. His heart was pounding so hard he could feel it and the noise of the crowd was so loud he could feel the vibration in his stomach.

Denis Menke was the batter. He tried to bunt the pinch runner, George Foster, over to second but fouled two attempts. After three balls the count was full and Menke fouled another one straight back. The pitcher held Foster on first with a couple of throws that made George dive back to the base. The Reds put on a hit and run and Foster took off but Menke fouled another pitch back. The crowd did not calm down but increased the decibels of their roaring. On the next pitch Menke hit a single to left field and Foster stopped at second.

"The Pennant is now at second base," Michaels announced with the assurance that something special was about to happen now that the winning run was in scoring position.

Almost certainly Darrel was going to get in the game. As Cesar Geronimo stepped up to bat, Darrel moved to the on-deck circle of this amazing platform—a Big League ball field in the ninth inning of a play-off situation when he could make a difference. The nation was watching. This type of situation is where every player dreams of producing the heroic hit to win the game, clinch the Series and get his name on the score card as the last hitter who drove in the winning run. With his lead-off hit and base running in the third inning Darrel already was responsible for the first run, a third of what they scored so far. A game winning RBI here and he might even be the Player of the Game, the utility player who becomes October's unlikely hero. It happens!

Dave Giusti pitched two balls to Geronimo. Bill Virdon, the Pirates manager, walked to the mound for a pitching change. Al Michaels said, "He's the coolest one in the stadium." Cesar swung and missed on the first pitch from Bob Moose and fouled a bunt attempt to even the count at 2 and 2. On the 2-2 count Geronimo hit it deep to right field and for a brief moment everyone screamed thinking it was gone, but took a moment to breathe when they saw Clemente settling under it at the warning track and make the catch. Foster tagged and headed to third base.

Now there were runners on first and third with one out.

"The Pennant is now on third base," Al called it like he knew George was going to score and win the game.

Darrel had been kneeling on one knee in the on-deck circle. He was praying. "Lord, you know I have always wanted this. Thank you for the opportunity. Please let me get a hit so we can win the game."

Bill Virdon came out to talk to the pitcher. For the Pirates there was no room for mistakes. Every strategy to prevent a run from scoring was in place. The outfielders and infielders moved in. The pitch selection was determined and the manager walked back to the dugout. Darrel waited beside the batter's box, took a few practice swings and soaked in the glory of the situation.

"Now it's my turn. I've got to get a hit." Darrel was feeling confident and knew he had what it took to drive in the winning run.

"It's three runs, eight hits and no errors for the Pirates. Three runs, seven hits and one error for the Reds," Michaels announced with a staccato cadence in his voice that couldn't wait for Foster to get to home and score the winning run. With the crowd roaring and everyone feeling that something special was about to take place, Darrel stepped to the plate.

"Moose is set and the first pitch to Chaney is low—ball 1."

Crowd noise filled in the space when Al was not talking. He didn't need to say anything. The volume swelled and told it all.

"Here's the pitch to Chaney, foul, straight back. The count is 1 and 1."

The next pitch was a pitch out. The Pirates thought the Reds might try a squeeze play. Wouldn't that have been a great way to win the game?

Darrel was one of the Reds' best bunters, so the squeeze would have made sense, except, if Darrel missed it and George got picked off, the winning run would no longer be only 90 feet away. It would also have prevented the risk of a double play, the main thing that Darrel wanted to avoid. But a hit, or just a sacrifice fly ball to the outfield, would drive in the winning run.

"Darrel waits. Moose gets set. Darrel from Hammond, Indiana. Batted .250 this year and platooned at shortstop with Davey Concepcion. Here comes the 2 and 1. Darrel pops it up. Alley goes back. Stennent comes in." Tension in Al's voice goes up in as it looks like they might collide and the ball will drop between them. "And they come together but Alley makes the catch. Foster has to stay at third. So Chaney can't deliver as he pops out to the shortstop."

He did not hear Al Michael's words "can't deliver" but Darrel felt it. He let his team down and himself too. This was his chance to get the clutch hit—a Big League play on a Big League platform. An opportunity like this only comes once in a lifetime. Darrel's disappointment turned his focus from the game inward, and his emotions boiled in frustration and anger.

When Darrel was batting every set of eyes in his dugout was on him. Pete Rose who drove Darrel in for the first run in the third inning, Johnny Bench who homered earlier in this rally, Davey Concepcion who competed with Darrel for the shortstop position and shared it with him this year, Sparky Anderson who managed Darrel in the minors and now in this grand game, along with every other teammate in the dugout and the bullpen. They all wanted their teammate to come through. They wanted it for him and the team as bad as Darrel did and when he returned to the dugout after making the second out, they would have smacked him on the butt, or pat him on the shoulder and told him to "stay with 'em"! A mark of a championship team is the way the players always root for each other.

But this time they couldn't. When a player is in a storm of rage and anger, it is better to just ignore him and let him work out his anger himself. Darrel threw his bat when he headed toward first, just in case the ball dropped. But when he knew the catch was made and he took his hard right turn back to the dugout, instead of jumping in ecstasy at first base surrounded by a pile of Reds' players celebrating a National League Championship and a trip to the World Series, a burst of bitter emotion controlled him. Angry with himself for not producing and at God for not answering his prayer and helping him, he kicked his glove and hat. They were sitting on the top step waiting for him, in case the game went to extra innings. To avoid flying debris the players scattered but kept their eyes on the field because Hal McCrae was coming in to pinch hit against Bob Moose and, hopefully produce what Geronimo and Chaney could not deliver—the winning run.

His kick was a direct hit. Thankfully he did not hit the cement step or he would have broken his foot. The hat flew over the dugout into the front row of the still hopeful and wild fans. His glove fell into a drain that was used to keep the water out of the dugout and off of the field. It worked hard earlier during the rain delay and had been left open.

Angry outbursts never accomplish good results. Even if they make a man temporarily feel better, he is in less a mood or place to produce until he calms down. Darrel had to calm down because the Reds were one batter away from extra innings if Hal couldn't knock in the game winning run.

Adding insult to injury, the fans acted in a "thanks but no thanks" gesture for the souvenir and they threw his cap back into the dugout. The drain pipe went three feet straight down below the floor of the dugout before it elbowed into the storm drainage system. At the bottom of this hole was Darrel's glove.

"I've got to get it."

But the action was on the field. All eyes, except Darrel's, were on Hal McRea, Bob Moose and George Foster—the Pennant Winning run on third base. The roar continued, but Darrel was distracted with his new dilemma.

McRae would either be the last batter in regulation or there when the game was won. George Foster was still 90 feet away, with an opportunity to win it for the Reds. Each pitch might be the one that ended the game. Foster was stretching his lead from third base and was ready to run on any contact. All the Reds, except Darrel, were at the edge of the dugout, ready to storm the field as victors in this baseball battle royal.

"The count is one and one. Bob Moose winds up, and the pitch... It's a wild pitch!" Al Michaels screamed as he broadcast. It was euphoria in

Riverfront Stadium. Hal was jumping up and down, waving his arm from the dugout side of home plate so George could score.

Darrel did not see it but he heard it. He was on the floor of the dugout with his arm stretched down into that drain pipe trying to reach his glove. Darrel's teammate, Jack Billingham, was holding onto the elastic waistband of Darrel's pants to keep Darrel from going down the drain—but Jack was watching the action on the field.

"Foster scores! The Reds win the Pennant!! The Reds win the Pennant!!!" The surprise bang-bang nature of a wild pitch and a score from third was faster than a hit that unfolds. The place went berserk. Jack dropped Darrel and joined the boys of summer as they instantly stormed the field in a jumping huddle of teammates who began this journey in February and now experienced the thrill of victory with the reward of another appearance in the World Series.

Darrel got his glove, even though it didn't matter for now. In just a few seconds he was one of the celebrants. The pop-out would have hurt a lot worse if Hal had made an out and the Pirates had won in extra innings. But that did not happen.

Championship teams learn how to win by helping each player maximize his talents and performance. Encouragement to overcome pop-outs is a necessity for a Big Leaguer. Darrel played in the World Series against Oakland just a few days later but with a new experience to add to his career. He was a lot wiser, and a better Big Leaguer because of it.

Bottom of the Sixth

THE RIGHT PERSPECTIVE HELPS EVERY MAN MASTER SELF

"No, in all these things we are more than conquerors through Him who loved us."
Romans 8:37

"You can have everything in life you want, if you will just help other people get what they want."
Zig Ziglar

I will "do" better when I can "be" better.

Most of my life, I got them backwards. That is a problem and is sometimes the worst problem.

What's wrong with Darrel wanting to be the hero and being mad when he wasn't? Is it a problem for me to take pride in the uniqueness of my church or to savor the approval of an affirming congregation?

Paul's direction to the Philippians, in the third verse of the second chapter, was to "do nothing out of selfish ambition or vain conceit," which seems impossible and downright impractical. Were Darrel and I practicing selfish ambition or vain conceit?

It all depends. If a man desires success, works hard for it and enjoys it with thankfulness, the fruit of his labor, there is nothing wrong with that. But if he is looking for the same accomplishment, whatever it is—to prove his worth, validate his identity or establish his significance, then he is doing it, at least in part for himself with a motive which is wrong. Even more, it is counterproductive and unnecessary.

Utility players and small church pastors are especially vulnerable although, in truth, every man is. That man does not often get the opportunity to be the hero, so he wants to make the most of it when the opportunity presents itself. Being the hero makes him feel like he is somebody and his value has been validated.

• • • • •

One of those times for me was Christmas Eve, when I got it backwards. But I must admit that was not the only time I made that mistake.

The era of church growth and mega churches was threatening to someone in my position, the pastor of a small church, who was trying to do something big in order to bolster my identity as a man and a pastor.

We were preparing for a Christmas Eve service during that seven-year cycle when Christmas fell on a Sunday. Our small church, only a few years old, had some people traveling while others were enjoying family visiting from out-of-state. In Castle Rock, Colorado, it seems that everybody is from somewhere else. We have people who are either going away for the holiday or they have people coming to visit at Christmas. These scenarios affect their Christmas plans, especially when it comes to attending a church service.

A few people wanted to worship on Christmas but could not come on Christmas Eve — how can you cancel Sunday services, especially on Christmas—Christ's birthday? Some wanted a Christmas Eve service but not a Sunday morning service because that was when the family always opened their gifts. Nobody wanted both and everybody had family traditions and plans.

It may not seem like a big deal, but to me it was. Both Christmas and Easter are when the church and the pastor better hit a home run or at least get a base hit. These holidays are like the playoffs. Christmas is one of those times when most people, even if they usually do not attend church services, celebrate the birth of the Christ-child and the wonder of God's love entering a needy world. At Easter they hear the winning message of the resurrection that conquers all, even death. These are times when faith and culture converge. Work stops and everybody has the same focus.

At Christmas, established churches have multiple services when thousands of festive people from the church and the community attend their services. Real animals fill their live manger scenes. Musicians sing carols, candles are lit and hearts are warmed at the thought of the gentle glow of a candle representing the Light of the world coming as a baby, wrapped in swaddling clothes and lying in a manger. Their parking lots overflow with cars, some filled with grandparents from back East, parents and kids. A little snow left over from a few days before and a starlit night, create the perfect Christmas experience.

Our service was also warm and welcoming but much smaller and simpler. Decorations were pretty but sparse. My church met in the gymnasium of an elementary school. A few of our youth would get to the service early and, under my supervision, set up luminaries in the parking lot; a few hundred bags with sand in the bottom and little candles would line the drive. The gymnasium-turned-sanctuary was filled with poinsettias and greens. The lights were turned down low. Christmas music was playing and a few of our volunteer musicians would help us experience a Holy Night. For our first couple of Christmases together we began to establish the tradition of going outside to light the candles—the school would not allow candles because of the fire hazard and the risk of wax dripping on the gym floor. We liked it outside in the cold, wading in the snow, seeing our breath under the stars, with the neighbors in the surrounding houses able to hear us sing "Joy to the World."

I was usually as nervous as a cat on a hot tin roof. How many would come? If some guests from the neighborhood came but only a handful from our church showed up, what will the visitors think? We need this to be good. It was not the bottom of the ninth inning but I felt the pressure to produce a winning event and on Christmas Eve, numbers were a key measurement.

Our church leadership had different opinions on when we should hold the Christmas service. I decided to have one 11:00 p.m. service, hoping to please those who wanted a Christmas Eve service as well as those who could not come early on Christmas Eve but wanted a Christmas day service. I was hoping that decision to be the right one. If it worked, I'd be the hero or at least a pastor who knew how to plan an effective Christmas weekend. If it went well, I would feel good about the service and happy for all who were blessed by it. I would also feel secure in my place as an effective pastor who led his congregation the right way. If not, then I would be disappointed that we missed the mark and the doubts of my leadership and questions of our church in the community would be uncertain, in my mind, if no one else's. After all, thousands are at the Presbyterian Church on the corner and at the Rock Church in the back of the neighborhood.

I have spent most of my ministry in such angst. On more Sundays than I can count, I would sweat the attendance, the music, PowerPoint, the offering, and how my sermon was delivered and received. That stress was not only because of my care and concern for the glory of God and the needs of the people, it mattered also for who I was and for my own perception of my ministry. Did we really matter to God? If we would just go away, would it make any difference?

Was this normal? Was I wrong? I wanted to do something great for God and for the people of the community. My personal fears were logical. Could this be "selfish ambition or vain conceit?"

The first events of our Colorado ministry had at least one common denominator with this Christmas Eve service—my need for success.

· · · · ·

We were invited to start a church in Colorado. Our lives up to that point were lived in the East. North and South was the way we thought, not out west. North Carolina, Virginia or maybe even Maryland would be a future home and a place to minister. Having lived in Pennsylvania, Ohio, Florida, and New Jersey, eastern locations made sense.

Susan was visiting her family in North Carolina and I was home in Lawrenceville, when I received the inquiry by phone. She was as shocked as I was when I told her that I just got off the phone with the guy who was in charge of church-planting for Colorado. He asked me to take a trip to check it out. Our former Youth Pastor told Steve about us. We felt that this was probably God's work in arranging these conversations and long-distance introductions. We had to check it out but it was a long way from everything familiar. Susan's sister, who overheard the conversation, simply said, "Get practical." We understood that reaction.

A couple of weeks later, we made the trip to Colorado and felt a strange and unexplainable stirring in our hearts, that this was going to be our new home and next ministry. It was not safe but it seemed that God wanted us to trust Him with this high-risk adventure. Only 10% of church startups called "parachute-ins", ever become established. That is when a church is started from scratch with no core group or mother church infusing the core group with talent and resources.

We said, yes to the invitation to move West and start a new chapter of our lives and ministry. It was time to start packing.

With the Ryder truck loaded, we climbed in the car and kissed our oldest son, Danny, goodbye and headed to the new and unfamiliar. Danny was eighteen, had a good job, a place to live, was involved in a great youth group and was going to Peru for his first mission's trip. It was the first time our family would not be living together, which did not help the emotions of moving to something new in a place which was different than any other place we had ever lived.

Colorado is a spectacular piece of God's creation but it is a different kind of beauty as compared to the tree-lined drives and wooded lots of Pennsylvania, North Carolina and Atlanta. The wide open spaces with few trees and the big, bluer-than-blue, always sunny sky—300 sunny days a year to be exact—reminded us every day in a thousand different ways that we were not in Georgia any more.

Our 30-hour drive from Georgia to Colorado included driving out of Georgia, into Tennessee and through parts of Kentucky and Illinois. We went all the way across Missouri and Kansas. Eastern Colorado was a total surprise with its flat, wide open spaces. Each mile seemed less familiar and it looked and felt unlike home even though it was going to be where we lived.

When we arrived, no one was waiting for us and we did not know anyone. Why did God call us all the way out here? Did He call us out here or did I just get the signals confused? What if something goes wrong at the house closing? We are so exposed and vulnerable with no place to go back to. If something goes wrong, what would we do?

We flew right through the closing without a single problem. So that fear was eliminated. It was before the economy tanked; at that time, we had perfect credit and enough money to pay the down payment on the house.

When a family gets into a new town, it is natural to get their bearings through the new job and friendships built in their church—maybe even before they get to know their neighbors. However, my church was my job and it did not yet exist. It was in the middle of summer and the kids were out of school. It felt odd to go to the grocery store or to a restaurant and never see a familiar face.

After the boxes where unpacked, it was time to get started with the church-planting venture. During the challenge of meeting people and inviting them to the vision I had for a church, my loneliness morphed into a confusing fear. Getting to something from nothing felt impossible and took a long time to develop. The "do-or-die" work pattern and lifestyle embedded itself in my mind and soul and affected me in every situation and relationship. It changed me and it was through that lens of fear and need that I met every circumstance and person. "Will this person be our friend? Will they share our desire for a new church?"

I was forty-five years old, too old for a failure, had a trusting wife, an impressionable son and a sweet little girl counting on me to succeed; we were out of our comfort zone. How could it be "selfish ambition and vain conceit" to want to get this new ministry up and running?

Certainly the insecurity was magnified because of the circumstances which preceded our departure from our former ministry. We closed the church we planted after our Princeton crisis. After thirteen years of experiencing provisions, building relationships, Vacation Bible Schools, board retreats, men's and women's Bible studies, Christmas programs, building programs, Sunday School classes—all while we were living life, having babies, raising our kids and rooting for the Braves—it came to an end. One Saturday morning, a consensus formed among our leaders. What God had started as Alpha, he was also Omega, bringing it to a conclusion.

Hopefully, it was the correct decision to close the church after thirteen years. We still had sixty wonderfully loving people but we were not getting bigger, only smaller. It was too painful to endure disappointing Sundays and the financial struggles after all that time. Maybe we quit. We hoped we were led by God who was closing one door and preparing to open another. To the best of our knowledge and understanding, we did what we thought He wanted us to do.

But it was heartbreaking to see the chairs, in which we sat during worship services, be hauled away in a truck for another church to use—at least it was a church and they would still hold people who were worshipping God, even if I was not their pastor. When the piano headed out the door with its new owner, a piece of us went with it, especially for my wife, our worship leader and pianist.

If someone would have tried to hold us back from any future ministry, even for a while, and say we needed healing and counseling, I would have resisted. I did not know the nature of my injuries or that what went wrong with my "doing", threatened my sense of "being".

This was, for me, a popping-out-in-the-bottom-of-the-ninth experience, and it affected all of my future at-bats.

Selfish ambition is subtle, logical and present. It has a corrupting affect, like files in a computer, which slow down the performance. Sometimes, it causes a crash.

Success feels good. Getting what a man wants and feeling able to make something happen or be a part of a winning team or a great accomplishment is very satisfying, affirming, and sweet to savor. Failure is painful, disappointing, and provokes doubt and self-loathing. Often, this lasts a lifetime and leaves, both a terrible aftertaste that every man wishes he could cleanse from his palate, as well as a stench he tries to remove from his nostrils.

So, naturally, I spent my life pursuing success and avoiding the pain of failure. Success was a plus. Failure was a minus. What they totaled equaled how I felt about myself—my thoughts of my worth, identity and significance. That affected the way I came to bat in all of the situations of my life, whether or not it was the bottom of the ninth inning of a League Championship game with the winning run on third base or a Christmas Eve service. Success, for me, was more than desirable, it was necessary. It was not just for the benefit of the result, but for the validation of who I was. That was toxic.

· · · · ·

Not many came to that 11:00 Christmas Eve service. I was depressed for a least a week. It was the second bluest Christmas of my lifetime—second only to the one after our departure from Princeton. If I would have had a cap and glove to kick, I would have kicked them too, but since I did not, I just kept kicking myself.

It was not counseling I needed to make things better, I needed a healthier sense of my "being"— my significance.

Patricia Raybon has written about a high school baseball player in her book, I Told the Mountain To Move—a compelling book on prayer from the perspective of her real life. In one chapter, she was attending a high school state championship baseball game with a close friend whose son was a star player on the underdog team.

"Please pray, Patricia." But, really, how do you pray for a sporting event? Patricia told her friend, "I pray that he be covered to play his best."

"But then during the night, I understood there was more. The Holy Spirit helps our feeble prayers, indeed. About 3 a.m., I was stirred awake. The house was dark. Dan (her husband) *lay next to me, sleeping, with even breathing.*

I eased the covers off, trying not to wake him. Then I padded down the hall to my little office. I turned on a lamp. I opened a prayer journal, found a clean page.

Then I sat there and waited. The best prayers have the fewest words—Martin Luther's reminder. I'm not sure that's always true. But tonight I would be a woman of few words.

Father, I am praying for Etienne (that was the boy's name). *Then I sat still. I would just listen. I would enjoy the presence of God.*

Then the Holy Spirit spoke.

And, yes, maybe God loves baseball. Getting us back home is his intent, after all. Besides that, however, the sport is a good game...

Does God hear such prayers?

I didn't know. But I knew this: The Holy Spirit offered a word for my praying friend's son. Moreover, it was a good and perfect word:

Tell the boy he's already a champion.

In fact, his whole team is a championship team.

They have fought the good fight. They have played like their good coach taught then. Year after year, when others doubted, they played the game with integrity, fairness and discipline. Better still, they played this good game with a good heart.

They practiced hard. Fought right. Played fair. Competed well. They studied to show themselves approved.

So, today, when they walk on that field — before the first pitch flies — they are champions.

Tell the boy these things. Then he can play with power and joy and the authority that comes from knowing he's already a winner.

And the game?

"The game will take care of itself." (From <u>I Told the Mountain to Move</u> by Patricia Raybon, Salt River an Imprint of Tyndale House Publishers, Inc., pp. 257, 258)

I wonder how my ministry and life would have been if I had confidence in my "being"—that I was a champion. Not a State champion or a National League champion but a winner in God's eyes. A winner in ministry measured not by external performance, or with visible and measurable results but by the love and promises of God.

Drama, with villains, failures and surprises makes a story interesting. I could have performed much better during the suspense of the ups and downs of life and ministry if my focus had been more on others and God with less of a need for personal success. He was there in His great faithfulness.

Our move to Colorado turned out to be a great one. The new scenery was only part of what God used to make all things new for us. We met wonderful people who stood by us in the new church planting adventure. This handful of families all became church-planters with us and, at a crossroads in our lives, Crossroads Community Church was born.

On my difficult Christmas Eve, the forty-or-so of us who were there had the opportunity to celebrate Christmas together. It was the perfect environment to experience the simplicity of the Christmas message. Except for the heavenly host of angels, the first Advent was a very humble event—even called the humiliation of God—with a small crowd which included a handful of shepherds and the young parents, Mary and Joseph.

The Christmas Eve service was not supposed to be about me experiencing success, measured in numbers compared to other churches, which would validate my ministry. The fact that God loved me was already established. My place in His heart was secure regardless of the attendance and my performance. If only I could have seen it that way, I could have enjoyed it and been more effective in showing the love of God that reaches to the humblest of circumstances.

My call to ministry in general, and His strategies in each of the exciting chapters of it, was His idea more than mine. I had made thorough and conscientious preparations to honor Him and to serve others. He was and continues to be active, working in and through me in ways which are eternal and immeasurable. He works in big ways and in small ways; in crowds, groups and individuals. He sees me as a champion and I need that perspective.

The same was true when we moved to Colorado to start the church. God was behind the project. He said, "… I will build my church and the gates of Hades will not overcome it." (Matthew 16:18) Everyday anticipation could have been from that perspective. Being part of His great plan of reaching this world was an honorable position. Discovery, not worry, was mine to enjoy and to experience every day.

When we closed the church in Atlanta, it was not the end of God's work or my place in His plan, although that is what I feared. When I left Princeton, it was easy to hear the voice of the accuser who said, "Something is wrong with you, Dan. You are disqualified for God's service." But God's voice said, "I still have a plan from this day forward—you are my champion. I knew all of these events before one of them came to be and I am going to work it all together for my good purpose and bring something good out of it."

A healthy perspective for every man is to focus on his "being"—his God-given significance. Humility is not losing his identity, but trading the self-promoting, performance-oriented identity for a God-given identity. Every man will have that opportunity many times.

In the worst and the lowest of times, whatever they are, God is there to say, "You are my champion. You are more than a conqueror. I love you. I have a plan for you." Those words of God are for every man, in every circumstance. When they reach into his soul and become his perspective on life, he knows he is significant.

The underdogs won the state championship baseball game because they performed like the champions they were. Every man will live up to the perspective that he has.

Every man can know he is in the Big Leagues and when he does he will perform like a Big Leaguer.

What's the Score at the End of the Sixth Inning?

What has been hit to you?
- When have you "blown-it" by missing an opportunity
- and causing something to go terribly wrong?
- How did it affect the way you viewed yourself?
- What was your reaction?

When you are up to bat what are you going to do?
- What can you do to separate who you are from what you do?
- How will your performance improve if your significance is not threatened?
- Who have you observed who gets this right in his/her life?
- Describe a healthy reaction when something goes wrong and the results are disappointing?

The Seventh Inning

Purpose

Turning a double play against the Mets.

Top of the Seventh

DARREL NEEDED TO BE READY WHEN THE GAME CAME TO HIM

"Just as a body, though one, has many parts,
but all its many parts form one body, so it is with Christ."
I Corinthians 12:12

"Be ready when the game comes to you."
Sparky Anderson

Cindy began to expect the worst.

"He is going to be in a bad mood again tonight. He only pinch-hit once for the pitcher in the eighth inning and he popped out. 0 for 1. He won't like that!" She could sense his frustration.

Darrel thought he needed to do something more. "Pinch-hit here, play a couple of defensive innings there . . . I'm better than that. I've got power, a glove and an arm. I've got to play more to get my average up. I'm gonna talk to Sparky and get some attention."

The frustration was part of being a Big Leaguer but for the last four months, it was forming into a crisis.

It started in Spring training when Davey Concepcion was starting to play all the time. Darrel wondered what was going on.

Platooning worked well the previous season. For Darrel, it wasn't as good as playing all the time but it was the next best thing. Davey would bat against lefties, Darrel would bat against righties. Darrel knew he would play a lot because the Reds were going to be facing a lot of right-handed pitchers.

The Reds finished the previous season with 95 wins, beat the Pirates in the National League Championship Series and went all the way to the Seventh Game of the World Series. Darrel played in all of the NLCS games as well as in four of the World Series games. Down 3 - 2 in the bottom of the ninth, the decisive game of the World Series, Sparky sent Darrel in the game to pinch-hit and get something started. He did not get a hit, but he got hit—in the knee. Take your base. The excitement was high and Darrel had the chance to be a hero and score the tying run. Unfortunately, he never crossed home. The A's won the Seventh Game of the World Series, 3 to 2, but Darrel gained the knowledge of what it feels like to be on base for the final out of a World Series.

Entering Spring Training, Darrel's first concern was to make the team. His next priority was getting to play and playing well. The more he played, the better he played. With the team finishing the 1972 season in the Series and Darrel hitting a respectable .250 average, compared to Davey's .209, he, at least, deserved a shot at the starting position. His chances were pretty good. At least, that's what he thought.

But change was brewing and people were beginning to notice.

"Chicago—The message came across loud and clear. It was the Opening Day of Spring Training, the start of the new year for the Cincinnati Reds.

Darrel Chaney was sitting by his locker as Davey Concepcion reported to camp—sitting and waiting. Concepcion came bouncing through the door and manager, Sparky Anderson, came over to greet him.

And what a greeting it was! Anderson threw his arms around the young Venezuelan in a gesture of affection. The scene was a warm one . . . . warm to everyone, but Chaney.

Chaney, you see, was supposed to battle Concepcion for the shortstop job on the Reds, the job vacated by Woody Woodward with his retirement. It was supposed to be a fair battle with each man starting equally.

But the scene in the locker room was the tip-off. Concepcion was ahead on points—Anderson was a Concepcion man. Chaney knew he'd have to do a whole lot to win the job." (Bob Hertzel, Cincinnati Enquirer)

With a World Series appearance the year before, the Reds were a major sports story at this time. Dozens of newspaper columns were following the drama of the shortstop competition.

Davey ended up playing every game and, the more he played, the better he got. His place as the Reds' #1 shortstop was looking more and more certain. And as Bob Hertzel wrote, Sparky Anderson liked him. It turned out to be for good reason. While Davey previously had performance challenges and some major attitude swings, he was a great defensive shortstop and his bat was improving. Sparky recognized the talent. It was almost as though he knew Davey was going to hit .287 with 8 home runs, 3 triples and 18 doubles, in 1973.

When a player like Darrel is one of the best his whole life and is competitive enough to make it to the Big Leagues, he does not want to sit on the bench nor does he expect to. When the team won and Darrel was riding the pine, there was the nagging feeling that "they" won, not "we" won. The guys who were playing all the time didn't think this way nor did they treat Darrel like an outsider, but he did not feel like he was helping the team.

However interesting the story was from the outside, inside Darrel's mind a battle was brewing over his future in baseball. What good is a player who never gets in the game? How long will I last if everyone who comes up from the minors takes away my position? Where is my place? Is this as far as I'm going? Is the dream over?

Watching baseball on TV gives a very simplistic view of a ballplayer's life. The spectator may get a small idea of the nerves which produce butterflies in a clutch-hitting situation. A competitive baseball player does not want to strike out, especially when the game is on the line. Carrying the desires of the whole team, the fans in the stands, and the fans at home on their living room couches, make the next 93 mph fastball the opportunity to be a hero or a goat. Baseball players live for that kind of tension. If they made it to the Big Leagues, they want to be in the game when it is all on the line so they can win it for everybody who cares.

But the intrigue that goes on with teammates, coaches, the manager, the front office decisions, the press, the fans, and the effects on the family and conversations at home—these are elements of the game which most fans don't know about nor pay attention to. To the player, it all converges inside his mind and his emotions. At times it reveals character flaws and he self-destructs under the weight of it all. Other times his inner strength connects with his physical strength to face these adversaries with a sense of destiny and purpose.

By 1969, Darrel had made it to the Big Leagues, but arguably too quickly. Sure, he wanted to be there, but a shaky start hurt his confidence and his chances. "Then all of a sudden, he found himself cast in a utility role and there was seemingly no way out. 'I was only 21 years old and getting the mark of a utility man. I didn't want that tag then and I don't want it now, at 24. I don't want it until I'm 34' he said." (Bob Hertzel, Cincinnati Enquirer).

But that is what Darrel had become. Davey Concepcion was the Reds' everyday shortstop.

For the first half of the '73 season, on game day, Darrel would come to the ballpark, work out, warm up, take batting practice and then sit on the bench. There were streaks when he went for weeks without seeing any playing time. He would do anything to help, even catching in the bull-pen when the pitchers were warming up. A pinch-hit opportunity or subbing for a few innings was a chance to get in the game, but it was rare and probably would be followed by two, three or four days, maybe even a week or two without playing time.

It seemed that the shortstop drama was over for the Reds but for Darrel, the decision which put him on the bench as a utility player, without the chance to earn a starting position, was taking its toll. Darrel's nickname was "Norton" because he sort of looked like Ed Norton on the hit TV comedy show, "The Honeymooners". Like his look-alike, Darrel had the ability to make guys laugh. His clowning was contagious and kept the clubhouse fun and the dugout entertained. But one has to be happy to be a good clown and Darrel was not happy. Darrel's frustration was evident, even on the bench.

"Cindy, the only way I'm gonna get in the game is if somebody breaks a leg," he complained on a hot July morning. "I'm going to talk to Sparky and see if I can get some more playing time."

The All-Star Game was July 24th. Sparky Anderson, the Red's manager was the manager for the National League team and five Reds were All-Stars. It was not a good first-half of the season for Cincinnati. June 30th they were eleven games off the lead. Before the All-Star break, it seemed like a good time to talk to Sparky. He had said, "My door is always open," so Darrel thought he might as well give it a try. It couldn't hurt, could it?

What if Sparky decided Darrel was only whining and ought to count his blessings just for being on the team? If he didn't think Darrel was any good, he could just release him to get him "out of his hair." On the other hand, if that was his plan, it might be better to know it and try to get traded or start looking for a job with the city of Hammond.

Inside Riverfront Stadium, the players' entrance was off the parking lot in the lower level. Just inside the entrance a large and comfortable lobby was available for players' wives. The players would go through that lobby, then through a door which opened into a hallway which went into the locker room—official personnel only. The Manager's office was on the left side of that hallway. The office was furnished with a desk, a conference table, an adequate amount of furniture with a few chairs and shelves, and his own shower and bathroom. He had a blackboard and a large bulletin board, utilized for planning and keeping his players focused.

Darrel did not have an appointment on Sunday, July 22nd, the last game before the All-Star break. Darrel was not in the line-up that day either. So, he mustered his courage and took the opportunity to speak to Sparky in his office.

The door was partially open and, showing appropriate respect, Darrel knocked. Sparky was sitting at his desk doing some paper work, probably working on his line-up or comparing his bull-pen to the Expos hitters. He was in his baseball uniform, Darrel was in his warm-ups. Sparky looked up from behind his desk.

"Can we talk a minute?"

"Sure, Darrel. Come on in. Close the door. Have a seat." He motioned to a seat at the conference table, then moved over there to sit down across from Darrel. Even while Sparky was moving his chair to sit down, he began, "I'm glad you came in. I've noticed your attitude has been off a little, lately, and it is affecting the guys on the bench. I don't want it to affect the team."

"Well, Sparky, I'm a little frustrated because I want to get some more playing time."

With Sparky and Darrel both sitting across from each other at the conference table, Sparky led the conversation.

"I'm glad you want in the game, so let's go, position by position, around the field and see where I can put you. Okay?"

At first, this seemed like a good idea to Darrel. "Alright. Let's see."

"I know you are an infielder, but you could play the outfield if we needed you to, so let's start there. Let's see how right field looks first. Okay?"

"Sure."

"Ken Griffey (the senior) is there and is having a great season. He has power, speed, and makes a great lead-off hitter. He might even be Rookie of the Year (he did have a great year, but Gary Matthews took Rookie of the Year honors). We probably should not make any changes there. Agreed?"

"Right."

"Cesar Geronimo is in center field. He is a gold glove winner with a good arm, power and a go get 'em attitude. Don't you think we should leave him there?"

"Sure."

"You might actually be able to play left field defense better than George Foster, but he does alright, don't you think?"

"Yeah, I guess so."

"But George is our best power-hitter. He might hit 50 home runs this year. That is not your strength, is it?"

"No, not really."

"On the infield, we have Tony Perez on first base. He's going to be in the Hall of Fame some day. Should I take him off of first base?"

"No way."

"You can turn a double play from either side of second, so I know you can play second. But Joe Morgan is there and he's another guy that has Hall of Fame potential. So doesn't he deserve to be there?"

Darrel was feeling ashamed for asking. This was turning out bad. Even as they were going around the horn, Sparky, not a man of words or gentleness, spoke strong and convincingly but not condescendingly or carelessly insensitive to the frustrated and confused 24-year-old Chaney. Darrel answered, "Joe's the best guy for second."

"I know you wanted short but Davey has done a darn good job at short. He's been selected to the All-Star team and his bat is coming around with power and a better average. So, what am I supposed to do here?"

"I guess Davey is in the right place for now."

"Pete Rose is at third. You know Pete. Nobody is ever gonna beat him out of a position."

"Right."

"And last, behind the plate is Johnny Bench. Guess what. He's gonna be in the Hall of Fame."

"I get your point, Sparky. Thanks for your time, "Darrel said as he began to slide his chair back from the table. He stood up with a sigh and a heart heavier than when he came in. It was obvious that he was not going to beat any of that superstar team out of a position.

"No, sit down and listen to me. Here is your purpose. If Pete gets sick, I will need you to play third. If Davey gets injured, you go into shortstop. If Joe needs a rest, you are the guy I go to. Do you understand? I need you. If I need a bunt, you are one of the best bunters on the team. If I have to pinch-run, you are one of the fastest and smartest runners we have. If we are going to be competitive, we need you to be the best utility player in the majors."

On that team, Darrel was the only guy who played for Sparky in the Minor Leagues with the AA Asheville Tourists. It didn't hurt that they had a history together. Darrel had confidence in Sparky's knowledge of the game and his assessment of his team's individual skills and potential. Sparky knew Darrel's skills and the intangibles—his love for the game, intensity, positive attitude, teachability and dependability.

Darrel was getting it and Sparky could see the enthusiasm returning. His body language changed from sitting compliant with his hands on his lap and his head hanging, to sitting alert, leaning forward, and looking straight into Sparky's eyes with hardly a blink. What Sparky was about to say would be some of the most motivational words Darrel would hear in his entire baseball career.

"Darrel, I want you to be ready when the game comes to you."

"Yes sir! I'll be ready," Darrel said as he reached his hand out and gave Sparky an I-mean-business handshake.

It was not the time for words, but for action. Sparky could see Darrel was a revived man with a new vision for the game. He returned the handshake, then went back to his desk as Darrel headed out the door and down the hall to the locker room.

Purpose has an amazing affect on a man's motivation. Knowing that being a utility player was his purpose and that he was a strategic part of the team which enabled every position to be its strongest, Darrel got ready for every game.

He was always one to work out, but his workouts became more intense. Before and after games, he would wear the rubber warm-up shirt so his two or three mile jogs would have maximum sweat and results. Workouts in the weight room increased his strength, but did not bulk him up or decrease his mobility. His humor and enthusiasm returned and so did the Reds' winning ways. Not that it was all about Darrel, but the second half of the season was a lot better than the first. They ended up winning the division with 99 wins.

As it happened, the game did come to Darrel; sliding into third base that day, Davey Concepcion broke his ankle and was out for the rest of the season.

Bottom of the Seventh

EVERY MAN NEEDS TO BE READY WHEN THE GAME COMES TO HIM

"Whatever you do, work at it with all your heart, as working for the Lord, not for human masters, since you know that you will receive an inheritance from the Lord as a reward. It is the Lord Christ you are serving."
Colossians 3:23, 24

"As a Christian considers the possibility of being a Christian glorified, often the reaction is… 'It is wonderful to be a Christian, but I am such a small person, so limited in talents—or energy or psychological strength or knowledge—that what I do is not really important.' The Bible, however, has quite a different emphasis: With God there are no little people."
Francis Schaefer, in his book, <u>No Little People</u>

Why doesn't a man dream of being a utility player?

It seems that a man believes that he is less than in the Big Leagues if he doesn't achieve superstar status or hold a lofty position at the top of his profession. Maybe he is thankful for his middle-management position, his place as a salesman or as the pastor of a small church. But doing his best at a lower position can seem like he is settling for less. Inside, something tells him that it is not enough to really matter.

During my rookie year in the ministry, I had my first real exposure to mega-church pastors and numbers. I was inspired and infatuated with them and began to measure myself, my ministry and my significance in contrast to these men and their ministries. A big new world had come into my view. Until then, simple-and-small was appropriate since my family lived in a small city, and in a small, paid-for house. We drove used cars and attended a small church. That was plenty good enough for me.... until I saw the big ministries and famous pastors.

At the time, I was a Youth Pastor in a solid church of about 350 people in Warren, Ohio. It was large by my standards and even there, I was over my head in responsibilities for which I was ill-equipped to conquer. Survival was my goal. Success was a dream.

Billy Graham's School of Evangelism was held in Cincinnati during a Billy Graham Crusade. Scholarships were offered so, with less than a year into full time ministry, I decided I wanted to see what this was all about. Until then, I had never seen a true celebrity, unless Dr. D. James Kennedy, a well-known Pastor, and Clarke Pinnock, a renowned apologist, counted. They spoke at my college during my freshmen year. I was so impressed with Dr. Kennedy's story, that years later, I preached most of his illustrations and could still do it, over 40 years later.

The line-up of speakers at the Billy Graham School of Evangelism was a "who's-who" of pastors and authors from large and prominent churches of the late 70's. I hadn't heard of Charles Allen or Kenneth Chafin before that day, but Robert Schuller was very popular and near the beginning of a long and prestigious ministry. Cliff Barrows led the singing and George Beverly Shea sang solos. Other speakers had written books and pastored and founded churches with thousands of members and attendees. I sat in awe of them. Susan and I together, sitting in an old, yet prestigious church in downtown Cincinnati, were hearing speakers talk about their experiences and insights in a way that made us aware that we were in the presence of greatness.

I will never forget what Charles Allen said, in his Texas drawl, as he spoke just before Billy Graham took the stage. He stood tall and, with a sly smile, he twanged out the words, "I feel in a terrible spot, following Kenneth Chafin and speaking before Billy Graham." He knew we were all waiting to hear Billy Graham up close and personal, instead of in a stadium or coliseum with tens of thousands present. "I feel sandwiched in between. But you know, I got to thinking, what's the best part of a sandwich?" I did not know preachers could be so entertaining. I could have listened to him and all the others for days.

Charles Allen's message, which included the need for pastors to support and encourage each other, complimented Dr. Chafin for the way in which he ministered to the "hoi polloi" while Dr. Allen worked with the "unwashed" multitudes—well, that's what he said.

A few moments later, I was standing in the courtyard during a coffee break when Billy Graham, led by security guards and others in his entourage, passed close enough that I could reach out and touch him. He wore a "Bear Bryant" style houndstooth fedora, I believe, to conceal his identity. It nearly took my breath away just to see the striking appearance of the man who has been the greatest evangelist in history.

Billy Graham had spoken to millions, including presidents, kings, movie stars, and the Pope. His evangelistic crusades reached countless people in multiple languages and in many countries. The other pastors had written books and pastored churches with thousands of members. Some, like Dr. Kennedy, started their churches from a mere 14 people and, with God's blessing, watched them grow to thousands.

Those great accomplishments, compared to what I had done, were staggering. Fresh out of Bible College, where I could barely finish my Senior-Paper and into my first year of Youth Ministry and marriage, both of which were more challenging than I had expected, I immediately adopted their status as my new standard of success and significance. I believed that if I endured and kept the faith, someday I would be that successful in ministry. I was uncertain as to how I would get there, but I was confident in my calling and I believed that if I followed God's leading and did not derail my career with a moral or ethical failure, I would make it. I had witnessed the Big Leagues of ministry and I knew that someday I would be there.

The journey forward couldn't be in Youth Ministry; that was merely a stepping stone or, so I thought. For a 23-year-old in the 70's, that was often the first step into pastoral ministry. So I did my time. I gave it my best, learned a lot from a patient and teaching congregation and, hopefully, touched a few young people with the hope that their lives were important to the God who loved them.

After a few years in youth ministry, I felt the urge to pursue a place with greater potential, so with itchy feet, I looked for my first church. I was called to a small church of senior citizens in south Florida. Retirees from the north who were done working and rural Floridians who resented the changes to their sub-tropical agricultural lifestyle made up my first church. They saw us as the kids we were and, sometimes, they treated us like kids who needed to learn a lesson. Other times, they enjoyed and appreciated us.

It was my observation that the church-growth era was ramping up at that time. Denominational leadership, and a lot of other guys like me, were all falling in love with big ministries, and success was verified by increases in dollars and growing numbers of members and attendees. Some referred to the measurement as "nickels and noses." Books, magazines and journals were about growth methodology, leadership skills, vision casting and targeted marketing, written by those who were in big and successful ministries. I gobbled them up so I could achieve their results.

Pastors who accomplished these things became the authors and speakers at conferences, workshops and seminars. They would encourage those of us in the trenches to emulate them and adopt their strategies and methodology so our ministries would grow, like theirs did. Although it was never said in so many words, I heard, "Then you will be in the Big Leagues."

In our country-turned-suburban little South Florida church, we worked hard sprucing up the tired church building with new paint and carpet, palm trees and sod-grass on the front lawn. I was a large part of the labor force on those projects. The parsonage, located next to the church, was the only house in any direction for at least a half-mile. When west

Delray Beach was rural and Military Trail was a quiet two-lane road, it was a serene setting—the little church with a fellowship hall attached for dinner on the grounds, and the manse next door to provide a place for the Pastor and his family to live. But the surrounding area experienced tremendous change. A convenient store and gas station was built next door and large, busy shopping centers sprung up on all four corners of the intersection. The once peaceful home was now located in the middle of it all.

Living there was like having a bedroom in a noisy mall—the only bedroom. People would ask us, "You live there?" When the gasoline storage tanks were refilled at the gas station, the gas fumes from the vent pipes filled our house with the putrid smell of petroleum. Consequently, we moved the parsonage—picked it up and moved it—to a lot in a neighborhood a mile or so away. It was an incredible sight to see the house on an unusual set of rollers and wheels, as the house-moving company drove our house down the street. I painted the house with a textured paint to give a stucco-like finish to the bruised and scarred walls of the cement-block house.

In addition to our hard work on the church's buildings, we had some good ministry there. Susan did some awesome things with the music ministry and hosted a top-notch women's missionary event at the Holiday Inn down on the beach. I learned Evangelism Explosion at Coral Ridge Presbyterian Church, and became a trainer of this program at my church. This is the program Dr. D. James Kennedy founded and that he talked about my freshman year of college and at the Billy Graham School of Evangelism.

One day we were studying Evangelism Explosion and doing our home-visiting. We called on a couple. Jean was home. We shared the gospel message with her using the Evangelism Explosion methodology. After the diagnostic questions, we shared the plan of salvation—God loves you, we are separated from God by sin, Christ paid for that sin with His death on the cross, (tetelestai, meaning paid in full), and we can receive His work by a simple prayer of faith and become part of God's forever family. Jean prayed to receive that work. Her husband Mel followed soon after.

Jean lost Mel to a heart attack a couple of years later and, alone as a new widow, she joined Child Evangelism Fellowship. Now elderly, she still travels the country to set up a booth at National, State and County

Fairs, to tell the same plan of salvation that I shared with her. She uses the Wordless Book. It has pages without words, but uses colors to describe God's love, the human need and the remedy that comes through Christ's work on the cross. Then she invites people to pray the prayer of faith with her. She gets amazing results.

Here is an excerpt from a recent letter from Jean, sent to me over thirty years after we visited her at her home. She is sharing the results of her ministry at just one of the Fairs. "October 2011… the Perry, Georgia National Fair… the gospel was presented to 4,569 souls. The Lord drew 1,234 of them to Him, including 384 children, 633 teens and 217 adults. Praise the Lord!!!"

At the time, though, I could not figure out how to be the leader I needed to be to take this group of people to the lofty goals of a big ministry that I envisioned. Neither could I see the success we *were* having as significant. So I was excited and eager to get a call to climb the next rung of the ladder. That was to get into a new ministry with all the potential to be a Big League ministry: an exciting new church in Princeton, New Jersey. As I described in the Fourth Inning, it was there that I had to persevere a huge setback. Once again, the hope of big ministry was deferred.

My new opportunity to start a church in suburban Gwinnett County, Atlanta seemed as though it might be the right opportunity to make it to the Big Leagues. We did not have tremendous growth in the formative years, but there was steady growth. Good things were happening and we were on the front of the Gwinnett County growth explosion. We needed a building to facilitate our ministry, but could not afford to buy land and build. So we sought a special use permit from Gwinnett County, to build-out space in a commercial building.

"You can't do that," I was told by the bureaucrat at the County's Planning and Zoning office. She was not helpful, but she was correct. Soon after that disappointing encounter, I met with a County Commissioner and informed him of our dilemma. He understood the problem and knew the appropriate solution. In two public hearings, the ordinance was permanently changed for the entire county so that going forward, churches could seek Special-Use permits to create a house of worship in buildings zoned for Office and Industrial Use. We got our Special-Use permit at the very next meeting.

Shortly after we got into that building, our new church, at the tender age of four years old, began to experience discord and inner conflict. My vision was for small groups and a large segment of our leadership preferred a Sunday-night service. My style of community outreach was not appreciated by the more traditional Christians. My tendency was to get along with people, I was conscientious and had founded the church. We emerged from nothing into a couple hundred people with an average attendance of 140. But the leadership decided it was time for me to go and they asked for my resignation after that terrible ambush meeting, that I described in the Third Inning. It did not seem to me that they were hearing from God. Certainly, I did not hear Him saying that. They felt so strongly about these issues and my inability and unwillingness to change, that one blisteringly hot July, this well-organized group left our church. I returned from vacation to a church half the size it was before. It resulted in broken relationships and a broken heart for me. I was now much farther away from my dream of Big League ministry.

Not knowing what to do, I kept moving forward. I smiled, worked hard and prayed hard. During the next two years the church recovered in many ways.

As we were almost back to where we were before that painful July, I began getting phone calls. "Pastor Dan, my company is transferring us. We will be moving out of state." "Pastor Dan, we will miss the church. We love you and our church family, but the time has come for us to go to the mission field." It culminated when, in a twenty-four hour period, three of my most hard-working, generous and supportive families informed me they were moving—two to North Carolina and one to Virginia. That summer, we lost a total of ten families. For a small church of just over a hundred people who were recovering from a split two years earlier, it was devastating. My wife was sad. I was angry and confused. "Why are we not getting where we wanted to go? Why are the Big Leagues so elusive?"

Darrel had his talk with Sparky. I had my talk with Jesus.

Darrel did not cry when he met with Sparky—baseball players only cry when they lose the World Series. It makes a nice camera shot to see a sad ball player with a towel over his head, indicating his disappointment.

I was in my office when I received the third phone call on that dark and disappointing day. No one else was in our nice, neat and clean church-in-an-office-building that day. I got up and walked into the sanctuary.

I needed to have an encounter with the God who called me, was leading me, and put the dream in my heart. So I cried. I cried tears and I cried out for some kind of explanation. "God, Princeton might have been another man's fault and maybe mine too for not knowing how to manage and resolve conflict. Maybe the church-split was at least partially my fault for not being the pastor others wanted me to be, not knowing how to lead or not going away like they wanted me to. But this is YOUR fault! You could have prevented this. You are opening doors of opportunity for people away from here. How am I supposed to build a church if you are leading people away? It's too hard to find them. Your plan must be different than mine!"

That was the time for me, perhaps as it was for Darrel, when I began to see that there might be a different point of view. So I prayed, "Okay, I know your way is best. Help me see it."

I didn't hear any audible voice, but something started to become clear in my thinking and feeling. Just as Darrel changed from feeling there was no place for him on the Cincinnati Reds to excited about the importance of his purpose, I went from crying in frustration to eager to hear a new plan and discover a fresh perspective for my future.

Initially, I was shocked with the reality that there was a different way to get things done and a better measurement for my significance. The reality produced excitement and joy because I discovered there was a specific role for me which would better fit me to God's purpose in His overall plan. It wasn't less, lower, higher or better than Billy Graham, Charles Allen, Kenneth Chafin and all the other mega-church guys, it was just different. My vision would be unique and strategic and would fill a role, accomplish a task which I was called to do that would help the Church and the people in places and in ways that only I could achieve. The world would be better and God would be glorified when I knew my purpose and my place on the team.

My purpose did not become crystal clear to me at that moment, but I was certain that I did have one and it was unique and strategic to God's plan. I believed I was going to be an encourager, particularly to people in small ministries or small pieces of larger ministries. Larger ministries did not mean less to me. I realized they were just one part of God's greater plan. The Billy Graham School of Evangelism people could catalyze ministry in broad and powerful ways that I could not, but I could reach people where they could not go. I could be part of the team and take the message to my place in the world with my voice, style and purpose. My position on the team is different and when I discover components of my purpose, I am more motivated and effective. I feel significant. I know I have made it to the Big Leagues.

Men need to know their purpose on the team too. Their life matters and what they do means something. If they are the utility player of their company, church or community, they need to be ready when the game comes to them. Men can know that they are in the Big Leagues when they are who God has made them. When they are where He has placed them. When they are doing what He has called them to do. Living and working there matters in immeasurable ways.

The Cincinnati Reds were the Big Red Machine as much because Darrel was the best utility player in baseball as it was because of the superior skills and athleticism of Ken, Cesar, George, Pete, Davey, Joe, Tony and Johnny. Those guys were better at being who they were because they had Darrel there when they needed healing or rest, a fresh set of legs or an encouraging word in the dugout, or a relief from stress because Darrel gave them a good laugh. The first place finishes, the National League Pennants, the World Series' trophy were as much Darrel's as theirs, not because he was the everyday shortstop, but because he filled a strategic role in which he excelled. He performed his role with competitive intensity, pride, and a commitment to be the very best he could be. Every day he could thrive in the drama of being a Big League ballplayer. This perspective took him to the top of his game and the top of the world when the Cincinnati Reds beat the Boston Red Sox in the 1975 World Series.

After the talk with Sparky, Darrel was ready when the game came to him and it did. I was ready for my game, after my talk with Jesus.

Every man's place on the team matters. His life has a purpose for when the game comes to him, and it always does. That's the Big Leagues.

What's the Score at the End of the Seventh Inning?

What has been hit to you?
- What job do you have now?
- Where is it in the pecking order?
- How do you like the work?
- How to you like the position?

You are up to bat. What are you going to do?
- How do you help the team with what you do?
- Why did God give you this job to do?
- Where can you adjust your attitude to improve your performance?
- What can you do to improve your game?

The Late Innings

Keeping The Score

The Eighth Inning

Immeasurable

Top of the Eighth

DARREL'S TOP-10 BIG LEAGUE SUCCESSES

"Now to Him who is able to do immeasurably more than all we ask or imagine, according to His power that is a work within us, to Him be glory in the church and in Christ Jesus throughout all generations, forever and ever! Amen."
Ephesians 3:20, 21

"Nobody can help being born common—but ain't nobody got to remain ordinary."
Satchel Paige

The late innings are where a lot of games are won or lost. Excitement builds. Keeping the score in these two innings reveals the success of Darrel and every man.

• • • • •

Bobby Cox won his first game as a manager for the Atlanta Braves on Monday night, April 10, 1978. With two outs and the tying run on first base, the game was won with a walk off home run. Darrel hit it!

The "Top-10 Plays-Of-The-Day" is a daily feature on ESPN's Sports Center.

Here are highlights Darrel considers his "Top 10" with the bat and the glove. There were a lot of good ones in an eleven-year career but these 10 reveal that he made some great plays in the Big Leagues.

• • • • •

10. **You are out!** The Reds were playing in Atlanta. Darrel was playing short and the go-ahead run was on second with two outs. It rarely works but when it does it is beautiful. The runner took his lead-off and Darrel got the signal. The pitcher turned, Darrel hustled behind the runner and over to the bag. The throw was on target, the glove was there and the tag was made. Inning over!

9. **Watch out for the stands!** It was a foul ball heading for the front seats of the stands behind third base and just past the bullpen pitcher's mound. In Riverfront Stadium in the 70's it was in foul territory but on the field—not behind the fence like it is now. Darrel got a good jump on the pop foul and was not going to let it drop. He was running at break-neck speed. Maybe it was situations like this that helped those words become a cliché. He tripped on the pitcher's mound going head first under a railing that separated the stands from the field. Batter's out!! He made the catch and hung on to the ball that he caught while sliding face first, just before he went into the stands.

8. **Not this time!** The Braves were playing the Mets. Darrel was the Braves' everyday shortstop. With the Mets batting, a sharp hit was driven between short and third. Darrel was playing deep but had to go

deeper and to his right. Muscle memory and quickness move faster than thinking. A shortstop has to react and Darrel did. Reaching across his body on a dead run away from first to make the catch he planted his left foot and then jumped with a twisting long throw to first for the out. It was a beautiful athletic play, the type that Troy Tulowitzki makes for the Colorado Rockies.

7. **Over the ivy!** For the boy from Hammond, Indiana, Wrigley Field was a sacred place. It was the home of the Cubs and one of the great ball parks of all time, unique for the ivy that covers the outfield fence.

Darrel was in his sixth year of the Big Leagues, including most of 1971 when he played in the minors. The Reds had 84 wins and were in first place going into this game with the sub .500 Cubs.

Darrel drove in the first run of the game in the top of the second inning with a line drive to right field that scored George Foster from second. In the third he grounded to first who doubled him up with a play to second and back to first, but Johnny Bench scored. Even when things went wrong they produced a good result and the Reds were ahead 4-0.

In the fifth inning, with two outs and Joe Morgan on third and George Foster on first, Darrel got to experience a lifelong dream. He homered over the ivy in right field of Wrigley Field. Seven to one was the score and the Reds went on to win 11 to 4. It was a five RBI game for Darrel.

6. **Big name play!** You know you are in the Big Leagues just by the names of players who are your competition. Bobby Mercer, the five-time All-Star was up to bat. The shortstop turned centerfielder had a 17 year major league career—most of them with the Yankees, but a two year stint with the Giants and three with the Cubs. Darrel was playing short and Bobby, who had power even though he was small—he hit 232 career home runs—lined a hit past the pitcher up the middle. Darrel dove to the left for the Big League catch and stopped a base hit by the great Bobby Mercer.

5. **Fireworks in Atlanta!** It was the fifth of July, 1976 for an 8:05 Braves game at Atlanta, Fulton County Stadium. Atlanta had been on the road for ten games—they won 5 and lost 5—and were home for the first time since June 24.

In Atlanta, July feels like summer and there is nothing like a short sleeve, balmy, southern night at the ballpark. The Braves were ready to play and the city was eager to finish their Bicentennial 4th of July celebration with the always fabulous fireworks display after the game.

During the off season Darrel was traded from the World Series Champions and the 108 wins, Cincinnati Reds, to the Braves who lost 94 games in 1975. Dave Bristol, the Braves manager made Darrel his everyday shortstop.

All of the 48,467 fans were accustomed to seeing the Braves lose and thought they were in for another night where the post-game show would give them their money's worth. The perennial playoff Pittsburgh Pirates scored two runs in the third, one in the fifth and sixth and two in the seventh. The Braves managed just one run through seven innings. Darrel started the bottom of the eighth by striking out and Pete Varney followed him with a fly out.

It looked like the Braves were going to go out with a whimper, but that's when the fireworks really began: that is, the ones on the field. Single, walk, walk, single, walk, single, wild pitch, walk. All of that means the Braves had batted around and scored four runs with three hits and four walks, all after two outs. Darrel was up to bat with the Braves down by one run. A base hit would tie it and potentially give the Braves the lead. An extra base hit would definitely put the Braves ahead. Darrel crushed it into the right field corner over Dave Parker's head and it was off to the races. Fans jumped to their feet and screamed like crazy. One run scored. Darrel was rounding first and heading for second. Two runs scored. Dave was finally getting it chased down and Darrel reached second. Three runs scored. Darrel headed to third. The relay came to third, Darrel slid, and the runner was safe! Darrel hit a three run triple and put the Braves ahead to stay.

Then, the happy fans could get ready for the other fireworks.

4. There she goes! Hitting Big League pitching is tough to do. Arguably Darrel came through the minors too quickly. His trip down to the minors in 1971 turned out to be a blessing in disguise. Near the end of his second year, before being sent down to Indianapolis, he was playing off the bench a lot and hit .232 for the season in 57 games. Darrel was always looking for the opportunity to gain more experience and prove he could be a contributing Big Leaguer.

On September 7, 1970 the Reds were in San Francisco for an afternoon game against the Giants. The high kicking Juan Marichal was pitching. He was in his tenth season of an illustrious sixteen year, Hall of Fame, career and this was one of his good days.

Good hitting makes for great pitching and the Giants gave him support. They got the lead with a two run first inning and scored another run in the fourth. Marichal was shutting out the Reds until the seventh when they scored two but the Giants got some insurance with three runs in the bottom of the eighth.

Darrel led off the ninth inning for the Reds. He went in to replace Davey Concepcion at shortstop after Angel Bravo pinch hit for him in the seventh inning. With a four run lead, Charlie Fox, the Giants manager was going to let Juan finish off the Reds and pitch a complete game. Darrel was excited to face the famous Big League pitcher from the Dominican Republic. He stepped up to the plate, took a couple of practice swings and stared into the eyes of Juan Marichal.

Juan was getting his signal from the catcher. Then he went into that wild wind up with his left leg straight up in the air and the ball in his right hand almost touching the mound. He fired a fast ball. Darrel took it for a strike, just to get to watch the delivery and wait for his pitch.

Batting left, Darrel was watching for another fast ball, maybe inside, and when it came he was ready and connected with the meat of the bat. It sounded like it and it was; the ball headed for the stands over the right field fence for a homerun! On the radio, Al Michaels called this one, "There she goes!" And Darrel got to trot around the bases for the first time as a Big Leaguer.

3. A great catch saves a No-No. A no-hitter rarely happens in the Big Leagues. As I write this book, only 233 have been pitched in all the games that have been played. Jim Maloney pitched one in 1965. On Wednesday afternoon, April 30, 1969 he had his good stuff and was putting down the Houston Astros' batters. By the top of the sixth inning he already had seven strikeouts. The first batter nearly ended his quest for a second no-hitter with a fly ball that almost dropped between the infield and the outfield, except that Darrel made a diving play to put out that batter. The game was well in hand and the Reds won 10-0. But the catch did extend the no-hitter. Maloney stayed hot with another five strikeouts and finished the game with no hits, to become one of a few pitchers to pitch more than one no-hitter in the Big Leagues.

2. Grand slam! There was no score as they began the bottom of the second inning. The first-place Cardinals were visiting Cincinnati to play the second-place Reds. Mike Thompson walked the leadoff batter, Davey Concepcion, to start the inning. Davey stole second base, so with first base open Thompson walked the next batter, Cesar Geronimo, and let them advance on a wild pitch while facing Bill Plummer. For the second time, first base was open and he walked Bill Plummer who was catching for Johnny Bench this July 7, 1974. With three walks, a wild pitch and no outs, Red Schoendienst went to his bullpen, and put Rich Folkers in to pitch, hoping to change the direction of this game before it got away from them.

Darrel was the batter.

After Folkers had taken his warm-up pitches, he was ready to face the number eight hitter who was a low risk for a home run, so he went after Darrel. Darrel made him pay when he drove the ball high over the right field wall and off the face of the second deck for his one and only big league grand slam.

The Reds would score seven more runs in the game, but the lead after the grand slam would have held.

1. Walk Off! Bobby Cox will be inducted into the baseball Hall of Fame. For 30 years he was a big league manager—26 with the Atlanta Braves, interrupted by four years with the Toronto Blue Jays, after his first five years with the Braves.

He was selected Manager of the Year once in the American League and three times in the National League. The Atlanta Braves won 14 consecutive Division titles beginning in 1991, were National League Champions five times and in 1995 won the World Series.

The first three games, for Bobby Cox as a manager, were losses. The fourth game was not going that well on a warm spring day in Atlanta. The previous year the Braves lost 101 games. Losses are painful and Bobby knew he had an uphill battle getting the Braves to become a winning team.

The Padres did not waste any time taking the lead and they led the whole game putting seven runs on the scoreboard.

The Braves would not go away though and got to within one run in the sixth. Both teams were scoreless through two outs in the bottom of the 9th inning. Darrel was playing off of the bench. After Joe Nolan pinch hit for Pat Rockett, the Braves' starting shortstop, Darrel, entered the game in the eighth inning. A ground ball was hit to Darrel for the first out of the eighth, but his biggest chance was going to be with the bat.

Time was running out in the bottom of the ninth. Biff Pocoroba made the first out with a fly ball. Dale Murphy struck out, for out number two. The Braves' third baseman kept their hopes alive with a single. So with the tying run on first and the winning run at the plate, Darrel got his first at bat of the game. Bob Shirley, the Padres closer only needed one more out, but he did not get it.

With a hitters count, Darrel drove the ball over the right field fence for a walk-off home run. Bobby Cox had his first win as a Braves manager.

• • • • •

Darrel had a self-deprecating habit. It is a common trait. Most men measure their value by comparison to others and by the parts of their dream that they have not achieved. It is easier to remember mistakes, than it is to remember successes. From that perspective a man never feels like he has made it to the Big Leagues.

Every man needs to take time and look at the highlights of what he has done. His "top ten" list will reveal a picture that is uniquely his and definitely the Big Leagues—God was there, things were accomplished and he mattered.

Bottom of the Eighth

EVERY MAN'S TOP 10 SUCCESS LIST

"I can do all this through him who gives me strength."
Philippians 4:13

"If you don't see yourself as a winner,
then you cannot perform as a winner."
Zig Ziglar

The highlight reel of an average guy's life may never appear on ESPN but it is important that he has one.

Darrel's highlights were from his Big League career in baseball, so I made my career "top ten" list.

Every man should put together his list. What it reveals will be surprising.

• • • • •

10. Ordination — I began 1979 with my Ordination work and test looming in front of me like a steep and impassable mountain. To make matters worse, I was devastated because of the Sugar Bowl outcome the previous day.

To receive an ordination is an honor and a responsibility beyond what I understood at the time. I sensed it was important but I was primarily following the protocols of my denomination. Ordain is to "Invest officially (as by the laying on of hands) with ministerial or priestly authority, to establish or order by appointment, decree, or law."

It is an important recognition given by established leaders of an organization who examine the ordinand to determine if he/she deserves this status as a result of adequate preparation and a clear sense of call of God in his life. For me, it involved two years of ministerial experience, additional book reports, mentoring and workshops, before I could be examined for ordination and then be publicly set apart for God's use in a public ordination service.

Following the rules and guidelines upon graduation from college, with a Bachelor of Science in Bible and Theology, I immediately sought a place of ministry and was called as a Youth Pastor to a church in Ohio. With zero experience but great enthusiasm, I took the calling into this wonderful, firmly established church which was very strong in ministry and enthusiastic for foreign missions.

My first day on the job was unforgettable. After I unpacked my car of all of my worldly possessions into the house which, after our wedding in one month, my fiancé and I were going to live in, I brought the remaining couple of boxes to the church. Contained in these boxes were books for my very first office. I placed them on a shelf or two, sat at the desk for the first time as a post-graduate, real life, had-to-produce adult. I did not have the foggiest idea what to do. There were no appointments on my calendar. As a matter of fact, I did not have a calendar. Fear flooded over me, so I did what any smart young man would do at a time like that. I closed the door, got down on my knees and prayed a simple prayer. "God help me." I really don't remember exactly what I said but I do remember feeling needy and getting down on my knees to pray.

Step by step and one experience at a time God led me and I began to get a few things going. The wonderful people in the church took me in and helped me get started. After being there three months, the senior pastor took a call to another church in California. Multiple staff churches were uncommon in those days so it was just the two of us in this church which had about 325 in attendance each Sunday. After he left, it was just me.

For the next two years when I was supposed to be doing my ordination preparation with all my book reports, workshops and mentoring, I was primarily trying to survive. The workshops were a welcome escape from the everyday challenges of learning how to be a youth pastor and developing a strategy for ministry. I was also adjusting to married life as my sweet southern wife, now married to a Yankee, moved to life in the north for the first time. If it were not for those record-setting winters with cold and snow, it would have been easier. The snow blowing under the door and the doorknob on the inside forming frost, gave her ample reason to wonder if marrying me was a good idea.

As we approached the end of 1977, I received a letter from the District Superintendent with a phrase I will never forget: "Get with it." I was young and impressionable, always wanting to please. I did not want to ruin my chances for success in ministry by screwing up this early in adult life. "The bliss of theory is no match for the mess of reality." I had heard that somewhere and I was finding out, in multiples, it was true. This was not college anymore, with all the friends, the fun and the potential. I was facing reality and the outcome was important. I was expected to produce.

In the next six months, I had to complete work which I had not finished in the past two years. With help from my mentor, I prepared a plan of action that would take me to the ominous oral ordination exam which I would take in front of the white-haired, deep-voiced, three-piece-suited examiners. As soon as the Christmas and New Year holidays had passed, I would get started in earnest.

On New Year's Eve, I was excited to begin watching my favorite college football team, ranked number one in the nation, with a 19-game winning streak on the line, try to win its first National Championship. I was excited and ready to do all my ordination work after the Penn State Nittany Lions beat Alabama's Crimson Tide. Maybe the game meant too much to me but with the famous goal line stand of Alabama, Penn State fans everywhere were dejected and disappointed when "we" finished six points short of the win. As for me, I was depressed. Life was difficult, I hardly knew what I was doing, I had a huge task in front of me and my team lost.

I knew I could not let a football game stop me so, putting my disappointment behind me I got started. One report at a time was completed. My mentor talked me through the questions I would need to thoroughly answer and support with scripture—questions such as, "How do you know God is a person?" Confidence which showed I knew what I was talking about and what I believed, was important too. Susan was my biggest cheerleader and practice examiner. We sat at the kitchen table in our apartment on North Road. She would ask me the questions, and I would give the answers.

The day of the exam finally came. She went with me to the District Office in Wadsworth, Ohio, and gave me a reassuring hug before I walked into the room to face the entire group of the Ordination and Licensing Committee. There were at least twelve examiners sitting around the conference table. I sat at the corner of the table facing these men, all of them at least twice my age, dressed in suits, who had more pastoral experience and Bible knowledge than I could have ever imagined. Maybe we were on the same team but it felt as though they were part of the obstacle standing in the way of me getting to my calling. They were probably nice guys, encouraging and helpful to their congregations but, to me, they were intimidating, ominous, and frightening.

The questions began and I aced every one of them. I could not wait for the questioner to finish asking, "How do you know God is a person?" I was nodding, as if to say, "Hurry up before I forget," and I began by giving the description of personality and scripture to support it. The exam went so well that they passed me in record time.

It was a Big League home run for the young pastor. My District Superintendent, preached a challenging message and my new senior pastor, prayed the prayer of dedication over me. I still have the cassette tape. My parents bought me a new black suit for this occasion (my wife really liked it). All the examiners came to my church, placed their hands on me and ordained me to the gospel ministry. The "Rev." I sometimes use before my name means much more to me today than it did then. It means I made it to the Big Leagues.

9. Culture Changes — The biggest challenge to moving the house that I talked about in chapter six, was the culture change it represented in the church and the community. It was the last vestige of the way things used to be with the cozy parsonage next to the little country church on the outskirts of town.

Joe came up to me after a Sunday evening service and said, "If you move that house, you will probably lose me." He was part of the old Florida which was agricultural, slow paced and casual, not touristy, glitzy nor white-collar-professional.

The community had changed in dramatic ways so, if the church didn't change, it could not reach the new people, with a different lifestyle. Also, the setting was different than it used to be and change had already occurred, like it or not. Decisions were forced on us.

I did not like conflict and I wanted everyone to be in agreement but we had to do something. So with a critic looking me in the eye in my first construction project in ministry, I had to make a Big League call. I chose to move forward. We did lose Joe, but we moved into a neighborhood that opened new opportunities and provided the church with a living arrangement for me and future pastors that was much more appropriate.

8. Rock the Town — Our pastors were meeting and praying about the reputation of the churches in the community. "Does the un-churched community see us as caring about them or only trying to build our churches for our own sake?" An idea formed: "Let's do something together which will show them we care. We are doing a lot for individuals and families but maybe a big project would be a testimony to our community."

At the same time, the Parks and Recreation Department of the Town of Castle Rock was wondering what they could do to get volunteers to care for the parks and open spaces around our town. These places are plentiful and important to Colorado communities. The town's icon, Rock Park, with its hiking trails, had been neglected for about ten years. People still walked up to the Rock but there were social trails where erosion had scarred the park and scrub oak had encroached on the trails.

Growth had improved the town of Castle Rock to be one of the best places to raise a family in the U.S. The park that was the town's icon did not properly represent this beautiful town on Colorado's front-range.

We decided to adopt Rock Park and the town eagerly welcomed us. A layman from another church provided the organization and I recruited volunteers. A two-year strategic plan emerged which included new trails, erosion control, steps, grooming of scrub oak, removal of noxious weeds, installation of fences and repair of the stone wall. Dozens of volunteers from churches around the community became "Keepers of the Rock" and the park was thoroughly refurbished.

The Town Officials were ecstatic with the results of our hard work. A few years later, in July 2011, when Family Circle named the town one of the best places in the country to raise a family, the park fit.

Most of all, the churches worked together in a volunteer effort which was a testimony to the town and to the church as to what could happen when we collaborate.

7. Large church platform — "Dan, would you be willing to lead our singles ministry for a while?" It was our first big church experience.

When our Atlanta house was on the market, the realtor gave us the name of realtor in Denver who could help us. It turned out that her husband was the executive pastor of this large, influential church. He welcomed me into their fellowship while we were in the gestation stage, before the birth of our church in Castle Rock. I was infatuated with big, important flagship churches which hosted thousands for worship each Sunday. They mattered more than my little work, it seemed, and, if I could be associated with them, my credibility increased. Their open arms surprised me.

I was encouraged to experience success in my year of serving in this church. Taking the opportunity to serve on this platform did more to encourage me about my own abilities and to see the weaknesses and strengths of each ministry.

I discovered I had Big League ability in a Big League church. It caused me to think, that maybe my ministry was the Big Leagues, even when it was in a smaller church.

6. Don't preach or you will be fired — Work outside of the church has been a necessary way for me to support my family since much of my ministry has been in smaller, financially-challenged ministries.

I was hired to be a Hospice Chaplain, serving in a way which surpassed my expectations of what Hospice accomplishes. During my training, the Lead Chaplain who hired me, looked and pointed at me while making a point to others in the room. He said, "If you preach to the patients you will be fired." My conservative, evangelical theology and my desire to lead people to Jesus, especially during the time they are sick and passing into eternity, caused me to recoil at this statement.

Very soon, however, I learned the wisdom and opportunity of this statement.

My view of ministry for many years was from the vantage point of the pastorate inside the church. I thought I had a good bedside manner in making hospital calls and that I preached an adequate, maybe excellent, funeral sermon. When I was in my church, I was a leader with the "home-field" advantage. People came because of what we believed. It was my job to proclaim it and to lead people in that direction.

But when I was in a clinical setting, I was the "visitor." It was my job to listen to people, honor where they were in their illness, their life situation and their faith. If they were interested in what I had to offer and they asked, I could tell them, pray with them and even explain the plan of salvation, but only if they wanted it. At the end of life when everything matters for all of eternity, this is the best method.

I discovered that this was the most effective method, even in parish ministry when people are alive and well. It was the way Jesus related to the paralyzed man when he asked, "What can I do for you?"

In a baseball game, all the innings matter but the late innings seem ultra-important. An error or a hit in the ninth inning seems more consequential than one in the first inning. Hundreds of times, I have come up to bat at the final moments of a person's life or in the first moments of their death and have been thankful to know the best way to relate to them and their family.

Hospice is the Big Leagues of ministry and caring enough to ask questions and thoughtfully listen is Big League evangelism methodology.

5. All 5's — Working in the business world is an experience every pastor should have.

Greg invited me into his boutique consulting, training and business development firm to train bankers in customer service and sales. This new experience for me included cold calls, setting appointments, traveling to the office of the credit union or bank president, from Oregon to Pennsylvania, and any point in between. I would listen to their needs and goals and, when appropriate, explain the sales development process, the best methodology for customer satisfaction measurement and offer to submit a proposal for how we could help them achieve a competitive advantage. Then I would deliver the workshop.

The customer loyalty and satisfaction drivers that we taught are principles of human behavior and response. A skilled use of them helps everyone relate in the best possible way in every situation.

I hated writing proposals and I had to be corrected multiple times. I did not like making cold calls either, although I did enjoy the challenge once I got started. Travelling to make sales presentations expanded my knowledge and confidence as I met bank executives and worked with them to develop their business. I loved delivering the workshops. I was encouraged to see that in the Big Leagues of business, even as a pastor, I could perform well. So well in fact, that most of my post-workshop-feedback evaluations were, on a scale of 1-5, fives! Fives were home runs!

4. A new skill — There was a lot of controversy in our town regarding a church construction project. Building a church on a parcel of land makes that land tax-exempt. Assembling Christians to worship, did not seem to impress the Town Council or the future neighbors of the church.

At the same time, a new daily newspaper, the Daily Star, was launched in our town.

Back when I was in Atlanta, a friend who was my first writing mentor critiqued my letters and newsletter columns with the knowledge of a professional writer who was both successful and accomplished in his craft.

I remembered everything he taught me to begin writing a column, "Faith Matters," for the paper. It was my job to find ways in which the church was of value to the community.

The first couple of weeks, when I was trying to write the column, I wondered what I had gotten myself into. Sandy, the managing editor, worked with me to help this column be different than a devotional or a report on an event. After about three weeks, a pattern came together.

This new project became a foundation to more writing. A few years later the Daily Star ceased to operate but the News Press and all papers in their network of newspapers continued to use my columns. The sky is the limit with new internet strategies for the paper, so I keep writing my columns that encourage and explain the value of the local church to its community. I am eager to see how far they go and how many they reach. When the opportunity to write was presented to me, I did not know if I could do it. But I am glad I tried.

I believe I was led to a vehicle for communicating what matters to me, in a way that is bigger and broader than I could have even imagined. It is a local paper, but writing is the Big Leagues to me.

3. The Kids Matter — I've read that Abraham Lincoln would not tip his hat to every adult but he would to every child. Adults are often VIP's but no child is. Not yet. Abe was asked, "Why do you pay them the honor, Mr. President?" His reply was, "You know who an adult is and what they have become but you never know who that child will become or what he will do."

His statement impacted the way I felt about children and church. They should feel important at church and they should like going to church. It should be a safe place where they learn lessons without a test and find mentors who will inspire them for life.

Ten years after I left our Atlanta ministry, I received a call from Nick. He was just a kid when I left. I considered his parents good friends but I did not spend any special time with Nick other than seeing him at church and when I was visiting at his home with his parents. He had some behavioral problems and, as he got older, he developed a serious drug and alcohol habit. His call came after he had lost some friends to death and prison. With his life in a tailspin, he called me and said, "You are the only adult I feel I can talk to." I was stunned. His dad was there for him,

I know, but something about the way I related to him back then let him know I was safe and capable of offering him some help as he attempted to turn his life around.

Sometimes, the biggest hits in life occur when you don't even know you are up to bat, especially with kids. A number of times, kids from my previous ministries would reconnect with me with e-mail or Facebook. When it comes to kids, everything you do is in the Big Leagues.

2. Alto means go — In Spanish, alto means stop. My friend John, nick named Alto, is flattered to see his nickname plastered on signs all over Mexico.

It was the Adopt-a-Family project for our Kiwanis Club in the Christmas of 2000. Alto and I were going to be delivering gifts which our club bought for a family who was going through a hard time. The dad was out of work and the mom was having numerous surgeries.

Alto and I met for coffee at the neighborhood coffee shop. It was the coffee shop version of Cheers for our town, where everybody knows your name. Jason, the owner, made it that way. I was a regular as I was trying to find a place to meet people. I had been in town almost a year and did not have anyone who had committed to join me in starting a church in Castle Rock. Alto and I sat at the table on the Castle Rock side of the coffee shop. Castle Rock was a beautiful sight looking out the glass walls beside our table.

After we waited through the line to get our coffee and reviewed our plan for delivering the gifts to Tim and Devne and their boys, Alto asked, "How is your church start-up coming?" I explained my present involvement in Colorado Community Church and my plan to begin some small groups as soon as I had some people. "My wife and I attend Colorado Community!" "Alto, would you consider becoming part of this project down here in our town?" Colorado Community was twenty miles away but well worth the ride with its excellent music, winsome preaching and dynamic leadership of a popular senior pastor.

The only reason anyone would give that up to come to an elementary school gymnasium with me would require God putting a call on their life, as He did in mine. When closing a sale, asking a girl out, swinging at a fast ball or inviting someone to change his life to join you in your venture, it is easier to not do it and live with the fantasy of "what if," than to go for it and experience the devastating failure of rejection. I did not want to risk it but I knew that if I did not, I doubted the reason I moved to this town, the calling I had, and even God Himself.

When we left Crowfoot, Alto gave me a hug and called me "Brother." He said he would go home and discuss this with his wife. It was not long after that, I was in their home with our first small group. It was a small group but a Big League highlight for me.

1. New Life — Going from unbelief to belief is a conversion which changes a person's whole being. Placing belief in Christ brings forgiveness, birth of a new identity and nature that ignites new possibilities and washes away old hurts and failures. At the very least, it provides the means to a new start. Helping people make that decision is my greatest pleasure. Watching their lives change for their good and for God's glory is the fulfillment of purpose which makes all the effort worthwhile.

Susan and I were learning how to share our faith with the Evangelism Explosion methodology in our first church. In our sixteen-week class, we memorized scripture and learned illustrations and a way to share our faith with the hope that people would understand their own needs as well as the extension of Jesus' gift to them through His death on the cross. We visited people, unannounced, who had attended our church and hoped to have the opportunity to use everything we learned. It was a canned approach but the motives were pure. If the people knew how difficult it was to reach out in this way, they would be sure we cared about them!

One particular day we were to go to the home of Jean. We finished our class, got in the car and drove to her house a couple of miles from our church in Delray Beach. I knocked on the door, she opened it and welcomed us in. After a bit of conversation, it seemed the opportunity was there to share the story of the Good News. As we began to share, her husband came home from work. He worked at the GM garage and did not have much to do with us but she did. She loved what we were saying and was responsive to the offer of Jesus' love and His forgiveness of sins. She prayed with us and thanked us for visiting. Later, her husband, who was eavesdropping and liked what he heard, also responded. They became great friends and active in our church. Jean works with Child Evangelism Fellowship of whom I wrote in Chapter 7.

This at-bat turned out to be a grand slam even though I did not know it at the time.

• • • • •

Most of my life felt like life in the trenches and not the Big Leagues. That is the way it is for most men. But it only seems that way. Writing your highlights is similar to throwing yourself an "It's A Wonderful Life" party. But do it anyway because, if you don't, they probably are not going to make another movie like that one just for you.

Some highlights are game-changers for you. They are accomplishments which have earned you a title, a plaque, or an office.

There is a set of highlights which were game-changers for somebody else. What you did made a difference in his/her life. These are the most rewarding but the least measurable. Maybe you even forgot about them until you stopped and wrote them down.

And there will be a few which changed your world. What you did made your company, community or family better off. Hopefully, you are appreciated but maybe not. Still, that does not matter. What matters is you came up to the plate or fielded the ball when it came to you. It will not make a spot on television but that is not the measurement.

Every man needs to know that his life matters and that what he has done makes a difference, even if nobody seems to notice. He will feel like a Big Leaguer and, if he really believes it, he will celebrate his life more. The next time he comes up to bat, he will dig in and get set because he knows he is in the Big Leagues and he has Big League ability for Big League plays.

What's the Score at the
End of the Eighth Inning?

What has life hit to you?

- Why is it more natural to remember our mistakes and failures than our success and accomplishments?
- What list(s) are in your memory about your life?

When you are up to bat, what are you going to do?

- Make your top 10 lists for your career.
- Then make one for your personal life and another for your family.

1.
2.
3.
4.
5.
6.
7.
8.
9.
10.

The Ninth Inning

Imperative

SAFE!

Top of the Ninth

DARREL'S PLACE
IN HISTORY

*"Your eyes saw my unformed body;
all the days ordained for me were written in your book
before one of them came to be."*
Psalm 139:16

"History will be kind to me for I intend to write it."
Winston Churchill

The World Series is one of the most significant annual events on the national calendar. It is not an official holiday, but each fall all eyes turn to baseball and the World Series trumps every other event. A competitive drama unfolds. New heroes are discovered. Old ones are immortalized. Come from behind victories are snatched from the jaws of defeat. Cities unite behind their team as the world watches two teams play a best of seven series to see who will be the champions of baseball.

It is the grand prize of the national pastime, the focal point for two cities and a memory maker for fans, young and old.

Every year since 1903 it has captured the attention of the nation except twice. In 1904 off the field competitiveness and bitter personalities led to teams which refused to play each other. In 1994, business and personalities interfered again. This time it was not John McGraw, the New York Giants' manager and his refusal to play against an "inferior" league and the disdain he had for the American League President Ban Johnson. It was a labor dispute between the management and players over revenue sharing and other ideas of how to make baseball more profitable, enjoyable and stable. There was anger and loss everywhere, but the biggest losers were the fans who were deprived of their pastime and the Fall Classic.

World Series anticipation begins when the player contracts go out in December and front offices fill in the gaps of their team with trades in the off season. Newspapers, magazines, radio and television report the trades and the potential they represent. Sports pundits debate the wisdom of the maneuvers. A pitcher has been traded for a power hitter. One team hopes to complete its pitching rotation to prevent runs while the other team attempts to create more offense. Both strategies are designed to help their teams play in the Post Season, hopefully all the way to the World Series. Last year's disappointment fades as the potential of the changes emerge.

Every team is hopeful when they assemble in Florida or Arizona to begin practice in mid-February. The northern cities, in the dead of winter, watch their boys of summer stretching on fields surrounded by palm trees. Maybe this will be their year. Cities want it, players feel it and managers strategize to make it happen.

For the Reds, anticipation had given way to expectation. They won 98 games in '74, 10 games ahead of the Eastern Division champion Pirates. But it was not enough to catch the 102 win Dodgers who lost the World

Series to the Oakland Athletics in five games. The year before that, the Mets beat the Reds in the playoffs but then lost to the A's in seven games of the World Series. The Reds did make it to the World Series in '72 but were the first victim of Oakland's three World Series wins in a row. Baltimore beat the Reds two years earlier in 1970. Their goal was unfulfilled.

The Reds were getting closer and Cincinnati was yearning for what it hadn't experienced since 1940. The talent, experience, winning records and close encounters churned the interest about this team with the confidence that a World Series victory, although elusive, was expected, even necessary for a team that would not be satisfied until they had achieved the conquest of the Fall Classic.

Opening day started a six month, 162 game quest to play in October. Win streaks and slumps separated winners from losers. Injuries created intrigue and complicated strategies with disabled lists and substitutions. Utility players and guys in the minors got their chances to play every day or get their call up to the Big League club. Wins and losses were calculated every day and the standings were posted on the sports pages and reported by the sportscasters of radio and TV. Records were set, no-hitters got pitched, grand-slams scored runs and stolen bases put runners in scoring position. Most days there were 15 games with all 30 teams doing their best to make it to the World Series or at least have an impact on who got there.

The Reds got right to work in 1975. It was almost over before it started. Their only hiccup during the season was in May when they lost six in a row and trailed the Dodgers by 5 ½ games. Their record was 18-19. They would not be satisfied with results that were far below their skill level. At the beginning of the season, Joe Morgan said about the Dodgers, "They just can't think they're better than we are."

After a couple of team meetings with pep talks from their Manager, Sparky Anderson, who said, "You are too good to be a .500 team," and teammates like Johnny Bench who said, "We got our pride up", they turned things around and never looked back.

"The magic number is Zero. The non-race is over. The Dodgers are dead and the Cincinnati Reds, for the fourth time in six years, rule the Western Division," wrote Bob Hertzel, the Sports reporter for the Cincinnati Enquirer.

His article continued, "The non-race came to a less-than-dramatic climax Sunday *(September 7)* when the Reds won their 95th game of the year, belting the San Francisco Giants, 8-4, before 34,415 in Riverfront Stadium. Five hundred miles away, in Atlanta, the Dodgers were rolling over and playing dead, losing to the Braves and were officially eliminated. It is hard to believe that a team with a 20 ½ game lead in the first week in September had a turning point in its season, but the Red's believed they had one *in May.*"

The Big Red Machine was churning toward the Pirates who had won the Eastern Division. Determination replaced desire months ago. "Displaying the courage and skill that had carried them all year, the Cincinnati Reds completed a sweep of the National League playoffs… scoring two tenth inning runs to defeat the Pittsburgh Pirates, 5-3, before 46,355 frenzied fans. The victory gave the Reds their third National League pennant in six years and won them the right to meet the Boston Red Sox in the World Series." (Bob Hertzel, Cincinnati Enquirer).

The Red Sox and everyone in Boston were ready to break the "curse of the Bambino". If Reds' fans thought their World Series drought was a long one, dating back to 1940, they got no sympathy from Bostonians who could not even remember their last championship in 1918—only 15 years after the first World Series.

After all the contracts, trades, practices and games, only these two teams remained and the first one to win just four games would be crowned World Champions. Every pitch of each inning was a battle between a batter and a team that tried to prevent him from being productive. Incrementally he tried to work his way around the bases and the battles continued with more batters and hard fastballs and breaking curve balls. Even the best batters lost most of the time, but when a few could put a rally together and advance all the way to home plate, runs would go on the score board, hopefully more than the other team could muster.

Boston fans are some of the most loyal and intense sports fans anywhere. Their New England Patriots of football were not winning in the 70's, but the Celtics won one of their NBA- leading 17 championships in the 75-76 season. A premier sporting event, The Boston Marathon was run for the 111th time. Fenway Park had been the Red Sox ballpark since 1912.

The "Green Monster", arguably, makes it the most recognized baseball field in the Big Leagues. In a city where Bunker Hill and Boston Harbor remind us of our nation's history, it was the perfect setting for half of a historic World Series.

It feels like a week-long holiday when a whole city catches World Series fever. The Reds were the pride and joy of Cincinnati. The Bengals had a great regular season record, but lost to the Oakland Raiders in the first round of the NFL playoffs. The NBA Cincinnati Royals, left town in 1972 to move to Kansas City. With the Big Red Machine playing in the World Series, sleep deprivation was the norm. Kids were sleepy in school and coffee boosted workers on the morning after. It was red everywhere in downtown Cincinnati.

Excitement spread throughout the whole country via NBC and their crew of broadcasters including Curt Gowdy, Tony Kubek, Dick Stockton and Joe Garagiola. They brought the games to over 35 million people who watched the play-by-play on their TV's in living rooms, college dorms, bars and hotel rooms. It was one of the most watched World Series ever.

Those who could get tickets to see the game inside the stadium experienced the spectacle surrounded by capacity crowds of cheering fans. They were eyewitnesses to history in the making. During a summer game the fans might allow their attention to wander. If they missed a play, they could hear about it, watch a replay and catch up somehow if they wanted to. But in the World Series, even the guy selling beer was paying attention. Foot traffic up and down the aisles was only because of necessity. Nobody wanted to miss a play.

To be a player in a game where his performance could change the outcome and affect baseball history is a level of existence that few of us will ever understand. All other ball games have ceased. No other teams are playing—he has surpassed them all. Every other team is among the spectators. On top of the baseball world, under the bright lights and on this grand stage, boyhood dreams have come true, athletic skills are displayed and passionate competition awakens every fiber, cell and emotion a being possesses.

Game One finally arrived and Boston was the home team. As in every World Series, the introductions took place as each player's name was called and he jogged from the dugout to a place with his teammates on the baseline. The subs were introduced first, followed by the starters and finally the manager.

Old Glory majestically waved in the breeze, only a few months from the bi-centennial of our nation's independence. Our nation's revolution started just a few miles from this ballpark. Rene Rancourt, the Boston Opera singer, performed a stirring rendition of the National Anthem and as he sang the final words, "The home of the brave" the crowd roared their approval.

Only those on the field could hear the umpire command, "Play ball!"

The World Series was under way. Game One was all Boston, to the great pleasure of the home crowd. The Reds' bats were silenced and they could not scrape up a single run. They were shut out, 6-0.

Even though it is a best of seven series, the Reds wanted to split these two games in Boston so they could return to Cincinnati with home field advantage, instead of a two-game deficit.

Game Two was a nail biter. Boston struck first when Carl Yastrzemski scored from second on a single to right field in the first inning. It was not until the fourth inning when the Reds' Joe Morgan scored from third on a fielder's choice hit to the shortstop. Both teams remained scoreless until the bottom of the sixth when once again, Hall of Famer, Carl Yastrzemski scored from second on a base hit. That was all the Red Sox could come up with, but the Red's put together a two-run rally in the top of the ninth as Johnny Bench and Davey Concepcion each reached home and the Reds took Game Two, 3-2.

Cincinnati was ready to bring the World Series to their town for Game Three and what a game it was. The Red Sox took a one-run lead and the Reds came back. They took a commanding lead, but Boston came back and the game went to extra innings. In the bottom of the tenth, the Reds pulled it out and with a 6-5 victory, took a 2-1 game lead in the Series.

Everybody felt the tension. The wives of the players sat together in the stands to root their husbands on. Even though they were not in the game, they would do whatever they could to help the guys win, whether or not the strategy made any sense. It is not just the players that get superstitious. These superstitions are not occult-type spells, but recognition of what was happening when something went right. So that it might work again, players and sometimes the wives, would try to do exactly the same thing so that good fortune would repeat itself.

Cindy Chaney and Jolene Billingham sat together for all of the games. During the fourth inning they made a trip to the Ladies Room and while there the Reds scored two runs. "Maybe they will score when we go to the bathroom. Let's try it next inning." Guess what? The Reds scored three runs. Cindy and Jolene missed a lot of the Reds' scoring that Series, because often when the Reds needed runs, they thought they would help by making a trip to the Ladies Room.

Darrel got into Game 4. The Reds got two runs in the bottom of the first to take a two-run lead but the Red Sox scored five in the top of the fourth. Fred Norman, the Reds' pitcher was keeping the Red Sox scoreless until the wheels fell off. Two singles, a double and a triple, including a wild pitch was enough for Sparky to make a pitching change. Pedro Borbon came in from the bullpen to get the remaining outs, but not before the Red Sox scored another run and led 5-2. In the bottom of the inning the Reds scored two more. Both teams were held scoreless for the remainder of the game.

Darrel's appearance came at the bottom of the sixth inning. Cesar Geronimo was on first but there were two outs when Sparky called on Darrel to pinch hit against Luis Tiant. Nothing doing. Darrel went down swinging for the third out. That is how the game ended: Red Sox five runs to two for the Reds with the Series now tied at two games each.

The Reds got the bats going in Game 5. They won 6 to 2. Darrel enjoyed this game from the bench. He would rather have been in the game, but he knew he was part of something special. His hero, Ernie Banks, never played in a World Series, so to be in his third World Series and feeling the drama in these games, he was going to enjoy every minute and be ready when the game came to him. His attitude in the dugout was contagious, spreading support and encouragement. This was not a time for self pity or self promotion. He did what he could to help the team, even from the bench, because every little thing helps.

There is more than one way for a player to keep his head in the game, even when he is on the bench. Ken Griffey had a few games where he was not hitting the ball. Merv Rettenmund was a backup outfielder in 1975 and was riding the pine with Darrel in Game 5. Carefully observing every pitch and hit and how each player was doing, they noticed that Ken was struggling a little. Just as Darrel said to Merv "Ken's not swingin' the bat very well," Griffey ripped one into the outfield. From then on, every time Ken came to bat, Darrel would get Merv's attention. Darrel moved around the dugout during the game, never in the same place for long. Maybe it was nerves, but he couldn't sit still. He was up and down the length of the dugout, sitting by and talking to other players. He would lean forward, catch Merv's attention from the other end of the dugout, look him in the eye and say, "Ken's not swinging the bat very well." Sometimes it worked. Sometimes it didn't, but they kept doing it (and the wives kept making trips to the bathroom).

The Reds led the Series 3 – 2 and they returned to Boston, after a travel day to play for Game 6.

Late inning plays seem more important. In reality, a run is a run and a catch is a catch, but when it comes down to the final opportunities when the consequence is apparent, the intensity of the moment increases exponentially as the drama unfolds. The same is true for the games that are late in a Series. Facing elimination heightens the tension. For the Red Sox, Bostonians and their fans everywhere, this was a decisive game. If they lost, it was over and the Reds were World Series champions. If they won, they lived to play another day and all the anticipation, preparation and games of a whole season would come down to one final Game 7.

This game with its late inning dramatics made it what the Major League Baseball network in 2011 considered the greatest baseball game of the last fifty years.

During the World Series the wives traveled with the team. Darrel and Cindy, Jack and Jolene Billingham and Bill and Robin Plummer enjoyed each others' company, and since they were earning extra money, they spared no expense in tasting some of Boston's best lobster and seafood after the games.

When the Reds arrived in town on Friday for Saturday's Game 6 and, if necessary, Sunday's Game 7 it was pouring rain. The tarp was not removed from the field so they looked for a place in town to practice. Their bus got lost looking for the small college where they would work out. It continued raining on Saturday, Sunday and Monday. Hanging out in the hotel with his wife and hitting Boston's best seafood restaurants was what the weather was best for, but it was bad for playing baseball. Game 6 was not played until Tuesday night. It was imperative that Boston win Game 6. After three rainouts, everyone was anxious to play this decisive game, and the drama quickly unfolded in the first inning.

Once the game got started, the top of the order for the Reds went down in just four batters. Ken Griffey reached on a walk. In Boston's at-bat, Yaz and Fisk singled and Fred Lynn homered to give the Red Sox an early three-run lead.

That was not the start Reds' manager, Sparky Anderson wanted. He believed a World Series win was overdue and the only thing that would satisfy this team and the Cincinnati fans was to finish off the Red Sox. Teams that win Game Six and live to play another day often win Game 7. Sparky did not want to give them that chance. He was feeling the pressure to win this Series and he did not want it to go to Game 7. If that happened, momentum would shift to Boston, the home team.

In the top of the third Sparky put Darrel in to pinch hit for the pitcher, Gary Nolan. It was Darrel's second time to see Luis Tiant. Knowing Tiant would be coming after him, Darrel jumped on the first pitch and got a hold of it. He hit it high and deep to left center field, but back on the warning track, at the edge of the Green Monster, Carl Yastrzemski made the catch.

The game stayed scoreless until the top of the fifth inning. In the fifth, the Reds rallied with three hits, one of them a triple by Ken Griffey, and one walk to tie the game as the Reds scored three runs. They scored three more, two in the seventh and one in the eighth to take a commanding six to three lead with only six outs to go for the Red Sox. But in the bottom of the eighth, Bernie Carbo homered with two on base and tied the score again.

With the score tied going into the ninth inning, the Reds went down in order in the top of the ninth, and the Red Sox got something going. They loaded the bases with no outs. A foul ball was popped near the stands in left field. Concepcion made the catch and Denny Doyle was tagging up on third. Don Zimmer was coaching third and could see that Denny was tagging but he thought he was faking it. "No, no, no!" is what Zimmer screamed at Doyle, but Doyle thought he said, "Go, go, go!" Doyle was out at the plate and the Red Sox went from bases loaded and no outs to two outs and runners now on second and third. The next batter grounded to third for a routine out and the Red Sox' hopes of winning it there were over.

No runs were scored by either team in the ninth, tenth or eleventh inning, but in the top of the eleventh, Joe Morgan hit a fly ball deep to right field. Dwight Evans made a running catch at the fence and saved a home run. Boston fans feared the worst, but each time the Reds had two outs, with everyone on their feet, the Red Sox fans cheered with relief as the third out arrived before any runs did. They survived and knew only one run would end the game and send it to a seventh and deciding game the next night.

In the twelfth inning, the same thing happened for the Reds. Once again they were held scoreless. Eventually this scoreless duel had to end. The leadoff batter was Carlton Fisk. Pat Darcy came in to pitch and was facing his first batter of the game. Fisk, a right handed batter, reached for the low pitch over the plate and hit it high down the left field line. Sparky Anderson did not even look at it, "I just prayed." Carlton said, "It seemed to stay up there five minutes and it needed my help." "He used body English to wave it over," was Curt Gowdy's interpretation. To Joe Garagiola, "It was like everybody in Fenway was trying to blow that ball fair." It was fair and it was a home run, one of the most memorable in all of baseball history.

The time was well after midnight in the East, but the Boston fans did not leave. For at least a half hour they cheered and hugged and embraced the special moment in baseball—this unforgettable moment in their lives. Even Pete Rose was so excited near the end of the game that he told Carlton Fisk at home plate, "This is the greatest game. I've played in a lot of games but this is the best! This might be the greatest game ever played and you and I are in it."

Sparky was discouraged after the game and believed the best opportunity to win it got away and now Boston was in the driver's seat. Pete Rose was one of the guys on the team that the other players looked to. Johnny Bench, Tony Perez and Joe Morgan all set examples of positive, can-do attitudes, intensity and professionalism. Their focus and confidence never wavered and it kept the Big Red Machine running. Full of enthusiasm and anticipation, Pete challenged Sparky, "We've got one more game to go."

Game 7 was decided by one run and it was also filled with excitement. The Red Sox had a three run third. But in the sixth the Reds scored two, another in the seventh and one in the ninth. The Red Sox came up to bat in the bottom of the ninth behind by only one run. These underdog ball players surprised everyone so far. Could the miracles continue? Could they do it one more time to end the curse of the Bambino and bring Boston a World Series Championship for the first time in 57 years?

With two outs Carl Yastrzemski came to bat, keeping alive the hopes of everyone in Boston. He was the one the Red Sox would have wanted at the plate in this situation. He did hit one high and to center field. The crowd for a moment thought lightening struck the same place twice, but as they saw Cesar Geronimo get under it, the hope for Boston vanished as he made the final out of this historic World Series.

• • • • •

Bowie Kuhn was selected as the baseball commissioner in 1969 to save baseball. In the 60's the popularity of baseball had begun to slip backwards. With Monday night football generating a new level of excitement for the NFL, it had, according to Bob Costas, "overtaken baseball as America's favorite sport." It was imperative that the glory be restored to America's pastime and the Fall Classic.

America had watched this World Series, had seen the personalities and experienced the excitement. George Will said, "The country was watching and the country was saying, 'We have taken a vacation from baseball, and it's time to come back.'"

Darrel was a seven-year veteran on the winning team. After the final out, celebration could begin for the victorious Cincinnati Reds, their fans and the City of Cincinnati. The jubilant huddle of World Champions jumped, screamed and embraced as they savored their victory on Boston's infield. Darrel was there and, later in the locker room with his team. He wears the World Series ring that reminds him, he was a part of making baseball history in the Big Leagues.

Bottom of the Ninth

EVERY MAN'S PLACE
IN HISTORY

*"And who knows but that you have come to
your royal position for such a time as this."*
Esther 4:14b

*"A small body of determined spirits
fired by an unquenchable faith in their mission
can alter the course of history."*
Mahatma Gandhi

This historic World Series made a difference in the world of sports. It had an impact on our nation by touching a countless number of lives. A resurgence in baseball was measurable via attendance numbers, TV ratings and merchandise sales. The increased interest in baseball, the impact on lives, including Darrel's, Cindy's, and all the participants, the crowds, the cities and in the memories and lives of the fans, are all immeasurable.

When life is about a sport, then the sport means too much. That's when it becomes the wrong thing.

But, when a sport helps us understand an aspect of life, develop our talents and character, provides a platform where a grander lesson is taught and learned, then it produces defining moments in an individual's life and sometimes affects the course of history.

In an article in the magazine, "Foreign Policy," Stephen Walt rated top world-changing sporting events which reveal the potential of sports to make a difference in world history. Here are five events with which we are familiar:

> *"**The Berlin Olympics, 1936.** Adolf Hitler uses the Olympic Games to highlight the superiority of the Nazi regime but his efforts are at least partly undermined when a black American, Jesse Owens, wins four gold medals.*
>
> *"**Ping Pong Diplomacy:"** U.S. Table Tennis Team Visits China, 1971. During the world championships in Japan, the U.S. table tennis team received an unexpected invitation to visit China and, shortly thereafter, became the first group of Americans to visit China since the communist takeover in 1949.*
>
> ***Black September at the Munich Olympics, 1972:** Palestinian terrorists seized, and eventually killed, eleven Israeli athletes at the 1972 Olympic Games.*
>
> ***South Africa Wins Rugby World Cup, 1995.** South African teams were barred from most International competitions during the apartheid era, a step which highlighted the regime's pariah status and helped undermine popular support for the policy. The post-apartheid team's victory in 1995 was a vivid symbol of South Africa's new beginning, symbolized when President Nelson Mandela awarded the victor's trophy to team captain, Francois Pinear, a white Afrikaner.*

The "Miracle on Ice": the U.S. Olympic Ice Hockey Team Defeats the Soviet National Team, 1980. Labeled the greatest sports moment of the 20th century by Sports Illustrated, the improbable defeat of a heavily-favored Soviet team by a group of U.S. college players arrived at a moment when many Americans mistakenly felt the Soviet Union was pulling ahead. In fact, the USSR was on its last legs, though its hockey establishment remained a powerhouse and eventually sent a lot of players to the NHL. (Stephen M. Walt, Foreign Policy, August 16, 2009, found online.)

In these historic sporting events, none of the main characters was there to change history. They just showed up to compete and gave their best performance. Circumstances which were bigger than they were, set a stage which multiplied the impact of their performance beyond what they could have imagined.

When Darrel drove that pitch deep to left centerfield, I'm glad (sorry, Darrel) that it did not go over the fence. If it had, the game, as it played out, would have ended in the bottom of the ninth inning with the Reds winning by one run, and the World Series in six games. It probably would not have been the best game of all time, albeit a good one, but baseball may not have received the spike that it needed.

Even though Darrel's performance was not everything he wanted it to be, it did have an influence on history. Historical events have many participants. Some win, some lose. Some are in the stands watching the game while others are at home cheering from their La-Z-Boy recliners while enjoying a bowl of ice cream. Yet, they are all connected in this event and each player in the drama is an element in the chemistry which produces the final product.

Many lists rate the most important historical events. They are open to interpretation. What makes one event more important than others is a matter of personal opinion but everyone considers these events of historic significance.

The Attack on Pearl Harbor, the event that lives in infamy. We remember it every December 7th. It galvanized the will of the United States to defeat the evil axis. **D-Day** and **Dropping of the Atomic Bombs on**

Hiroshima and Nagasaki, saved the world from aggressive enemies but ushered in the danger of nuclear annihilation.

The Bolshevik Revolution in 1917 changed Russia forever. It also changed our world by launching Marxist communism as a powerful ideological force with military threat and force behind it. **The Cold War** resulted, and dominated world politics for over half a century.

The terrorist attacks which changed our feeling of safety are identified by the date: **9-11.**

Recognizing Israel as an Official Nation in 1948 is the epicenter of world politics as the Arab, Israeli and Palestinian conflicts shape oil prices, terrorism, economies and human rights issues.

The Stock Market Crash of 1929 showed a developing world how fragile and superficial wealth can be and how important economic health is.

Almost 40 years later, **The Moon Landing** was a great scientific accomplishment inspiring imagination and hope for conquering new frontiers, with scientific minds and cooperation.

Throughout these events of history, the great majority of participants were not planning on making history but suddenly became involuntary participants in cataclysmic circumstances which enveloped them. Their reactions made a difference within the event. Even when people were victims of atrocities, they put a face to the event so that within every statistic a human soul was represented, giving immeasurable and eternal worth to the event.

The magazine, "The Atlantic Monthly" interviewed 10 eminent historians in order to assemble a list of the 100 most influential individuals in American history. While I was impressed by the accomplishments of these individuals, looking at their accompanying pictures, I was struck by their humanness. Every one of them had to wake up with messy hair, morning mouth and deal with other unsavory but necessary bodily functions as they began their day. They were tempted with doubts and perplexed by questions, I'm sure. They had skeptics, competitors and enemies who opposed them, some from oceans away while others only had to look across the kitchen table. Normal vulnerabilities and needs, such as sickness, fatigue, hunger, loneliness and fear, pestered and tempted them.

Here is about one-third of the list with its very brief synopsis of the monumental contribution of the influential person, as given by "The Atlantic Monthly."

Richard Nixon (1913-1994) He broke the New Deal majority, then broke his presidency as a result of a scandal which still haunts America.

Sam Goldwyn (1879-1974) A producer for forty years, he was the first great Hollywood mogul.

Jonathan Edwards (1703-1758) Forget the fire and brimstone: his subtle eloquence made him the country's most influential theologian.

George Gallup (1901-1984) He asked Americans what they thought, and the politicians listened.

John Brown (1800-1859) Whether a hero, a fanatic, or both, he provided the spark for the Civil War.

George Herman "Babe" Ruth (1895-1948) He saved the national pastime in the wake of the Black Sox scandal, which permanently linked sports and celebrity

Cyrus McCormick (1809-1884) His mechanical reaper spelled the end of traditional farming and the beginning of industrial agriculture.

Sam Walton (1918-1992) He promised us "Every Day Low Prices," and we took him up on the offer.

Lewis and Clark (1774-1809; 1770-1838) They went west to explore, and millions followed.

James D. Watson (1928-) He co-discovered DNA's double helix, revealing the code of life to scientists and entrepreneurs alike.

Louis Sullivan (1856-1924) The father of architectural modernism, he shaped the defining American building: the skyscraper.

Horace Mann (1796-1859) His tireless advocacy of universal public schooling earned him the title "The Father of American Education."

Bill Gates (1955-) The Rockefeller of the Information Age, in business and philanthropy alike.

Frederick Law Olmsted (1822-1903) The genius behind New York's Central Park, he inspired the greening of America's cities.

Harriet Beecher Stowe (1811-1896) Her Uncle Tom's Cabin *inspired a generation of abolitionists and set the stage for civil war.*

Jackie Robinson (1919-1972) He broke baseball's color barrier *and embodied integration's promise.*

Jonas Salk (1914-1995) His vaccine for polio eradicated one of *the world's worst plagues.*

Ronald Reagan (1911-2004) The amiable architect of both the *conservative realignment and the Cold War's end.*

Mark Twain (1835-1910) Author of our national epic, he was *the most unsentimental observer of our national life.*

Henry Ford (1863-1947) He gave us the assembly line and the *Model T, and sparked America's love affair with the automobile.*

Thomas Edison (1847-1931) *It wasn't just the light-bulb; the Wizard of Menlo Park was the most prolific inventor in American history.*

Martin Luther King Jr. (1929-1968) *His dream of racial equality is still elusive but no one else did more to make it real.*

Benjamin Franklin (1706-1790) *The Founder-of-all-trades: scientist, printer, writer, diplomat, inventor, and more.*

Thomas Jefferson (1743-1826) *The author of the five most important words in American history: "All men are created equal."*

George Washington (1732-1799) *He made the United States possible, not only by defeating a king, but also by declining to become one, himself.*

Abraham Lincoln (1809-1865) *He saved the Union, freed the slaves, and presided over America's second founding.*

Whether or not we agree with what they did or consider their impact a benefit or a detriment, we can see, in these auspicious lives, the embodiment of behaviors which every man can possess.

They were ordinary people who did extraordinary things. What made them memorable was what they achieved. Before they did it, they were regular people. Many faced poverty and came from humble circumstances. Each had to grow up, learn, discover his or her place, respond to opportunities and relate to others, personally and professionally.

They were people with an idea. Through their living experiences, they allowed thoughts to germinate. Time to think, explore, ask, research, and discussion gave birth to new products, methods, conditions and solutions. When these new ideas or products were introduced, they were radical and seemed ridiculous to the listening crowds.

They were all people of action. If the problems were too big, complicated or entrenched in the fabric of the culture, to be changed by one person, they wrote something to affect the thoughts of readers and influence the masses. Their decision(s) directed others and created laws. When something was needed that did not exist, they would not be satisfied until they designed, researched, invented and produced something new.

They were people who took risks. Failure, rejection, or even death was more likely than success and each paid the price. Accomplishment of their purpose was more valuable than their comfort or safety.

They served others. Perhaps some of them fulfilled a dream or were rewarded with wealth and fame because of their contribution. But, most importantly, all of them produced something for other people. They saw needs, politically, socially, aesthetically, mechanically, technically, etc., which fueled their motivation and stirred their thinking.

They were people with a conviction. They possessed a strong belief that their action was necessary. Quitting was not an acceptable option. Fervor and intensity affected their ethic.

They did not know the magnitude of their contribution. Maybe they thought what they were doing was big and, certainly, it was important but the magnitude of their contribution was beyond measure or imagining.

Usually, historic events and their main characters seem too important or complicated to aspire to. They are bigger than life, grand and spectacular. They make our lives and efforts seem small and trite as if we are mere drops of rain in a hurricane of torrential downpours. They are the Big Leagues. The temptation for me is to think, "I am in the stands, reading history books but not making history."

In attempting to believe that God has a plan for our lives, we often miss the reality that timing is part of his design. We were "knit together in our mother's womb, fearfully and wonderfully made." The unspoken truth is when that happened, it also mattered. God's love for us gives us our value but His design with our gifts, talents, passions and interest are strategically given for a time and a place. We are made for a specific time and for specific events in history.

Looking at the world around me, I wonder why I am alive and in ministry now.

The past 30+ years of my ministry was primarily in small and new churches, but it has been in the church growth and mega-church era.

With all the emphasis of church growth and the publicity of the mega church, 90% of the churches in America are still small. Fifty percent of Christians still attend small churches and large churches use small groups of many kinds to help people grow through relationships.

There is an army of small churches and local pastors caring for half of the Christians in our country. Am I alive for this time in history so that I can help them know they are in the Big Leagues, too? Can I be an encouragement to those in small places of ministry?

Healthcare is a volatile issue at this time in our country's history as we debate how to care for the uninsured and the approval of nationalized healthcare. Is it God's providence that I am in Hospice, as a chaplain, when people are realizing that the vast majority of what a person spends over the course of his lifetime for medical care is done in the final weeks of life? Can I help by encouraging people to discover the compassion and comfort of a form of healthcare that is less expensive but makes the end of life more livable as well as more loving and dignified?

Like so many of the historical events in sports, our world and the lives of influential people, I may never know how great my contribution is or how the actions of my life will change history. Like Darrel, I need to come up to bat and swing at the first pitch. When I believe I am alive today, not by accident, but as a part of God's plan, I can begin every day knowing that my life is important and I am in the Big Leagues.

In sports, ministry, politics, business, music, education, writing, families, where you go tomorrow and what happens around you, the actions you perform, the idea you pursue, the product you produce, the song you compose, the problem you solve and the injustice you address, there will be your presence and you will change the course of history.

It is imperative that every man knows his life matters and that what he does will shape history. He is already in the Big Leagues.

What's the Score at the End of the Ninth Inning?

How are you fielding what life hits to you?
- What is going on in the world today?
- How have the conditions of the world affected you?
- When have you been a part of an historical event?

How has your hitting been?
- Why are you alive today?
- Consider your age, education, family and place you grew up to see what is unique about you.
- What ideas, skills, talents, resources and opportunities do you have?
- How will you use them to help somebody? Address a problem?

Extra Innings

Winning The Game

The Tenth Inning

Eternal

Top of the Tenth

A BIG LEAGUER ENCOUNTERS ETERNITY

"Since, then, you have been raised with Christ, set your hearts on things above, where Christ is, seated at the right hand of God. Set your minds on things above, not on earthly things."
Colossians 3:1,2

*"Aim at Heaven and you get Earth thrown in.
Aim at Earth and you get neither."*
C.S. Lewis

The pressure is on in the extra innings. Every play is critical to the final score. Intensity increases. These three innings are about the ultimate issues and winning the game.

• • • • •

There are times when you need to be in two places at the same time. But you can't.

"Hello."

"Darrel, it's Larry." There was no such thing as caller ID back then, and Darrel was taking the phone call at the ballpark. Larry knew how to get a hold of Darrel at Busch Stadium.

"What's going on? Is everything okay?"

Darrel and Larry got along fine and still do, but it was very unusual for him to call Darrel while he was on the road. The Reds were playing the St. Louis Cardinals in a Saturday afternoon game and he caught Darrel at the ballpark after the game.

"No, it is not okay. Mom has cancer."

It was bad enough that she had cancer, but while Darrel was traveling the country with high hopes for a great future, his family was at home dealing with matters of life and death. Ellie was diagnosed in 1972. Breast cancer felt like a death sentence.

"How bad is it? Is she going to be okay?"

Carlos and Ellie, Darrel's Dad and Mom, had been dealing with this alone at first. They went to the doctor for the exam about the lump in the breast and did not tell the boys until some further diagnostics had the doctors certain that it was cancer. They began planning for a mastectomy with lymph node removal if there was any sign that it had spread. Before the mastectomy they would biopsy the lump in case it was a benign cyst, but that was unlikely. With surgery scheduled, it was time to tell the children.

Larry was home so he was the one they called first. He was the oldest, even if only by eleven months. With news this bad, it was a logical choice to tell Larry first. Darrel was not only fearful for his mother's future and what was going to happen to her, but he felt guilty that he was not there when he was needed the most.

"It is breast cancer, Darrel. Mom is going to have surgery and if it goes as expected she will have radiation after that. We will hope and pray for the best."

"Is there anything I can do?"

Darrel was torn. As a utility player trying to establish his place on the team, he knew he could not leave the team for days or weeks. In those days, there was a lot less compassion for players whose mothers were sick. He needed to be tough and focused. He knew he had to stay. Yet, this is mom and she could die.

"I can't believe Christmas might have been the last time I will see her healthy." Darrel was stunned. Cancer sends shock waves through every family it attacks. Everything is confused until the dust settles, but when someone is away or on the road, like Darrel was, and trying to get established on a competitive team at a Big League level, the dust stays stirred for quite a while.

There is no class that teaches a man what to do when a cancer diagnosis comes into the family. If there was, nobody would take it because they don't want to believe it is going to happen to them. This happens a lot, but always to other families.

Cancer is a condition that, under the best of circumstances, requires a series of diagnostic procedures and usually surgery. It is followed by radical treatments that attempt to stop the recurrence or the spread of the disease and are followed with exams that hopefully bring the news the cancer is in remission. After a minimum of five years the patient might be considered cancer free.

The toll it takes on the entire family financially and emotionally is expensive, extensive and sometimes catastrophic. This was the situation the Chaney family found themselves in as they faced an uncertain future with decisions and events beyond their knowledge, experience and control.

"Thanks for calling, Larry. Keep me posted. Let me know how the surgery goes. Promise? Call me right away!" Darrel leaned against the wall with the big black pay phone. With a sigh, he put the receiver back on the hook, ran his fingers through his hair and slowly began to walk to the hotel.

"Darrel the bus is pulling out."

"Go ahead," he waved and grunted, barely loud enough to be heard. He was not in the mood to be in a bus with a bunch of rowdy buddies who were in good moods.

He walked to the hotel with both of his hands stuffed deep into his pockets and his eyes focused straight ahead, not looking to the left or the right. The St. Louis Arch and the people he was passing were of no interest to him. Every possible scenario was swimming through his mind. Finding solutions to any of them was impossible, but he tried to solve them all or at least come up with some options.

Bill Plummer, Jack Billingham, and Dennis Menke were coming out of the Chase Park Plaza Hotel lobby when Darrel entered the revolving door. "Darrel are you joining us for dinner?"

"Sorry guys, not tonight."

"Darrel, are you alright?" Jack asked. It did not take a psychologist to determine something was bothering Darrel.

"My mom's got cancer. She's gonna die. I've just got to be alone for a little while."

"Sure thing Darrel. Hey man, we're really sorry. Let us know if there is anything we can do." "Thanks. I'll be alright I just have a lot to think about right now."

• • • • •

Sundays are work days for baseball players. They do not get to attend church services because of their games, so a chapel service is offered in the locker room for the guys who want to come. They do come, and like a Sunday church service, they attend for different reasons. Some come because it is a tradition they ought to fulfill. It is part of a weekly ritual they need to feel they have made every preparation for being a great ball player. A lot of guys come to get God's help. "Maybe if I show up at chapel, say a prayer and ask for God's blessing I will play better." "I need all the help I can get and I believe in God and want His help too." A few guys are devout in their faith and they want to honor God with this simple worship and feed their faith on the Scripture of the day and the words of the chapel speaker.

Most teams have a Chaplain who invites speakers from around town to share a brief devotional. The speaker is instructed ahead of time, "You are there for the players, not to get autographs or have photo sessions. Just share a simple message of faith and inspiration, read a scripture and say a prayer. I will introduce you and conclude. You have about 15 minutes for each team. We will do the visitors first and then the home team. Thanks for coming."

With those instructions, a lot of speakers share a simple Gospel message. They tell the guys the Christian faith is more than a belief in God, but a relationship with God. When we recognize our need for Him and admit that we have sinned and fall short of His goodness, by a simple prayer of faith, we invite Him into our lives.

Darrel's faith had cooled down to nominal. Being a good Catholic boy, he went to church a lot of times and believed that God was real, that Jesus died for his sins, that there was a Holy Spirit and good behavior was rewarded and bad behavior was punished. He attended the chapel services out of respect for God and his faith, but baseball was his passion and his best efforts went into becoming a baseball player. Faith might be of some help, but it was compartmentalized into one more ingredient of many that made up Darrel. Faith was not about a relationship with God that could be present in every area of his life.

• • • • •

Darrel pulled the key out of his pocket and unlocked the hotel room door. He reached inside the door and placed the Do-Not-Disturb doorknob hanger outside. He did not want housekeeping or teammates knocking on the door. This was serious and he needed time and space to think.

Tossing his sport coat on the bed he walked over to the window and just stared at the town of St. Louis. His eyes might have seen it, but his mind was not processing what he saw because he was still trying to come up with a solution to comfort the dark ache, fear and dread in his emotions. He turned away from the window nervously paced back and forth. With his hands behind his head he stared through the ceiling wanting to see

God offering help that was beyond anything Darrel could come up with or this world could offer.

It is good to have a foundation of faith and reminders like chapel services even if you wander away from it for a while. There is a place to come back to. It is like a faith account has been set up and it has been sitting there waiting for you to draw against it. Without totally understanding, yet needing and hoping there was more, Darrel fell to his knees right there in his Chase Park Plaza Hotel room.

Kneeling between the beds Darrel prayed, "Lord, I have never done this before, but I really need You and I know it. I ask You to forgive me of my sins and come into my life. I want to be close to You and have You in my life. Would You take my life and lead it and help me live in a way that pleases you? Help my mom and dad. We really need You now. Amen."

God did not give Darrel's mother cancer so that he could get Darrel's attention. Our planet is cursed and contaminated by sin. Bad things happened to nice and good people. Storms hit, earthquakes shake, volcanoes explode, wars rage and diseases ravage. But, it is during bad times that many people come to a realization of their own inadequacy and look for help from God. When they do, they find He is there and cares about them and is pained by their suffering. In love and through His sacrifice on the Cross, He reaches out to them to be present in their lives and bring hope and redemption to their life and situation.

When the crisis passes, some people forget their encounter. But for many, it is more than temporary help or a cry of need; it is an openness to be converted by God in a way that is real and life changing. Problems do not go away and plenty of doubts and questions persist, but something lingers that has made the person and life different. That is the way it was for Darrel. He got up from that prayer a changed man.

He was going to need the strength that came from above because his worst fears were about to come true. The Chaney's lives were never going to be the same again.

Darrel was finding his place on one of the very best teams in baseball history. After a year in the minors, four years in the Big Leagues and in a season that gave Darrel playoff and World Series experience, mom was battling cancer. Her cancer surgery was radical and her battles through chemo and radiation took years. The family held out hope that she would beat it. She was hoping too, and enjoying her son's development as a Big League ballplayer.

Ellie worked to keep her spirits up for her family. The vomiting, fatigue, pain and expense that accompanied the treatment to keep living made it hard to do the things that were important to life. But the value of a faithful husband and the love shared, the meals enjoyed and routine times of having him come in the door after a day of work at Sinclair Oil, increased in value with the thought that they may all be lost. A sunset or a rainy day have special meaning to a cancer patient. Watching her children begin adulthood and the joy of grandchildren was a treasure of immeasurable value to a devoted mom with cancer. If the disease would take her, she did not want the treatment to rob her of the experiences she could squeeze out of every day.

Watching her son play on a Big League team would make any mom proud, but Ellie savored every experience with love and wonder. It was a special treat when she saw Darrel on TV and a call from the kids was never an interruption.

"Hello", she would answer the phone with a wisp in her voice. Her mood sounded good, but the forced air showed she was not herself.

"Hi Mom, it's Darrel." He tried to stay upbeat. It was hard to know how to respond. It was important to care but it might make things worse if he noticed the changes. So, he did the best he could to act like it is the way he wanted it to be instead of the way it was.

"Hi Honey. I saw you on TV last week. I'm sorry you didn't get a hit that time, but your team won."

"Me too. But I will next time. Keep watching. How are you doing?"

"I'm doing alright. I feel tired and the treatments make me sick, but I will get through it. Don't worry about me. You keep up the good work. I am proud of you."

In the 70's, pay phones needed the correct change for long distance phone calls or a collect call, when the person receiving the call pays an even higher price, is required. Darrel could not call every day, but he tried to call at least every week. When the Reds were home he could do better.

"I am praying for you Mom. I love you. Keep watching."

Darrel's positive personality and his competitive athleticism served him well to get him to the Big Leagues. Facing the challenges of career vulnerabilities and his mother's uncertain future required the development of his character. Nurturing his faith by attending Chapel Services, reading his Bible, praying in a disciplined way and finding teammates that shared his faith molded Darrel into the life of Christ.

For a few years it seemed like the treatments worked. For the most part, Ellie got her energy back. Her hair grew back and the whole family was encouraged with the hope that this painful chapter was over and they had all survived.

Then in 1978, the news every cancer patient fears, hit the Chaney family. There was a recurrence and the cancer had spread. There were metastases in the bone with a large tumor the size of a grapefruit in the back. More surgery was required to take some bone from her hip and put it in her neck.

Over the next year, with Ellie's condition worsening, the pressure was getting to Carlos. She could not do her usual responsibilities. Pain management was critical. Darrel was traded to the Atlanta Braves in 1976 and he was playing a lot with them through 1979. During baseball season he had to be with the team so Larry and Mary Kay, Darrel's sister, helped as much as they could, but nothing was enough.

In December of 1979, Carlos had a heart attack. Three arteries were blocked and the surgeons performed a triple by-pass. Five days before Christmas both Dad and Mom were in the hospital. At least it was the off season so Darrel was home for this episode.

Christmas may be the worst time for bad events. Memories of the past, the joys of being together and the hopes of a future converge with the greatest holiday of the year. All the stores are bustling with shoppers buying their Christmas gifts. They find their way beneath the Christmas tree decorated with lights and tinsel, filling the house with the fragrance of pine. Cookies, eggnog and hot spiced apple cider welcome family and friends who gather to celebrate the birth of the Christ child. The Chaney's always attended Midnight Mass together to hear the story of the Savior who left His throne in Heaven to come into a dark world and save the people from their sins and sorrows.

Carlos and Ellie were released from the hospital just before Christmas. She was too sick to go to church, but the family tried to make it feel like Christmas. She wanted to be with her family and she gave it all she could to be part of the opening of gifts.

The kids did the shopping and decorating as they tried to save this sacred family tradition. Darrel did not want to burden his mom with the news that he had been released from the Braves. He was considering a few options with the Mets and Pirates, but at his age he did not want to start all over and it would have meant more bench time and finding a place on well established teams. He would probably retire from baseball, but for now his Big League concerns were for his mom and dad.

Ellie did more than she should have in trying to open gifts. It was before she was bedfast so she had walked to the living room to be with the family but had to return to her sick bed. The pain had gotten out of control. When she returned to the bed she was crying, moaning and screaming in pain. It was impossible to wish each other a Merry Christmas and a Happy New Year under these circumstances.

She hung on for a few more months. Morphine helped to manage the pain but in May, Ellie's earthly life ended and the Lord who came that first Christmas, came to take Ellie to live forever in the place he had prepared for her.

> "Do not let your hearts be troubled. You believe in God; believe
> also in me. My Father's house has many rooms… And if I go
> and prepare a place for you, I will come back and take you there
> to be with me, that you also may be where I am."
> **John 14:1-3**

Darrel laid his mother's earthly body to rest the day after Mother's Day in 1980. He had to begin the journey of grief in this next chapter of his life. Grief is learning to live with a piece of you missing. Darrel had two big parts of his life missing.

Most important was his Mother, but soon baseball would be gone. The dream had come, provided many great experiences, but now it was over.

And now, the one who brought him into this world who loved and nurtured him and was one of his biggest fans was also gone.

*"Nothing can make up for the absence of someone whom we love,
and it would be wrong to try to find a substitute;
we must simply hold out and see it through.
That sounds very hard at first, but at the same time it is a great
consolation, for the gap, as long as it remains unfilled, preserves the
bonds between us. It is nonsense to say that God fills the gap; God
doesn't fill it, but on the contrary keeps it empty and so helps us to keep
alive our former communion with each other, even at the cost of pain."*
Dietrich Bonhoeffer

A relationship with God is more than having someone who gives a man what he wants or takes away his pain.

He wants to know the infinite, sovereign, eternal God and be known by Him so he can live in a relationship with Him. Then a man can experience God's presence and guidance in every situation and experience. God is present and powerful in the mysteries, heartbreaks, failures and victories in a man's life.

Darrel's prayer between the beds of the Chase Park Plaza Hotel responded to God's offer of the relationship that will last forever. Beyond baseball, Darrel experienced the hope of eternal life and the daily presence of the eternal God, and he got a complete new perspective to life's Big Leagues.

Bottom of the Tenth

EVERY MAN'S ENCOUNTER
WITH ETERNITY

"For God so loved the world that he gave his one and only Son, that whoever believes in him shall not perish but have eternal life."
John 3:16

"Most men lead lives of quiet desperation and go to the grave with the song still in them."
Henry David Thoreau

Men, in our busy, can-do, always-stay-positive, get-'er-done, American culture, are usually focused on making a living and having some fun.

But in his heart he feels like there is more. He knows there must be a reason for what he is doing and why he is here. Whether he identifies it or not, he is longing for God, the infinite, the eternal.

In the book Heaven, Randy Alcorn writes, "We are nostalgic for everything that is implanted in our hearts. It is built into us, maybe even at a genetic level. We long for what the first man and woman enjoyed *in the Garden of Eden,* a perfect Earth with perfect and untainted relationships with God, each other, animals and our environment. Every attempt at human progress has been an attempt to overcome what has been lost in the Fall" (From Heaven, by Randy Alcorn, Tyndale House Publishers, p. 77).

Thoreau, in his famous quote, "Most men live lives of quiet desperation and go to the grave with the song still in them," may have believed that most men never satisfy this longing. He certainly thought most men died before they discovered the source of fulfillment and significance.

Every man can experience God and live in the sweet spot of the significance God gives him. He might literally come to his knees, like Darrel did, or he might come to the humble place in his mind and heart when he bows and admits his need of God and opens his life to the presence and work of God.

Often it takes a profound loss that produces a severe crisis to grab a man's attention and turn him from the normal things of life to an urgent search for God. Even for the man who believes in God and is experiencing Him, the hard times can clarify his belief and make the eternal more real.

• • • • •

I enjoyed knowing Ginnette as our next door neighbor and the first convert of our new church. Her gift of hospitality was a rare and remarkable blessing in a neighborhood where everyone moved in from somewhere else. She could put a beautiful dinner on the table, surround it with diverse guests, clean it all up afterwards and make it all look easy. She was happiest when her house was full of people, and we enjoyed being included in those people. That we became one of her good friends when she initially was resistant to "preachers" and preferred barking dogs for next door neighbors, is what made her hospitality that much more pleasant. Her dinners were interactive events around a raclette—a cross between a fondue and an indoor grill, where everyone reached, talked and laughed. Her laugh had a burst of enthusiasm and volume that was infectious.

The welcome center she set up at church and the dinners she would host for visitors and new members set the bar for a church which learned how to enjoy fellowship.

We were talking to Tom in the front yard on the Sunday afternoon the Hayman fire started. The largest wildfire in Colorado history had started in the mountains just west of us. Our new church's first baptismal service was at the Butterfield Park pool and our Church in the Park was a glorious service except for the blue haze and strong smoky smell. The fire would burn for more than a month and, when the sky turned brownish yellow and the view of the sun was filtered so much that it was safe to stare at it, we knew something bad had started. Tom and Ginnette were going to be baptized that day as a testimony to their new faith in Christ but Tom decided to wait until Ginnette could be with him and they could do it together. She was in the hospital after a knee replacement surgery.

"Ginnette had a stroke today," he reported in his usual understated style and his strong French Canadian accent.

"Really?!?" Susan asked incredulously. She was much more alarmed than Tom but maybe it wasn't as bad as it sounded, or he just did not understand.

Tom was a financial officer for an Australian explosives company which is linked to the mining industry in Colorado. People who work in finance are often quiet in their demeanor, with a matter-of-fact, go-by-the-numbers approach to life. This doesn't mean that they are like that on the inside but if you were to judge by appearances and demeanor, you would say that nothing bothered them.

Tom and I stood at Ginnette's bedside the next day when she returned from a test of some kind. She was barely responsive and I didn't know if she was anesthetized or if something was wrong. I had made hundreds, maybe even thousands of hospital visits as a pastor and I did not like the looks of this situation, so I took the liberty to help Tom by asking some questions of the hospital staff. Soon I had a Patient Advocate helping us find some answers. Actually, our only satisfaction was that she started looking for the answers and would get back to us. We were hoping that Ginnette would sleep this off and be much better the next the morning.

Walking out of Aurora Medical Center, 50 or so miles from the fire, the smoke was much worse than the day before. It felt apocalyptic as the fire spread toward us in dangerous and record-setting speed.

Early Tuesday morning, my cell phone rang. Tom was sobbing. "Dan, please pray. Something is terribly wrong. They are taking Ginnette to ICU."

I cleared my schedule and went to spend a day filled with disaster. The fire was out of control with zero-percent containment, the sky was darkened with smoke and we were informed that Ginnette's situation was out of control, too.

"There is nothing we can do." the neurologists told us.

"Ginnette might not make it," I told Alto, one of our closest friends who was a leader in our new church. "Would you call our church family and get our small group here to support Tom."

"Oh, Dan! No!! This is awful. I will call and get back with you on who can come and when."

Early that evening, their daughters Vicki and Stephanie, who had just arrived from Canada, and Tom and I met with the doctor. They had graciously allowed me into their sacred space.

"There is no hope," she told us as gently, yet as plainly as she could. "Two blood clots passed through a hole in the heart and went to the brain causing the brain to herniate. The swelling and the damage is catastrophic. I'm sorry. You need to make decisions on whether or not you want to continue life support."

Our friends had gathered. Some brought food so we could stay for the vigil. Everyone cried and prayed. We loved Tom and Ginnette and the pain we were feeling was compounded by the anguish Tom was going through.

"Dan, I trust God but I don't understand Him." He confessed.

"I know Tom. I don't understand either. I am so sorry."

I did not understand and didn't even know how to pray. "God, the doctors can't do anything. Would you prove Your might and power and heal Ginnette's brain." Instead of a heartbreaking death in our young church, this would be an inspiring healing to raise her from her death bed. That was the most victorious solution and plan in my mind.

Meanwhile, the Hayman Fire raged, spreading and devouring more of the beauty of Pike National Forrest. The stench of smoke was everywhere, thick enough now that embers were dropping in our neighborhood. The fire was about 20 miles away.

It was Wednesday when the ventilator tube was removed. None of my experience in hospital visits prepared me for that event. I stood by her bed in the ICU, with Tom, their daughter Stephanie and the medical staff. The medical staff unfastened the tape and slid the ventilator tube out of her mouth. Would she keep breathing or would she pass quickly? I believed we were doing the right thing but a shred of doubt nagged at my mind. But I resolved, if God wanted to heal her, He did not need a ventilator and if He wanted to take her, it would not keep her.

It was out. The room was silent and we watched and waited. She was breathing on her own. All anyone could do was wait and hope.

The national news arrived in town to cover the fire. Governor Owens proclaimed, "Colorado is burning." Several fires were out of control around the state. Thousands of fire fighters had flown and driven in from around the country to battle the blazes. The biggest and most unusual fire was near us. Castle Rock is south of Denver and the fire was west of us and down toward Colorado Springs.

Evacuations had begun. Many others were on stand-by. All of the Front Range of Colorado was in a state of emergency.

At the hospital, we were too. We were waiting. A couple of days passed and there was no recovery nor was there death. "These things can take time," they told us. But, we didn't know what it meant or what to do.

It was Sunday again. Excitement from our first baptismal service, with the celebration of many testimonies of new faith was muted by the confusion of acute grief. What would my sermon be that morning? As the service approached I remained stunned and confused. When I reached the sidewalk near the glass doors of Meadow View Elementary School, our house of worship for over five years, Julie met me with an expression of utter shock. Her lips quivered, chin puckered and eyes filled with tears. Silently, we looked at each other in stunned disbelief of how our world changed that week.

The next morning at 1:00 the call we were expecting came from the hospital.

"Hi, Dan," Stephanie said softly. "My mom died." It was over. Ginnette was gone. God did not answer any of our prayers the way we wanted Him to. Now our young church had to start planning the first funeral service.

The service was full of tears, laughter, and a message of hope in eternal life. Mercy Me's song, "I Can Only Imagine" asked what it will be like when we see Jesus.... "surrounded by Your glory, what will my heart feel, will I dance for you Jesus or in awe of You be still?" Ginnette was the first person from our church to know the answer to that question and, for a few minutes, we found comfort in that glorious thought and the hope of Heaven for all eternity.

Trying to follow her example of hospitality, the reception at her house was a feast of hors d'oeuvres, meats, cheeses, breads, fruits, vegetables, desserts, fine wine, teas, coffee—all in abundance and beauty. She would have been proud and loved that every room in the house was packed full of people. Cars lined the street on both sides. All of our neighbors, her colleagues from work, and the church community joined Ginnette's family for a celebration of a life that we all loved.

The fire was a week old but just getting started in claiming 138,000 acres and 133 homes. And our grief was just getting started. I had no idea how to deal with grief which conquers a soul just as fire burns dry ponderosa pines.

Ginnette's daughters had to get on with their lives. Tom had to go back to work. Our church was a little over a year old and we had to get up and move on.

Carrying rocks uphill would have been easier.

Using faith incorrectly can cause more damage than comfort, even though the facts may be correct and the motives are pure.

It is normal to say, "She's in a better place". We believed that and Heaven was our hope but we were not there. Even worse, our place was sadder, lonelier, and full of more questions than we had two weeks earlier. We wanted her with us and we wanted her to be planning our next big event so we could watch her impress our guests with flavors and fragrances of food which thrilled every palate. "She will be helping prepare the Marriage Supper of the Lamb that we will all enjoy in glory," we said with an odd mixture of humor and hope. But how would we live until that time?

I discovered what a large a part of my life she was. Watching Colorado sunsets from our back deck was something Susan and I would enjoy, but now, it would trigger the sadness that we could not revel in the beauty with our next door neighbors, Tom and Ginnette, like we did on many previous summer evenings. Flower boxes overflowing with well-watered, groomed and pruned assortments of some of Gods' finest handiworks were now going to be neglected and empty on her back deck. Those empty flower boxes stirred a darkness within me that was worse than the sorrow. This situation was wrong. The loss made no sense and there was no way to replace her or what she did and every meager attempt fizzled pathetically. When I saw her widowed husband pull into a dark house after a long day at work, the sorrow spread from his house to ours.

How our church would deal with the grief was beyond any of my talents or knowledge in ministry. I was part of this culture which deals with grief by denying it, and trying to fill the void by being busy and moving ahead, confident that things will get better. I believed the lie that "time heals all wounds," so I sought to get on with life as fast as I could, filling every aching moment with a diversion of work, play, the noise of a TV or the sounds of Praise Music to help the pain go away.

When the crisis came into my life, and into the life of the people I was leading, there were parts missing in my strategy to deal with it.

Serving as a Hospice Chaplain about ten years after Ginette's death, exposed me to experiences and training which opened my eyes to the crisis that comes from a death. I was very naïve about grief. If I had known back when Ginnette died, what I know now, I could have better helped my church family and I would have experienced God's comfort more and understood the eternal more accurately.

The crisis that comes from death comes around too often. Hopefully I would find some of the pieces that were missing when I went through Ginnette's death. Thanksgiving of 2009 we made a trip to Pennsylvania. We sat in the living room of my Mom and Dad's little one-bedroom apartment at the independent living facility.

"The doctor says I probably have only a couple of months," Dad told us.

I was sort of expecting it and worried what would happen to Mom and how my brother, Jim, in Atlanta, and I, in Colorado, could care for her. For a couple of years, Jim visited them every month and even more often as Dad's health declined, all while holding down his computer programming contracts in Atlanta. His efforts were sacrificial and abundant.

Dad's determination to care for Mom doubled the time the doctors expected him to live, but, even at that, we knew he would not last long. Near the end, I came for a week so Jim could take a deserved break and get back to his family and work.

When I walked in the door of the apartment, Mom was not the same. She was confused and demented. Some things she could understand but in her confusion she repeatedly asked, "Is Dad dead?" After a brief hospital stay, Mom was admitted to a nursing home. They were wonderful people who cared for her. Kind roommates and neighbors made it bearable but this dear lady who loved to bake pies, mow grass and teach Sunday School, should not end up a demented soul maneuvering her wheel chair around a nursing home hallway all hours of the night.

Dad died a week after Mom went to the nursing home. His job of caring for his wife was finally completed, so he could go. Mom passed on, two months and two days later.

I had not lived closer than 200 miles to them since I went to college over thirty years earlier. I knew their deaths would sadden me but I was surprised at the extent of my grief. One day I saw a herd of elk and wanted to call Dad, but realized he was not going to answer. Another time a World War II B-17 bomber flew overhead and I had one of those moments of tears and deep melancholy.

The bereavement experts from my Clinical Pastoral Education and my hospice, warn of these feelings, confusion and other reactions in the normal grief process. They also ease the grieving person toward the need to experience the pain of grief.

Unlike any of the previous grief episodes in my life, instead of avoiding the uncomfortable or hurrying past the awkward and uncertain thoughts and sadness, I took time to face them by devoting time to contemplate the worth of Dad and Mom and the reality of my loss.

I actually felt more alive, not because there was *not* pain, but because there *was*. The loss I felt was because of how much they meant to me and

I could celebrate the value and impact of their lives. I realized what I was feeling was a normal, human emotion. I was fully alive by allowing myself to experience it.

The low points in life are as important as the high points. Maybe more important. Big League baseball is not just about grand slams and the World Series, but it is also about outs and losses, slumps and losing streaks. Life is not just about sunny days, happy times and feeling good. The way one deals with loss helps them prepare for gain. We can only go as far up as we go down.

Any loss—a job, a dream, a business, a marriage, physical strength, etc.—can be the catalyst to this discovery. Maybe the men Thoreau was referring to have the tendency to flee the pain or fill their lives with activity, like I did after Ginnette died.

But God is present. More than taking the pain away He will reveal Himself and the hope that there is more, and it is not more of the same broken product, but it is in a place where all is made new and it is for eternity. Dealing with our crises and losses by spending time facing the reality of them and experiencing the pain, provides the environment to discover deeper meaning to everything we have, the spiritual part of our identity and the thirst for the eternal. In these circumstances, God will reveal His presence.

Randy Alcorn in his book, Edge of Eternity, borrowed some of C.S. Lewis' thoughts and verbiage when he wrote,

"This is it...the country for which I was made! At last, the real world! I've been born. All my life on Earth was but a series of birth pains preparing me for this. This is joy itself. Every foretaste of joy in Shadowlands was but the stab, the pang, the inconsolable longing for this place! How could anyone be satisfied with less than this?' (Quoted in Heaven, Randy Alcorn, p 16)

Whatever a man's circumstances, however deep his pain, when he has faced his losses, felt his pain and given himself to God, he will find his way through because God promised, "If you seek me with all your heart, you will find me." Then a man will live in the confidence of his God-given significance with security in the eternal and he will know he has made it to the Big Leagues.

What's the Score at the End of the Tenth Inning?

What has life hit to you?

- Who have you "lost"?
- How did you handle the grief in your life?
- What have you done to seek God?

In the bottom of the inning, what are you going to do when you are up to bat?

- What can you do to face the losses of your life?
- How will you seek God?
- How will a strong sense of the eternal benefit you?

The Eleventh Inning

Destiny

Giving 100% for his new team, the Atlanta Braves.

Top of the Eleventh

DARREL'S LIFE CHANGES

*"And we know that in all things God works for the good of those
who love him, who have been called according to his purpose."*
Romans 8:28

*"All this teaches that the happiness of God
is rooted in his utterly unique power and authority in the universe.
He is the 'only Sovereign,' and therefore he is the* happy *Sovereign,
because there is none than can frustrate what he aims to do
according to his good pleasure."*
John Piper in *The Pleasures of God*

"Your services are no longer needed by the Atlanta Braves."

Three strikes and you are out.

It was a fast 15 years since the Reds' Tony Robello and Dale McReynolds visited the Chaney's and offered Darrel a contract. In 1981 they were hard words to hear, for Darrel, who had devoted his life and given his best to a dream, a sport and an organization. Suddenly and unexpectedly, life as it was known had come to an end.

Questions swirled in Darrel's mind. "What is next? How do I continue? Is there something wrong with me? What am I going to do now?"

• • • • •

"And in sports news," the radio broadcaster announced, "The Reds utility player, Darrel Chaney has been traded to the Atlanta Braves for outfielder Mike Lum."

Strike one.

Darrel was driving when he heard of his trade on the car radio.

Just a few days earlier he was talking to Dick Wagner, Assistant General Manager in the Front Office of the Reds. During the first baseball strike, the buck was passed to Darrel to represent the team. Being the Player Rep was not as glamorous as it sounds. There are a lot of meetings and risks of being misquoted and misunderstood, but it does take a player deeper into the personnel and workings of the business of baseball.

After seven years he had come to accept the value of being a utility player. A machine needed to have good parts at every position including the bench and he worked hard to be ready when the game came to him.

"You aren't going to trade me are you?" Darrel quipped.

Darrel and Cindy were comfortable in their house. Cincinnati felt like home after the many moves of the early years. So when he heard it on the radio it set off a random series of thoughts and emotions.

"Oh, no! What if Cindy hears this before I tell her?"

Immediately he tried to analyze the situation and the unanswerable questions swirled in Darrel's head. "What does this mean? Am I of no value to the Reds? Are they just getting rid of me? Or do the Braves want me? Am I going to be a huge improvement to one of the worst teams in baseball? Will things turn around in Atlanta? What will it be like to live in Atlanta? Crime rate is high and there are some rumors about how bad the schools are. Is this the beginning of the end for me in baseball?

The Braves lost nearly a hundred games the year before. It would be a transition from first to worst—World Champions to basement dwellers.

Darrel did manage to get home before Cindy heard the news, but as soon as he walked in the door this was the first thing on his agenda.

"Hi Honey. We need to talk."

"We're moving?"

"You heard?"

"No! We are? Really? Where? Is it final?"

"I can't believe it. I heard it on the radio. It's right though, I called Bob Howsam our GM and he confirmed it. Bob is a good guy, I have a lot of respect for him. He seems to think it is going to be a good thing for me because I will have more of a chance to play."

"When do we need to move?"

"Right away. Well, as soon as possible after Christmas I guess. I have to get to West Palm Beach for Spring Training in February. We can go through Atlanta and look at some apartments and see if we can find a good place. We are going to have to start packing."

"Wow," Cindy said with a deep sigh as she sat down to let it sink in. "This is a shock. I'm not sure where to start. I've never even been to Atlanta."

Job relocations disrupt every area of one's life and impact every relationship. In the uncertainty of Big League baseball there is a distinct possibility that all the energy to move to unfamiliar surroundings will be very temporary.

Darrel and Cindy organized a list of needs, responsibilities and desires.

First, get their house in Cincinnati sub-leased. Then they had to pack and find a new place to live. It needed to be a neighborhood where Keith could grow up, attend good schools and find a safe place to play. Friends for Darrel and Cindy would be nice too. They had to find a moving company and make the actual move to Atlanta, drive the car and do this in six weeks before spring training in South Florida, all the while hoping that Darrel would be successful with his new team and get an acceptable contract with adequate income.

It was the week before Christmas when the trade came through. It hit their holidays like a tornado. Everything was in a state of confusion, but a familiar voice on the phone brought some clarity to the new situation.

"Darrel, the phone is for you."

"Who is it?"

"I don't know. He didn't say and I forgot to ask him."

"Hello."

"Darrel Chaney! It's Dave Bristol. Are you ready to come to Atlanta?"

"Dave Bristol! Great to hear your voice!! It looks like we are back together again. It's been a good ride since that first year in Cincy. How are you doing?"

"I'm doing great and looking forward to good things in Atlanta. I am glad you are going to be a part of it. You have always been great to work with so I want you to be my everyday shortstop. Marty Perez is going to move to second. You've got the right stuff and I want to turn things around in Atlanta."

Dave managed the Red's before Sparky Anderson did and he was the manager who brought Darrel to Cincinnati for his rookie year. A few years later their paths crossed at third base in Montreal. They both remembered the exchange. Dave asked Darrel how it was going and Darrel said he was doing well except he wanted to play more. Something must have been in the works to lead Dave to say, "Be patient."

Darrel could get excited about this news. There was a good reason to move plus their first big need was met. They found a renter for their Cincinnati house, Larry and Joyce Shepard—the Red's pitching coach and his wife. The Chaney's got a shot of new enthusiasm to enter the next chapter of their lives.

They packed, labeled and stacked their boxes to be loaded on the truck. The move was coming together except for one small accident. Cindy reached for a can that was on a high shelf. It fell, conked her on the head and gave her a nasty cut. It hurt like heck and about knocked her silly. Blood matted her hair, ran down her face and stained her shirt. Darrel took her to the emergency room to get half a dozen stitches, so they stopped packing for that day.

With everything packed and loaded they piled in the car and said good bye to Cincinnati as home and headed south. Their destination was

West Palm Beach. Along the way, they stopped in Atlanta, scouted some apartments, found a good one and made a deposit. Dave Pursley, the team trainer for the Braves, took out Cindy's stitches. One person and experience at a time, they began to adjust to a new team, city and relationships.

That year Darrel played in 151 games, batted a respectable .252 with one home run, twenty doubles, eight triples and 50 RBIs. The bad news was the Braves lost 92 games and finished last. His former team won 102 games and swept the Yankees in the World Series. The Braves were in a rebuilding mode and Darrel was only one piece of a much larger solution. For four years they would be in last place and would have to wait until 1982 to have a good season. That is when they won 89 games, finished in first place in their division, but lost to the St. Louis Cardinals in the NLCS, 0-3.

As a Brave, Darrel's pay increased. His starting pay was $32,000 which was better than his best pay in Cincinnati and for the first time he secured an agent. High School friend Paul Stivers had begun a legal practice in Atlanta and offered to be Darrel's agent. Maybe he could improve Darrel's situation. That turned out to be a good move as Darrel got a three year contract for the first time in his career. As the salaries of baseball players were beginning to rise, Darrel enjoyed some of those benefits. His new contract was $55,000 for the first year, $65,000 the second and $75,000 his final year.

If baseball playing on a winning team was the only determining factor, it would have been a bad one. But there were other things to consider. Beyond his increased playing time and income, Darrel and Cindy found Atlanta a great place to live. They left the apartment, got a house and explored many opportunities that would extend beyond baseball.

Everyone knows a Big League career is not going to last forever. For the first time an injury put Darrel on the disabled list. The bone spur on his heel never really got better. Sometimes he played through the pain and was batting .300 in the last couple weeks of the 1979 season, but the natives were restless in Atlanta. Bo Bock was stirring up trouble on his radio show blasting the ineffectiveness of the Braves and complaining about "old" guys, like Darrel. Bobby Cox was beginning his thirty-year run as a Braves manager, but the beginning was ugly. To be an older player with an injury possibly meant the end of Darrel's Big League playing days.

At the end of October a letter came in the mail from the Braves. Adding insult to injury, $.36 postage was due. "Thank you for your service to the Atlanta Braves baseball club but your services are no longer required. We wish you the best in your future endeavors."

Strike two.

• • • • •

In today's world, eleven years in the Big Leagues, at even at minimum of $424,000, a man and his family could live comfortably for the rest of their lives, unless they blew it all on fast living and poor investments. Darrel's wages were respectable in 1979, but while he might have hung up the spikes, he was not able to stop working, nor did he want to.

After his release from the Atlanta Braves, calls came from the Mets and Pirates with an invitation to Spring Training, but they were conditional. He had to earn his spot on one of these established teams. The contract Darrel had with the Braves had expired meaning there were no salary guarantees plus playing out of New York or Pittsburgh would require another move. Atlanta, in the suburbs near Stone Mountain, provided a great place for the Chaney family to live. Great weather, new schools, beautiful houses, modern shopping and neighbors with southern hospitality encouraged Darrel and Cindy to grow roots and establish them for the long haul in the booming city of the South.

Change is inevitable, but it mugs you like a thief in a dark alley. It is not impossible to prepare for, but with so many unknown factors, it is difficult. Transition times between jobs are important, but for Darrel there was not much time to lick his wounds. He had to leave a setting with relationships and responsibilities that fit his skills, personality and dream and say good-bye to a situation that was familiar, satisfying and richly fulfilling. It is hard to imagine another set of people and opportunities that could be as good, let alone better.

Two doors down the street were Frank and Sue. Frank, a former Georgia Tech football player, and Sue, with her talents at decorating, hospitality and working with Frank in the development business, made them natural friends for Darrel and Cindy. Adventurous and energetic in business, life and faith, the two couples started a friendship that continues to this day.

Frank wanted Darrel to join his development team and specialize in the new field of corporate relocation. Gwinnett County was on the verge of becoming the fastest growing county in the United States. It would reach that status and stay there for much of the 80's and into the 90's and would turn from a rural north Georgia county into one of the most robust counties in greater metro Atlanta and the nation. It became a cosmopolitan melting pot of businesses from across the country and around the world. The opportunities for development and corporate relocation were endless. Frank paid for Darrel to attend Real Estate school.

A call came from Ted Turner's office before Darrel could get any traction in the real estate world. Turner Broadcasting System was going to begin broadcasting the Braves as America's Team by making them the first Big League team on cable. People everywhere would be able to watch every game of the Atlanta Braves. Darrel got to stay in baseball, with a $32,000 contract for two years, not as a player but as an announcer. His new team included Ernie Johnson, Pete Van Wieren and Skip Caray as the new broadcast team for TBS and the Atlanta Braves.

Real estate would have to wait. Darrel knew the value of being good at playing more than one position in baseball. So somehow, someday he would discover the value of real estate training. Being able to do more than one job is like having the skills to cover more than one position. It's money in the bank for when you need it.

"Darrel, what are you going to do when you are done playing?" The question was common, but when it was asked and who asked it was not. It was Cincinnati Reds broadcaster Al Michaels back when Darrel was establishing his place on the Big Red Machine. "You have a good voice. I think you could become a broadcaster." So Darrel, taking his Big League utility player work ethic into everyday life, and following the recommendation of a great sportscaster, he got his third class operator's license from the Columbia School of Broadcasting. That made him ready for when the broadcasting game came to him, and it did.

A live post-game show, along with play-by-play, was Darrel's gig for two years. After the game, he was the guy on the field with a microphone who grabbed the MVP of the game to ask him how he did it. "How did it feel to score the winning run? Did you know it was gone when you hit it? Was it the pitch you were looking for?"

The fast pace made the job interesting, dynamic and fun. Sometimes Darrel would get set on one side of the field. With a one-run lead it looked like the visitors were going to win so he would get set up, have his questions prepared for one player and then the game lead would change, the home team would win and he would have to get to the other side of the field, change his questions, get his camera crew in place all during the brief wrap up by the guys in the booth and a commercial break.

Darrel understood hustle so scrambling around was no problem. Problems came only a couple of times when his interviewee didn't speak English and their answer did not match his questions. The guys upstairs thought it was hilarious when Rufino Linares, the Braves' left-fielder and sometime pinch hitter, in very broken English and an accent too strong to understand, talked about his catches and the pitches he faced when Darrel was asking about his home-run and how it felt to win the game. With their microphones turned off they laughed and howled as Darrel was struggling to understand what Linares was saying and sweating, down on the field in front of the live TV audience, wondering if anyone listening could make better sense of the answers than he could.

Life was good. The income was not much but it was a paycheck. Work was fun and it was baseball. He and Cindy, frugal and good money managers, put a little away to help them through the transition from Big League player to former Big Leaguer so broadcasting had them in a good place with long-term potential.

TBS was breaking new ground going national with the Braves on cable. The eccentric owner of TBS, CNN and the Atlanta Braves, Ted Turner, was visionary and creative. His methods forever changed the way things were done in television news and sports ownership. A media mogul and visible character, jumping on his train could take Darrel to some desirable destinations.

Half-cocked, apathetic and negative are words that would never describe Darrel Chaney. Every at bat, every game, every team, every level, every time, he left it all on the field. Broadcasting would be no different. This ground floor experience was an opportunity loaded with potential. Some day Darrel's words and voice could be recognized along with the likes of Vin Scully, Harry Caray, Jack Buck and Tim McCarver. When dreams are pursued, the destination is often beyond the limited knowledge of the present.

Al Thornwell, an assistant to Ted Turner, came to Darrel at the end of his contract in 1982. "We are making a change. We are letting you go. We think you can make a better living working for someone else."

"This comes as quite a surprise. Is there something else I can do? I'd like to stay in baseball and the Braves organization. Maybe coaching in the minor leagues? A different role on the broadcast team?" It was not the first time Darrel's talents, skills and desires could not be fully utilized. Competition for his position and lack of appreciation for who he was and what he could produce were barriers that he lived with for all his years in the Big Leagues.

"No, there is no place for you in the Braves organization. Your services are no longer required."

Strike three.

• • • • •

What does a Big Leaguer do when he strikes out?

He gets frustrated. No Big Leaguer likes to strike out. The goal is to produce with a hit. A strikeout takes the team one-third closer to the end of their opportunities. If it is the final out of the inning, any runners left on base are stranded. If it is the final out of the game, the whole team loses. Maybe the loss was not the batter's fault, but his strike out failed to keep their hopes and chances alive. This strikeout felt like the last out of the game.

Getting traded, released and fired is frustrating. Anger, doubt and fear find fertile ground in these situations. It is dark territory a man must pass through.

He learns from it. Maybe he was fooled on a pitch. Next time he would be watching for that. The hitting coach saw something in the swing of the bat or the stance in the batter's box. Adjustments would be made. Every at bat improves timing so he would be that much better next time. The best batters make an out 70% of the time. This is an out that is now behind him, improving his percentages that the next time he is up to bat, he will get the hit.

Experiences cannot be wasted. The skills that were developed to do one job have transferable components. Take the lessons learned to the next job. Admit the mistakes made and avoid those landmines in the future. Remember the people you worked with because you need to follow the golden rule and they will probably show up somewhere down the road. Recognize God's work in molding your life and conforming your character as He directs your steps by closing and opening doors. This is a lesson you need in every area of life.

He comes up to bat again, more determined than ever to get a hit. When a batter lets a strikeout get into his head, he is headed for a slump. The sooner he comes back to the plate determined to get a hit, the better.

A batter has to wait for the team to bat around before he gets his next at bat. Between opportunities there is the time to shake off the frustration and apply the lessons. In a game, it is waiting for eight batters. Or maybe he has to wait until the next game. The timing in life is different, but there will be another at bat and a man needs to get ready for it.

• • • • •

Darrel was out of baseball, at least as a professional. He would attend reunions and share his acquired wisdom in the Major League Baseball Players Alumni Association. Every day, in different career settings and with a fresh set of teammates, he would need to use all of his experiences and faith to meet his new challenges.

A few days after being dumped so abruptly and completely by the Braves, his good friend and neighbor, Frank, dropped by the house to offer some consolation and encouragement. He had seen Darrel's firing in a newspaper column. Jim Royer and Dick Peischel at Royer Realty did too and invited Darrel to join their company. Another ground floor opportunity, this time as Vice President of Relocation was available. The earlier training was just waiting to be used and Darrel applied it with intensity. Darrel thrived with the Royer job for six years when a national company, Corporate Transfer Service, gave Darrel another opportunity to expand his world. He traveled from coast to coast helping people who were going through major changes in their lives. Some were moving up in the company and others were moving to a different town because their work, but they were all experiencing the challenges that come from taking a family to a new place and beginning a new phase of life—a road Darrel had traveled.

Life in the Big Leagues is temporary for every ball player. Some retire and others are released, but no one plays forever. Once a man has made it to the Big Leagues, whatever he does, wherever he goes and whoever he is teamed up with, if he has worked through his frustration, learned life's important lessons and stepped up to the plate again, he will always perform like a Big Leaguer because that is who he is. Even more, God has been working it all together to make him into the man of God's purpose and help him fulfill his destiny.

Bottom of the Eleventh

EVERY MAN'S
LIFE CHANGES

"Commit to the LORD whatever you do, and he will establish your plans."
Proverbs 16:3

"The lot is cast into the lap, but its every decision is from the LORD."
A Proverb—16:33—by, King Solomon

Every man experiences the disorienting events of job and career changes. Many include relocations to new houses and cities. Some are complicated by divorce, death of a partner, friends and loved ones, a life-changing illness or a trauma regarding a child.

Inside the crucible of tumultuous change, it is normal for a man to question his significance, doubt his abilities and not feel as though he is in the Big Leagues. He may question his worth as a man.

Change is unavoidable. My parents' lives were stable and they were as entrenched as anybody could be. Dad worked for Lycoming, the manufacturer of small airplane engines, for over forty years and most of that in the service department. He and mom lived in the same house for fifty years, which dad had built. They both enjoyed seeing their parents grow old. Grandma and Grandpap Hettinger lived into their 90's. Grandpap died six months short of his 100th birthday. He lived in every year of the 1900s.

Beneath the appearance of stability and throughout the working years of my dad's life, I saw the concern he carried, that his job would disappear and that he would not be able to care for his family. His industry was more vulnerable than the auto industry. Layoffs were common and every few years there were labor disputes and strikes. After he retired, he worried that the funds paid into his pension would be squandered, similar to what happened to the innocent people who lost it all at Enron. If circumstances did not change, the possibility that they could was unsettling to a faithful and strong man.

Even when the setting stays the same, the people in it age, friends die, others move away and very little remains the same.

I called Dad on my last Sunday at Crossroads, the church we started in Castle Rock. To step down from that church was the most difficult decision I ever made. Susan was going through some health issues while battling depression. I had exhausted all of my efforts and ideas to grow the church. As heroic as it was to bring a church into existence from nothing, I could not get it to grow beyond a barely viable small church. The people did not want us to go but Susan and I did not have, at that time, the energy or know-how to get it to the next level, so I fired myself and without much of a safety net.

"Hello?" Dad had a consistent way of answering the phone where his voice went up slightly at the end, like he was asking a question. That was almost always followed by him lightly clearing his throat.

"Hey Dad, today was our last day. It was a wonderful service and very affirming. It made me feel like we did some good work and made a difference in people's lives."

"I'm glad it went well. I have some news too."

Maybe he did not tell me before because he knew we were going through changes and did not want to distract us. Maybe he just wanted to wait until it was final to tell me so I would not meddle in his business. He liked to be in control of what he did and, sometimes, did not appreciate my interest or want my suggestions. In either case, what he told me was going to be a huge change for our family.

"We have a sign in the front of our house. It says 'sold'."

"Wow! That is a surprise. What are you going to do?"

I had mixed feelings. The cozy little country home on 2-½ acres of land was getting to be too much to handle. They kept it neat-as-a-pin. The grass was always mowed and flowers bloomed around the back yard in the summer time. In winter, they kept the driveway shoveled or cleared with a snow blower. Three severe floods nearly destroyed their neighborhood and, each time, put them in peril but they survived, repaired the damage and recovered. Now, however, if anything happened that was even a minor injury or illness, they were vulnerable, so I was relieved they were going into an apartment in an independent-living facility.

For me, even though I was away from that house my entire adult life, it was a stable reference point from which I could measure my progress and development. It was also a happy and safe place to which I could return. In some ways, I wanted to get away but, in the most important ways, I enjoyed coming back to it. It would no longer be there for any of us.

This news signaled big changes for a family who managed to avoid them for so many years. It was odd at first to visit Dad and Mom in a little apartment and join them for meals in a dining room with other residents their age.

But, by far, the biggest changes came when Dad's leukemia took his life and Mom moved up the hill to the skilled nursing facility. It taught me that no one is in total control and there are changes which come to us, whether we like them or not.

I was amazed and proud of my parents' courageous decisions and decisive actions when major moves confronted them. Their changes were more than a job description, a change of scenery or different friends. These were changes for the final stage of life. When the door of their house in which they raised their boys and spent their married years together, was literally closed behind them, they walked through the new one in front of them. When that one closed, Dad walked into the door of his Heavenly Father's house where a place was prepared for him. Mom walked into her nursing home, then two months later she made her final move to meet her Savior, where she was reunited with her daughter who died at two weeks old, and her husband.

Unlike Dad and Mom, there were a lot of moves in my life, but I believed that successful work would take me to a destination where everything was stabilized into a secure and comfortable existence. The more elusive that place became, the more I recognized that "normal" meant continual change.

About a year after we left our church, Crossroads, I crossed paths with Russ, a colleague in ministry and also a friend. We met in the parking lot of a grocery store. He was the Lead Pastor in one of the prominent churches in our town. At that time, they were looking for someone who could start small groups or anything that helped people connect in meaningful relationships. I called the next day and asked if he thought it was something I could do. We were both surprised and excited at the potential.

At the end of my first full week at my new job, the church had a ground-breaking ceremony for the construction of a new sanctuary. After many years of pastoring new churches that met in places such as a Jazzercise studio, a car-lot showroom, office buildings and schools, it was exciting and fulfilling for me to be on the staff of a church which had a building and was going to have a beautiful and spacious new sanctuary. But that was the smallest blessing of working in that church. The congregation was receptive and responsive to my ideas and initiatives. I broke out of the small church setting and was thriving in this church of approximately 1,000 people, with 500 - 600 in attendance each Sunday.

When we introduced a campaign featuring our small groups or when the pastors were on vacation, I would deliver the sermon. It was the best setting in which to preach. The new sanctuary was wider than it was deep, so the congregation felt close and intimate. It was inviting and comfortable with the new furniture, soft lights, floor-to-ceiling stonework beside a magnificent hand-made Celtic cross in front of the sanctuary. The beauty was an understated elegance. I tried to be as interesting as the congregation was. Many congregations today are homogenous; either everyone is old or young. This church was a collection of all ages, mostly professional and active people whose lives were dynamic and productive. Yet, they were willing to share their struggles, needs and failures.

The new sanctuary was not only beautiful, but also expensive; the weight of the mortgage stretched the budget to uncomfortable extremes. Skilled and diligent efforts went into financial planning and every expenditure was analyzed so that all the resources could be maximized and ministries would not be curtailed. As a staff pastor, I believed my job would be the first to go if staff cutbacks were necessary. In churches, there are not many other areas to cut.

Still, I was surprised when Russ came into my office after I had been there three and a half years and told me, kindly, but directly, "I'm sorry Dan, but we are going to have to cut your position. The money is just not here and we don't have the growth we hoped we would have."

I felt a surge of adrenalin go through me in a blush of awkwardness. It was important that I had the right attitude but, initially, I was confused at my new situation. It would not be honest or honoring to the church if I was cavalier, nor would coming unhinged in anger or panic be a testimony of Godliness and trust.

I was tempted with anger and, on the opposite side of the coin, self-loathing.

"How could they let me go with all that I am doing? They will regret this! Whose decision was it anyway?" I was not guilty for feeling angry since there was validity in those thoughts, but they were unproductive and selfish, so I am glad God spared me from falling into the trap of bitterness.

The other side of the coin was, "What's wrong with me? Why can't I really succeed at anything?" Forced change often results in wrong measurement.

In reality, continuation in a job does not necessarily mean success nor does leaving mean failure. Sometimes change comes from success which exceeds the position, but never does it prevent future opportunities.

Thankfully, I recognized these extremes and verbalized them calmly the next time Russ and I talked. I wanted to be open and honest. He listened and we both were sad at the changes yet hopeful that something good would come from it. Through God, it always does.

During the time I was at this church, a complementary job and supplemental source of income came my way as a chaplain at a hospice in the Denver area. I never dreamed of being a hospice chaplain. It was a position that was not on my radar in any way. Parish ministry was something I understood but clinical ministry was a style and a place that I had never explored. Initially, I sought it because I needed to supplement my income but, once there, I discovered it fit with my gifts and calling as well or better than any other role I had in ministry. I found it to be an arena which was fertile with ministry opportunities and populated by smart and compassionate people.

Hospice opened up a whole new world to me. Ministering in a clinical setting set up new boundaries and taught me the skill of listening. My Clinical Pastoral Education instructor helped me understand the difference between the home-field of parish ministry in contrast to the clinical setting, where I was the visitor.

The church-growth era in the last 30-40 years of church history has focused training on leadership, growing congregations, and focusing our message with marketing techniques. Often, the strategic necessity of caring for individuals was missed or I did not learn it. Caring for individuals is what chaplains do. They perform their ministry of presence and compassion in desperate and difficult circumstances and they do it better than any colleague I have had in parish ministry.

I love the church and believe it is God's passion and project. My ministry there has been enriched by lessons learned in the clinical world.

When I work at Hospice, I live the dream of coming up to bat with a decisive World Series game on the line, two outs and two strikes. As I stand at the bedside of a soul who will imminently be passing from this life to the next, or when I am supporting a spouse, family, or friends of one who has just passed and they ask me to share the message of God's grace and the hope of Heaven, I feel as though I just hit a home run in the Big Leagues. I don't hear the crowd cheering my game-winning hit but the scriptures assure me that I am surrounded by a great cloud of witnesses and, when each one comes to the Savior, all the angels in Heaven rejoice. I imagine some of these patients greeting me upon my arrival at the gates of Heaven, similar to players surrounding home plate in a walk-off home run.

As doors closed on one chapter of my life and ministry, another one opened. Thankfully, God was faithful to me and led me forward in personal development and ministry advancement. When I look over my life and observe all of the changes, I see events, intensely concentrated with God's presence and goodness.

My good friend in ministry, Tom Melton, was the first person to tell me, "What is most personal is most universal." In that wisdom I believe the phases of Darrel's and my experiences are common to men everywhere.

I got frustrated.

In spite of God's faithfulness, I did not enjoy the disruption of my life or the interruption of my plans as a result of these changes.

Potentially negative ramifications included but were not limited to lack of income, negative blemishes on my resume, and loss of respect by my family and friends. Fear radiated through my whole being just like a burn and could not be denied nor ignored.

Doubt was as big and bad as fear but it was more subtle. It could be missed or even swept under the rug. Just as termites silently eat away the integrity of a wood structure, doubts were eating away at my confidence and significance. "What mistakes did I make?" "I thought this is what God led me to do. Did I get the message wrong?" "There must be something wrong with me. Things don't work out the way I want them to." I might have been playing hardball but I did not think I was a Big Leaguer. For a time, in each event, I felt like a loser.

When angered, some guys react quicker than others. The damage which often comes from outbursts of anger and fits of rage frighten me. I refrain from those acts and instead, internalize the frustration. That, however, turns out to be fuel for the fire of fear, fertilizer for the seeds of doubt.

I learned from it.

It is natural to look for a destination where everything is stabilized into a secure and comfortable existence. That takes no effort but, after all of life's turbulent experiences, it is painfully clear that we will not find our stability in calm and unchanging circumstances. Surprisingly, God does not give us the peaceful circumstances we ask for. Instead, he offers Himself in the circumstances. The man who finds God, is a man who has a foundation which can withstand the storms of change.

I learned that life is full of dramatic change and that it is painful but the pain does not need to be fatal. If the characters of the Bible could not avoid exiles, shipwrecks, imprisonments, battles and struggles which turned their lives upside down, chances are I am not going to either. I can resist change and build a fortress around myself for protection but change will catch up to me, even if it is in the later years, as it did with Dad and Mom.

Paul's encouragement to the Philippians taught me an important lesson. "Now I want you to know, brothers and sisters, that what has happened to me has actually served to advance the gospel." (Philippians 1:12) Got it! What has happened to me has taken me to numerous places, introduced me to more people and expanded my world beyond anything else I could have planned. It did improve me but in addition, these experiences expanded my ministry and helped accomplish more for God.

Few people experienced more dramatic changes in their lives than the Biblical patriarch, Abraham, "who believed God, and it was credited to him as righteousness... So those who rely on faith are blessed along with Abraham, the man of faith." (Galatians 3:6, 9) I pray my faith will increase so I will trust God as he leads my life.

When I look back, I see He was in every situation, but so often I was looking at the situation instead of looking for Him. My prayer was for things to get better or be different. I learned that God cared about my circumstances so I should first pray that I will know His love, be confident in His care and experience His presence. When He is big in my life, the changes do not seem as big and unmanageable.

I will come up to bat again. And again!! And again!!! And each time with greater insight and determination to be more productive.

This book is intended to help every man realize his significance in God's sight and know he is in the Big Leagues. Regardless of the changes in his life, as my brother has encouraged me, "God has an A-Plan for your life from this day forward."

Rediscover your dream. Find a hero who will encourage you to pursue it. Keep plowing through the ambushes, setbacks, one-year contracts, and blown opportunities. Understand your place on the team. Celebrate your successes. Discover your place in history. Embrace the eternal through God's grace and face your pain and grief. Survive the changes in order that you can keep hitting and discover your destiny.

Your life matters and you are is in the Big Leagues.

What's the Score at the End of the Eleventh Inning?

What has life hit to you?

- What have been major changes in your life?
- How many of them were forced on you against your will?
- Where did those changes take you?...Geographically? Professionally? Emotionally? Spiritually?

What are you going to do?

- Look again at the major changes in your life and identify where God was during that time?
- List the benefits of those changes?
- What changes are in your future?
- Why can you feel secure as you face your future?

The Twelfth Inning

Infinite

Making and immeasurable impact.

Top of the Twelth

DARREL'S GREATEST ACHIEVEMENTS

"For when you did awesome things that we did not expect,
you came down, and the mountains trembled before you.
Since ancient times no one has heard,
no ear has perceived, no eye has seen any God besides you,
who acts on behalf of those who wait for him."
Isaiah 64:3, 4

"The life of the generous person gets larger and larger."
Written after his wife's passing, while confined
to a wheel chair and living in a nursing home.
Paul McMahill

Life is like a baseball field. It feels so big and it goes on forever.

The view from behind home plate expands into a spacious outfield as the perpendicular foul lines start at home plate and extend hundreds of feet into the outfield. The left field line in Boston's Fenway Park measures 310'. Right field is 302' and center field is 420' deep. At Chicago's Wrigley Field the left field line is 355', center is 400' and right field is 353'. Regardless of the uniqueness of the outfield fence, the effect is the same. No other athletic field or court has this unique shape, which creates a vast expanse of grass, with a home run fence that only limits the defense. The further the ball passes over the fence, the more exciting and spectacular the home run. There is no limit, but it all starts at a 17" place call home plate.

Other sports have end-zones and base-lines. Put a toe on that line and the player has exceeded the limits of the game. But the distance of a baseball field is unlimited.

Darrel's life is like that field. What started in a small way in Hammond, Indiana, increased every year. It continues to enlarge in immeasurable dimensions. Some of his greatest hits, never made it into the Big League box scores, but their impact is still expanding.

"Hey Darrel!! Darrel Chaney!!!" The voice was shouting out across one of the vast concourses of Hartsfield International Airport in Atlanta.

Darrel stopped and looked at the large African-American man waving at Darrel and making his way through the crowd. His friendly smile invited Darrel to turn to see who this guy was and what he wanted.

"Darrel. You don't recognize me do you?"

"I'm trying, but I'm sorry, I don't."

"Well, that's okay. I'm Arthur Neal. I was a kid when you knew me. I was a batboy for the Braves."

"Wow! Great to see you again. How are you doing and what is going on in your life?"

"Do you remember when you invited me to Baseball Chapel?"

Since Darrel's conversion, at the time his mother was diagnosed with cancer, he made the Baseball Chapel a priority each Sunday. It was a good substitute for church services for the Big Leaguer. After the Scripture reading and prayer, when the guest speaker was finished with his message, often, an invitation was extended for the ball players, to respond to God's amazing grace through Christ's work on the cross. Just because it was short, in a locker room and with a bunch of guys in various stages of getting dressed for the game, it did not mean that decisions of eternal consequence did not take place.

The Braves had a road trip to Cincinnati that included a Sunday game. This particular time they invited the batboys to make the trip with the team. Nick the Greek Pirovolos was the speaker for Sunday's chapel service. His story, "Too Mean to Die," testified that his gangster, gambling, fighting, imprisoned life was radically changed by his conversion to Christ. If God could reach into the life of a guy trapped in a lifestyle of crime and entangled with relationships that required it, then maybe baseball players could imagine the power of God making a difference for them too.

Nick was in a small room right next to the locker room, waiting for the team to arrive. Darrel went through the locker room, telling each of the guys and announcing loud enough for everybody to hear, that Chapel was today, it was going to start soon and today's speaker was going to be a good one.

Darrel invited everybody, even the batboys. This batboy accepted Darrel's invitation.

At the end of the speech, with heads bowed and eyes closed, the speaker asked if anyone wanted to make the decision to open their life to Christ. "If so, raise your hand."

Chapel was finished and the players shook the hand of the speaker and thanked him for coming.

The Bat Boy went back to his work with the equipment manager, but before he finished his job, he stopped for a minute to talk to Darrel. "Darrel. Thanks for inviting me to chapel today. I want you to know, I raised my hand and asked Christ to come into my life."

"Hey that's great!! I'm glad you came and really happy you did that. Now, why don't you tell some people what you did. That will help it to be more meaningful to you and will be good for those you tell. You can even tell the Cincinnati guys if you want to."

Until this day in the airport, Darrel did not know the expanding impact of that day.

"Yes. I do remember. Nick the Greek was the speaker that day and you raised your hand and opened your life to Christ. That was a long time ago. How long has it been?"

"That was 1976 and its 1998 now. I guess that makes it around 22 years ago. No wonder you wouldn't recognize me."

Darrel and Arthur, stood face to face in the airport, put their luggage down and celebrated the moment with smiles and good feelings that come from the realization that God did His infinite work through their brief encounter.

"Well, I have stayed with it. I am a Pastor and have my own church in Fayetteville, Georgia."

"No kidding??!! That's great. I am so glad to hear it."

They headed off in opposite directions to catch their flights, but not before they affirmed each other with a brotherly hug. In the noise and busyness of the Atlanta Airport, Darrel learned that one of his most important successes in the Big Leagues took place before the game in a small act, a simple invitation that produced infinite and immeasurable results.

Like the baseball field opens wide and spacious from the narrow space of home plate, this small act expanded far beyond anything Darrel could have thought or even imagined at the time.

· · · · ·

Today, Darrel has the gift of experience. He looks back and realizes the reality that his dream came true. Disappointments, setbacks and struggles did not prevent it. But he sees that beyond the dream a bigger story was being written. Baseball was the means, not the end. It was the platform, not the message. And the message is not over and will never end. It spreads wider than the outfield grass and keeps growing with more opportunities.

· · · · ·

In a small Catholic Church in the North Georgia Mountains, Darrel and Cindy attended Sunday Mass with their grandsons. As is the custom of that church, each service a few people are selected from the congregation to carry the Gifts to the front of the sanctuary to be consecrated. Tithes and offerings from the congregation along with the bread and wine to be used for Holy Communion are the sacred gifts. The Chaneys were asked if they would be the Carriers of the Gifts for this Mass. Gladly they accepted, but Cindy bowed out and thought that it would be better for Darrel to do it with his visiting grandsons. Austin, Chase and Connor, 14, 11, and 9 preceded a very proud grandfather. Each carried a Gift and Darrel, standing behind the middle grandson, placed a hand on the shoulders of the boys standing on the left and right.

Home runs made Darrel dance around the bases, but this event brought tears to his eyes. His legacy of a Big Leaguer found its highest purpose in influencing lives and glorifying God. That is unlimited.

· · · · ·

Darrel did not have a Hall of Fame career and he was not one of the superstars on his teams. Trips to the Minors, one-year contracts, games viewed from the bench, pop-outs in the bottom of the ninth inning, trades and releases attacked his feeling of significance and tempted him with doubt and discouragement.

Yet, Darrel's faith brought him to a relationship with Christ that connected him with the eternal. Changes beyond his control were under the direction of a covenant-making and covenant-keeping God, who directed each step. Years after baseball, the experiences shared and the lives touched continue to grow far beyond the fence of the outfield.

· · · · ·

Every month he touches hundreds of lives, in speaking engagements with a variety of audiences as wide as a Big League outfield. He gets to inspire kids at the Boys and Girls Club, the little leaguer with the Big League dream at the Habersham Little League, lecture to college students on baseball skills and attitudes at Emory University, and motivate the professionals in the Maple Capital Management Group at a private dinner party. He still gets to hang out with his Big League colleagues, like former manager, Bobby Cox, in charity golf tournaments. Darrel enjoys and makes the most of every opportunity. Now he believes he is significant and what he does makes a difference and lives are positively impacted at each event. The Big Leagues are bigger and greater than a temporary career in baseball.

Significance is not just a different category of things that a man does. There might be some truth to that, but true significance comes from knowing who he is in the eyes of God. That reality affects his behavior and the value of everything he does. Every experience draws him closer to God and opens his eyes to the fact that each experience is used by God in ways that surprise and fill him with wonder.

The big things matter, but so do the little things. Each person, circumstance and event has eternal consequences. Even when baseball is over, the Big Leagues continue for the significant man and his significant life with infinite results.

Bottom of the Twelfth

EVERY MAN'S
INFINITE RESULTS

*"However, as it is written: 'What no eye has seen,
what no ear has heard, and what no human mind has conceived—
the things God has prepared for those who love him—
these are the things God has revealed to us by his Spirit.
The Spirit searches all things, even the deep things of God."*
I Corinthians 2:9, 10

*"Many men have been changed by the world, but the man
who knows his significance is a man who can change the world."*
Dan Hettinger

When I see God's love for me and realize that he made me with a design for this time in history, I understand the significance of my life. Each event in my life is unlimited in potential and I know I am in the Big Leagues.

· · · · ·

"Where did the Christian faith enter our family?" My brother Jim was driving to church one Sunday when the question occurred to him. It is a reality that is easy to take for granted.

Dad paused and considered, "Who was the first in our family to come to faith and how did that happen?" Then it occurred to him. "Mrs. Overdorf, a stout German lady, who lived by the railroad tracks in Newberry, Pennsylvania, invited Mother to a prayer meeting at the West-End Christian and Missionary Alliance Church."

That church was located across the street from Memorial Park with a direct view of Bowman Field, the second oldest Minor League Baseball field in the country.

We do not know what happened there. There was no big announcement and, from the view of everyday life, nothing seemed to change. It was simple little meeting, where a handful of ladies got together to pray about their needs. This was the place where my grandmother made a decision with an impact that would never end. She confessed her need of the Savior and opened her life to the presence and power of God's love and leadership.

Her husband followed and so did their two children, Bob and Marcia. They married and cultivated the Christian faith in their families and their children, a total of four, who also became believers, raised their children in the love and instruction of the Lord. It is my privilege and duty to perpetuate this legacy through my family.

The witness for Christ, through action and word, in some big, but mostly small ways, which has come through our family, is immeasurable. This is not because we are special people who have done extraordinary work, but because God sees all of His children as significant—in the Big Leagues—and that includes us. He does not waste a single move and that is where I receive my motivation and eagerness for the future.

As I contemplate the impact of an individual's "home-plate-sized" action, I imagine Mrs. Overdorf in Heaven. The scriptures teach much about rewards. Maybe she walks to the ARM (Automated Reward Machine), the heavenly version of the ATM, to check her Reward Account Balance.

If she did nothing else in life, her impact on our family begins to populate her page. My dad's impact on his Sunday School student, Bob, and his life and years of service teaching kids in church, appears. The thousands of people who Jean led to Christ at fairs all over the country, fill the screen and add one line after the other, because many of those people also influenced lives and they are a part of Mrs. Overdorf's spiritual legacy. Fruit from the ministry of this book shows up and, it includes, not only those who read the book, but those who are influenced by those who read the book.

The spiritual impact of her life was more than she could have ever imagined. Mrs. Overdorf stands in Heaven, looking at her Reward Balance in utter amazement. With a celebratory scream she says, "I only invited one simple, unassuming lady to a women's prayer meeting. How did I get all of this reward?"

• • • • •

Getting a foul ball at a baseball game is a rare souvenir. I remember my first one. It was a Minor League game. My brother, Jim, and I were watching the Williamsport Astros, with their Big League hopefuls, Shane Hummel and Bobby Peefle and a bunch of other guys who never played baseball in the Big Leagues—but they were heroes to us. A foul ball was hit straight backwards over the stands. Since the exit and entrance to Bowman Field was open and unguarded, I took off running around the outside of the stadium. In the parking lot, behind the bleachers and grandstand, there in plain view, was my prize and first foul-ball-souvenir—a new, white, official New York/Penn League game ball. So other eager hands would not knock it loose, I took hold of it with a full hand grab. As I stood and held it in front of my eyes, rotated it in my hand with my finger tips touching across the threads, I could hardly believe that I obtained this cherished prize.

In similar fashion, after I had my "talk with Jesus" and began to discover a different way of measuring my significance and ministry success, I started to notice the prize of immeasurable results. It was the Big League of discoveries for me. I had found the promise of God for me and His work in and through me at times and in ways that I could not even ask or imagine.

• • • • •

A long time friend sent me an email. We had not talked for twenty-five years. At first, I did not recognize his email address because his name was accompanied with a woman's name that was different than the wife I remembered. He and the wife I knew, Jan, were in my church in Delray Beach, Florida. He was reading A.W. Tozer and was reminded of me—a connection I am proud of, but hardly worthy of. However, I will take any compliment I can get, so that is the way I took it. I was so excited to reconnect with this great friend from many years earlier.

His message stated, "I lost Jan in 2005 to cancer and liver failure. We had a great 31 years of marriage but she had a progressively worse set of health and pain issues." It was terribly sad news for me to hear. Jan was my first secretary. Even though she was new in the faith, she understood that a little church needed a great nursery so she also volunteered for a couple of years, by watching the babies during the worship services.

His email revealed the name of his new wife and next place of usefulness. "I married Mary Ellen about a year after Jan died. After 38 years in banking, we were looking for an opportunity to serve God in mission work. Not pressing on doors - just ready in heart, if He opened the door. He did that while we were on a short-term trip in July, 2010. So now we are in the Dominican Republic. Yesterday was spent doing laundry and making beds and balancing the base store cash - a little different than running a bank, but counting and handling pesos is a lot like dollars..."

I had to call Dick at his new address, because an e-mail was not enough. It was curious to me how a career banker would end up working as a missionary in the Dominican Republic and I wanted to express my condolences for the loss of his wife.

Our conversation started about Jan. She suffered for years with many surgeries and near-death experiences. After an infection entered her blood stream she developed sepsis. An expensive and experimental treatment worked and she recovered but, not long after, she had a setback. Too sick to go home, not sick enough for the hospital, she was admitted to a nursing home—a sad place for a woman in her late 40's. She had a fall and went back to the hospital. Then there were complications. There was nothing more the doctors could do. They suggested Hospice.

"Honey, do you know what that means?" he asked Jan and she nodded weakly. They cried together and he prayed for Jan. She was peaceful. Quietly, he headed for the door and heard Jan praying. "Dan, she was praying for me. She just got the news she was dying and she was praying for me." His voice trembled in gentle, tearful affection. "I fell in love with her all over again."

"Dick, I am proud to call you my friend." I was calling from a coffee shop so I tried to conceal my emotions. To hide my tears, my elbows were on the table with my hands, holding my head. I spoke the words into my phone that was lying on the table in front of me. I was hearing him, loud and clear, through my ear-buds.

"Dan, you are more than my friend. You are my spiritual father!" I was humbled and overwhelmed with the honor of being considered the spiritual father by a man of his spiritual maturity.

I remember the day he responded to Christ after a sermon which I delivered. It was a small Sunday morning service in a little church with a young and inexperienced pastor preaching a forgettable sermon. But it reached beyond anything I could ask or imagine. And it keeps going.

$$\bullet\ \bullet\ \bullet\ \bullet\ \bullet$$

The outfield grass beautifully spreads hundreds of feet wide as the foul lines stretch like raised, open arms, from the small, 17 inches of home plate.

Mrs. Overdorf's reward continues to grow. So does Grandma's, Dad's, and mine. They are infinite.

Rewards were not Mrs. Overdorf's goal, nor Grandma's, Dad's, nor mine. Even though the Lord promises rewards for those who serve His church and do His work, that word often distracts from the main point. The point is, the significance, value and impact of a life is much bigger than we realize. It extends infinitely beyond anything that we can ask for, imagine or measure.

• • • • •

My dad came home from lunch one day when I was a little guy, and he brought hoagies from a Catholic Church fundraiser. They were selling them at his office so we were treated to the best submarine sandwiches in the world. There is still no place in the country where you can buy a hoagie, also called a sub, like the kind you get at places like Joey's Place, in Williamsport, PA.

While the family was gathered for Dad and Mom's memorial service, I convinced my son Danny to get one of Joey's Italian subs. It is a two handed meal. Both hands grip the fresh baked, hoagie roll containing lettuce, tomato, peppers, onions, provolone, capicola sausage, Genoa salami and prosciutto. The "I'd-have-to-kill-you-if-I-told-you-the-secret recipe" of homemade Italian-herb dressing, plus extra mayonnaise, that squirts over the fingers and out the end of the overstuffed roll, provide the finishing touches.

Danny looked at me in amazement after he worked to stuff that perfect blend of textures and flavors into his mouth. "This is the best hoagie I have ever tasted."

I had no doubt.

• • • • •

Life should be that way. Full of experiences of every kind, so abundant that it takes all a man's being to embrace it and, even when he does, and some of it falls apart, he just keeps taking it in and living a Big League life, one at-bat at a time and making an impact on the world. The results of his labors are infinite.

The lifelong dream, matured and refined, continues to guide and motivate a man. Heroes fan the flame as life's battles threaten to extinguish it. But all the time, God knows each man and reaches out to him so he will know and be known by God. Then he has made it to the Big Leagues and discovered the source of his significance. Under God's leading and blessing every little home-plate-size event, each relationship, every job undertaken, is unlimited in its potential and the result is beyond measure, a home-run, which extends beyond the Big League outfield. His significance is established, his life gets bigger, what he does matters and his impact is infinite. The world is different because he was alive.

• • • • •

I was called to the bedside of a man in a nursing home. He had lived a full and robust life in Colorado, enjoying fly-fishing for trout in the mountain streams. Active in his faith and church, he brought children to church so his wife could fulfill her greatest pleasure of teaching them in Sunday School.

The Lord took her home first. Paul's health declined significantly and he spent his last months in a nursing home in the Colorado foothills. Grief occurs with every loss. There were many losses—health, mobility, an active outdoor lifestyle and the love of his life.

A Bible was conspicuous next to his bed along with a copy of <u>Heaven</u>, by Randy Alcorn. His son, proudly shared with me, his love and admiration for his dad. He had been reading through a journal that his dad had been keeping since he lost his wife and was confined to a wheelchair and bed in a small room of a nursing home.

I was not sure I should read it, but I did not want to be discourteous when the son offered it to me. Many pages were full of hand written Scriptures, prayers and daily experiences of struggle and blessing. It fell open to the page with the quote, "The life of the generous person gets larger and larger."

Here was a man who had discovered significance apart from circumstances. In the lowest of circumstances, he was going to use his valuable life to touch those around him, and he lived with the satisfaction that his life was not getting smaller, but was getting bigger.

While I was there, a steady stream of people came by his room to pay their respects. His testimony impacted me and I share it with you and his legacy infinitely grows.

That is the way to die. It is also the way to live. His circumstances did not control him. His life transcended them.

• • • • •

Many men have been changed by the world, but the man who knows his God-given significance, understands that his life matters. His potential is infinite. He is a man who can change the world.

What's the Score at the End of the Twelfth Inning?

How are you fielding what life has hit to you?
- When have you felt that your life is not important?
- What has been the way you have measured your worth??

When you are up to bat, when the game is on the line, what are you going to do?
- Take an inventory and count the immeasurable ways God has worked through your life.
- How will you change the way you look at opportunities in the future?
- Knowing your life matters more than you know, what will you do next?
- How will a strong sense of the eternal benefit you?

ABOUT THE AUTHOR

Dan Hettinger lives in Castle Rock, CO with his wife Susan and daughter, Angie. Dan and Susan have been married for over thirty five years. For their entire ministry they have been involved in ministry, mostly in churches with Dan as the pastor and Susan as music and worship director. Dan now serves as Founder and President of the Jakin Group, a ministry of encouragement to men, Pastors and Christian workers. He also serves as a Hospice Chaplain, at Hospice of Saint John and Susan works as assistant to the director of Women's Ministry at Greenwood Community Church. Their sons Danny and Andrew are married. Danny and his wife Kelly live in New Philadelphia, Ohio, with their son Gram. Andrew and Brittany live in Austin, TX, and are expecting Dan and Susan's second grandson, Hayes.

To schedule Darrel and Dan for speaking engagements log on to

www.DarrelChaney.com.

CPSIA information can be obtained at www.ICGtesting.com
Printed in the USA
LVOW07s1926150913

352514LV00002B/4/P